COGNITIVE-BEHAVIOURAL INTEGRATED TREATMENT (C-BIT)

COGNITIVE-BEHAVIOURAL INTEGRATED TREATMENT (C-BIT)

A Treatment Manual for Substance Misuse in People with Severe Mental Health Problems

Hermine L. Graham
University of Birmingham, UK

with

Alex Copello, Max J. Birchwood, Kim T. Mueser,
Jim Orford, Dermot McGovern, Emma Atkinson,
Jenny Maslin, Mike Preece, Derek Tobin & George Georgiou

John Wiley & Sons, Ltd

Other Wiley Editorial Offices

John Wiley & Sons Inc., 111 River Street, Hoboken, NJ 07030, USA

Jossey-Bass, 989 Market Street, San Francisco, CA 94103-1741, USA

Wiley-VCH Verlag GmbH, Boschstr. 12, D-69469 Weinheim, Germany

John Wiley & Sons Australia Ltd, 33 Park Road, Milton, Queensland 4064, Australia

John Wiley & Sons (Asia) Pte Ltd, 2 Clementi Loop #02-01, Jin Xing Distripark, Singapore 129809

John Wiley & Sons Canada Ltd, 22 Worcester Road, Etobicoke, Ontario, Canada M9W 1L1

Wiley also publishes its books in a variety of electronic formats. Some content that appears in print may
not be available in electronic books.

Library of Congress Cataloging-in-Publication Data

Graham, Hermine L.
  Cognitive-behavioural integrated treatment (C-BIT) : a treatment
approach for substance misuse in people with severe mental health
problems / Hermine L. Graham, with Alex Copello . . . [et al].
    p. cm.
Includes bibliographical references and index.
  ISBN 0-470-85437-5 (cloth : alk. paper) – ISBN 0-470-85438-3
(paper : alk. paper)
  1. Dual diagnosis. 2. Cognitive therapy. 3. Mentally ill–Alcohol
use. 4. Mentally ill–Drug use. I. Copello, Alex, 1957- II. Title.
  RC564.68G737 2004
  616.86′0651–dc21
                                                    2003010743

British Library Cataloguing in Publication Data

A catalogue record for this book is available from the British Library

ISBN 10: 0-470-85437-5 (HB) ISBN 13: 978-0-470-85437-2 (HB)
ISBN 10: 0-470-85438-3 (PB) ISBN 13: 978-0-470-85438-9 (PB)

Typeset in 10/12pt Palatino by Dobbie Typesetting Limited, Tavistock, Devon
Printed and bound in Great Britain by TJ International Ltd, Padstow, Cornwall
This book is printed on acid-free paper responsibly manufactured from sustainable forestry in which at
least two trees are planted for each one used for paper production.

To Ida Bentley

CONTENTS

ABOUT THE AUTHORS

Dr Hermine L. Graham is a Consultant Clinical Psychologist in Birmingham and Solihull Mental Health (NHS) Trust and a Lecturer at the School of Psychology, University of Birmingham. She previously worked as Head of the Combined Psychosis and Substance Use (COMPASS) Programme in Northern Birmingham, UK. In a managerial and clinical research capacity she developed and evaluated an integrated treatment and service model for people with severe mental health problems who use alcohol/drugs problematically. She has published articles within this area and provides national and international consultancy/advice on service and policy developments for this client group. Her clinical and research interests include the application of cognitive therapy for people with combined psychosis and substance use. She has co-edited the book *Substance Misuse in Psychosis: Approaches to Treatment and Service Delivery* (2003), published by John Wiley & Sons, Ltd.

Dr Alex Copello is a Consultant Clinical Psychologist, Service Director for the Birmingham NHS Substance Misuse Services, the lead professional for the Trust Addiction Research and Development Programme and a Senior Lecturer in Clinical Psychology at the School of Psychology, the University of Birmingham. His research and clinical interests include the impact of addiction upon families, the evaluation of services for alcohol and drug users and their families both in primary care and specialist settings and the use of qualitative research methods. He has been involved in international cross-cultural research, assessing the impact of addiction on families in Mexico, Australia and, more recently, Italy. Alex is one of the principal investigators on a MRC funded United Kingdom multi-site study evaluating alcohol treatment. He has been involved in developing a social network based treatment that has been evaluated in this study. He publishes regularly in a number of scientific journals and has co-authored the books *Living with Drink: Women Who Live with Problem Drinkers* (1998) and *Substance Misuse in Psychosis: Approaches to Treatment and Service Delivery* (2003).

Max J. Birchwood is Director of the Early Intervention Service and Director of Research and Development for Solihull Mental Health (NHS) Trust and Professor of Mental Health at the University of Birmingham, UK. His clinical and research interests have centred around the development of methods of promoting individuals' control over their psychotic symptoms, including the application of cognitive therapy to psychotic symptoms, as in acute psychosis, and the recognition and control of early warning signs of relapse. He has published widely in these areas and is a prominent figure in this field. His books include *Psychological Management of Schizophrenia* (1994), *Cognitive Therapy for Hallucinations, Delusions and Paranoia* (1996), *Early Intervention in Psychosis* (2000) and *Schizophrenia* (2001). He is currently involved in the development of community based early intervention for people with psychosis across the UK and is patron to the National Schizophrenia Fellowship in the UK.

Kim T. Mueser, PhD is a licensed Clinical Psychologist and a Professor in the Departments of Psychiatry and Community and Family Medicine at the Dartmouth Medical School in Hanover, New Hampshire. Dr Mueser received his PhD in Clinical Psychology from the University of Illinois at Chicago in 1984 and was on the faculty of the Psychiatry Department at the Medical College of Pennsylvania in Philadelphia until 1994. In 1994 he moved to Dartmouth Medical School. Dr Mueser's clinical and research interests include the psychosocial treatment of severe mental illnesses, dual diagnosis, and posttraumatic stress disorder. He has published extensively and given numerous lectures and workshops on psychiatric rehabilitation. He is the co-author of several books, including *Social Skills Training for Psychiatric Patients* (1989), *Coping with Schizophrenia: A Guide for Families* (1994), *Social Skills Training for Schizophrenia: A Step-by-Step Guide* (1997), *Behavioral Family Therapy for Psychiatric Disorders, Second Edition* (1999) and *Integrated Treatment for Dual Disorders: A Guide to Effective Practice* (2003).

Jim Orford trained in Clinical Psychology at the Institute of Psychiatry, London, and later obtained his PhD at the Addiction Research Unit at the Institute. His career has involved substantial commitments to the development of services for people with addiction problems, and the training of clinical psychologists, both in Exeter and later in Birmingham. Apart from a special interest in the addictions, and particularly their impact on the family, about which he has researched and written extensively, his main field of interest is community psychology. In 1992 Wiley published his *Community Psychology: Theory and Practice* and in 2001 the second edition of his *Excessive Appetites: A Psychological View of Addictions*. He is currently Professor of Clinical and Community Psychology in the School of Psychology at the University of Birmingham, and is Head of the Alcohol, Drugs and Addiction Research Group at Birmingham University and Birmingham and Solihull Mental Health NHS Trust.

Dermot McGovern has been a Consultant Psychiatrist in the NHS for the past 18 years. He has always had an interest in people with severe mental illness and currently works with both an Assertive Outreach team and an Early Intervention in Psychosis team in Birmingham and Solihull Mental Health Trust. His main research activity has been in the area of the epidemiology, diagnosis and management of schizophrenia.

Emma Atkinson is an Occupational Therapist who worked with the COMPASS Programme from 1999–2001, developing occupational therapy based groups and interventions for people with severe mental health problems who use alcohol and drugs problematically. She previously provided occupational therapy input into community based mental health teams for adults and older adults and currently resides in Australia.

Jenny Maslin is currently training as a Clinical Psychologist at the University of Hertfordshire. Previously she worked as Research Psychologist with the Combined Psychosis and Substance Use (COMPASS) Programme. Her research interests centre on psychosocial aspects of problem substance use, with a particular focus on life stage issues. In addition to a number of publications she has co-authored the book *Living with Drink: Women Who Live with Problem Drinkers* (1998).

Mike Preece is a Clinical Nurse Specialist who has worked for the COMPASS Programme for three and a half years. He has experience of working as an alcohol counsellor and on a busy inner city primary care mental health team. Currently he is in the final year of a Masters Degree Programme in Community Mental Health. Mike is responsible for facilitating and developing Cognitive Behavioural Integrated Treatment in one of the Community Based Assertive Outreach Teams. He takes a lead role in organising and developing training based on requests made to the COMPASS Programme by other services. Since joining the COMPASS Programme he has gained experience in teaching nursing students at Birmingham University and multi-disciplinary staff across the Trust.

Derek Tobin is a Clinical Nurse Specialist working in the COMPASS Programme in Northern Birmingham Mental Health Trust. His background is in mental health nursing with experience of working with people who experience severe and enduring mental health problems in the community. He is currently involved in the COMPASS Programme's Research Project: Evaluating Cognitive Behavioural integrated Treatment. Within this role he is responsible for facilitating the development of this model within one of the community-based Assertive Outreach Teams. He is currently developing the COMPASS Programme's consultation liaison service based on a brief intervention which supports staff within mental health and substance misuse services to work with clients with combined severe mental illness and drug and alcohol problems. Since joining the COMPASS Programme he has completed a BSc (Hons) degree in Mental Health Studies. He is also involved in teaching pre- and post-registration nursing students at Birmingham University and the University of Central England.

Dr George Georgiou is a Consultant Psychiatrist at the Addictive Behaviours Centre, Birmingham UK, and Honorary Senior Clinical Lecturer in the Department of Neurosciences, University of Birmingham. He initially trained as a general practitioner in Medicine before undertaking a career in psychiatry and addiction. Recently his work has focused on the treatment of patients of co-morbid substance misuse and either physical or mental illness. This includes work with people who are undergoing liver transplant, as well as the application of techniques developed in the addiction field, both pharmacological and psychological, in this group of patients.

AIMS OF THE BOOK

This book is designed to provide guidelines to clinicians (mental health/ addiction) for the treatment of problematic drug/alcohol use in their clients with severe mental health problems. The C-BIT treatment approach was initially designed for use in settings that provide some assertive outreach, although components can be used with clients in settings where such outreach is not possible. While the majority of the book describes a treatment approach called "Cognitive-Behavioural Integrated Treatment (C-BIT)", in the first section we seek to set the scene by outlining some of the background issues concerning substance use and mental health problems. In this section, we summarise the prevalence rates of substance misuse in people with severe mental health problems, the impact of alcohol and drugs on mental health and social functioning, and an introduction to why and how cognitive-behaviour therapy has been applied to this client group.

Part Two of the book will take you through the C-BIT approach in a step-by-step manner. It will guide you through how to deliver interventions appropriate to your client's stage of engagement with you. Illustrative case material is used throughout, and techniques are suggested to tackle obstacles to behaviour change that may arise during the course of treatment sessions.

The final section of the book will address some of the key issues involved in the process of implementing integrated treatment.

ACKNOWLEDGEMENTS

We thank all the clients and clinicians who contributed to the developmental process of this treatment approach and manual; the Northern Birmingham Mental Health Trust staff for their continued support; the COMPASS Programme Steering Group members for its commitment to the development of evidence-based practice for this client group; Jacqui Tame and Nina Balu for their untiring secretarial support, in preparing this manual; and the COMPASS Programme team members for their ongoing support in disseminating this work (Jenny Maslin, Derek Tobin, Mike Preece, Emma Atkinson, Joanne Wall, Sarah Badger, Isla Emery and Emma Godfrey).

PART ONE

INTRODUCTION TO COGNITIVE-BEHAVIOURAL INTEGRATED TREATMENT (C-BIT)

Chapter 1

ISSUES IN WORKING WITH THOSE WITH COEXISTING SEVERE MENTAL HEALTH PROBLEMS WHO USE SUBSTANCES PROBLEMATICALLY

THE NATURE OF COEXISTING SEVERE MENTAL HEALTH AND ALCOHOL/DRUG PROBLEMS

Although there has been an increasing awareness of problem substance use in clients with severe mental health problems (that is, "dual diagnosis"), it continues to be underrecognised in the psychiatric population. Even when treatment providers correctly identify substance misuse, the treatment response has often been inappropriate and ineffective. The result of inadequate assessment and ineffective treatment of these clients is a poor course of illness, including more frequent relapses and rehospitalisations, the increased costs of care and containment being borne by families, clinicians, law enforcement, society and the individual.

Effective treatment of this client group and improvement of their long-term prognosis rests with clinicians and treatment providers working in collaboration with clients and their carers. Clinicians thus need to be familiar with current knowledge about alcohol and drug use in the psychiatric population.

Prevalence of Problem Substance Use

The Epidemiologic Catchment Area (ECA) study of over 20 000 people in the USA found that 47 per cent of those with a diagnosis of schizophrenia and 60.7

per cent of those with bipolar disorder had substance use problems in their lifetime compared with 16.7 per cent in the general population (Reiger et al., 1990) found lifetime prevalence rates of alcohol use disorder of 43 per cent among clients with a diagnosis of schizophrenia, and higher rates for those with schizoaffective disorder (61 per cent), bipolar disorder (52 per cent) and major depression (48 per cent). Studies in treatment settings in the UK have tended to look at 1-year prevalence rates. For example, Graham et al. (2001) found that 24 per cent of clients with a severe mental health diagnosis were identified by their keyworkers as having used substances problematically in the past year. Menezes et al. (1996) identified a 1-year prevalence rate of 36.3 per cent among clients with a functional psychosis. Studies in the USA, have typically found recent rates of substance misuse in this population of 25–35 per cent.

Studies of the prevalence of substance use problems in people with severe mental health problems have shown significant variations. A number of contributory factors have been highlighted (Weiss, Mirin & Griffin, 1992; Warner et al., 1994). These include variations in the method used to assess substance use, the time period used (for example, problematic use in the past year versus problematic use over the course of the lifetime), diagnostic criteria for mental health and substance use problems, and the setting where substance use is assessed. Nonetheless, the studies all point to higher rates of problematic use of alcohol and drugs (abuse and dependent use) among those with mental health problems than the general population.

Types of Substances Used

The substances typically misused by people with severe mental health problems include alcohol, cannabis and stimulants (cocaine/crack and amphetamine). The question of whether people diagnosed with certain mental health problems are more prone to misusing particular types of substances has been the topic of much debate. Early reviews suggested that people with schizophrenia were more likely to use stimulants problematically than clients with other mental health problems (e.g., Schneier & Siris, 1987). However, more recent and larger studies of the prevalence of specific types of substance misuse in clients with a variety of severe mental health problems, including the ECA and the National Comorbidity Survey (NCS) (Kessler et al., 1996), have failed to replicate this finding (Kessler et al., 1996; Regier et al., 1990). The evidence suggests *availability* is the primary determinant of which specific substances are misused (Mueser et al., 1992), as opposed to the subjective effects. It is important not to overlook the fact that a very high proportion of clients with severe mental health problems smoke tobacco (de Leon et al., 1995; Hall et al., 1995; Hughes et al., 1986; Postma & Kumari, 2002). Due to the limited information currently available about the use of tobacco in this population or its interaction with mental health problems, tobacco use will not be addressed in this manual.

Demographic and Clinical Correlates of Substance Use Problems

Understanding which clients with severe mental health problems are most likely to have problems with alcohol/drugs can facilitate the early recognition and treatment of these clients. A number of reviews of the demographic, clinical and historical factors associated with this client group have been carried out (e.g., Dixon, Goldman & Hirad, 1999; Drake & Brunette, 1998; Mueser et al., 1995). A number of demographic character-istics are correlated with substance misuse. In the main, the same characteristics that are related to problem substance use in the general population are also related to problem substance use in people with severe mental health problems. These include being male, young and single, and having lower levels of education. The clinical correlates include poor engagement and adherence with treatment. Additional correlates related to the personal history of individuals that have been identified include initial better pre-morbid social functioning, antisocial personality disorder (ASPD), family history of substance use problems, trauma and post-traumatic stress disorder.

The Impact of Substance Use Problems on Severe Mental Health Problems

It has been suggested that people with severe mental health problems who use substances problematically often experience greater adverse social, health, economic and psychological consequences than those who do not. These consequences are said to be exacerbated by the problematic use of substances (Drake & Brunette, 1998; Mueser et al., 1998a). Problematic substance use can lead to an increased risk of relapse and rehospitalisations (Hunt, Bergen & Bashir, 2002; Linszen et al., 1996; Swofford et al., 1996). The strongest evidence linking symptom severity and substance use is the effect of alcohol on worsening depression. The risk of suicide is significantly increased in persons with a primary substance use problem (Meyer, Babor & Hesselbrock, 1988), as well as in individuals with schizophrenia, bipolar disorder and major depression (Drake et al., 1985; Roy, 1986). This risk is compounded in persons who have severe mental health problems and use substances problematically (Bartels, Drake & McHugo, 1992; Torrey, Drake & Bartels, 1996).

Substance use problems among this population are associated with increased "burden" on family members, as well as interpersonal conflicts with relatives and friends (Dixon, McNary & Lehman, 1995; Kashner et al., 1991; Salyers & Mueser, 2001). Financial problems often accompany chronic substance use, as clients spend their money on drugs and alcohol rather than essentials such as food, clothing and rent. In addition, substances or craving for substances can contribute to disinhibitory effects that result in aggression and violence toward family, friends, treatment providers and strangers (Steadman et al., 1998; Swartz et al., 1998; Yesavage & Zarcone, 1983). The combined effect of problematic substance use on family burden, interpersonal conflict, financial problems, and aggression and violence often renders these clients highly vulnerable to housing instability, homelessness and exploitation (Drake, Wallach & Hoffman, 1989; Pickett-Schenk, Banghart & Cook, 2003). Furthermore, problematic substance use can result in illegal behaviours (such as possession of illegal drugs, disorderly conduct secondary to alcohol/drug use, or theft or assault resulting from efforts to obtain drugs), leading to high rates of incarceration (Mueser et al., 2001). In addition to the clinical, social and legal consequences of problem substance use, severe health consequences are also common. Substance misuse may contribute to risky behaviours, such as unprotected sex and sharing needles, that are associated with HIV and hepatitis infection (Cournos et al., 1991; Razzano, 2003; Rosenberg et al., 2001a,b).

MODELS OF COMORBIDITY

As we have previously mentioned, people with severe mental health problems are at much greater risk of developing problems with alcohol/drugs than people in the general population. What accounts for the higher rates? Understanding the factors that contribute to the high rate of comorbidity may provide clues useful in the treatment of this client group.

Kushner and Mueser (1993) have described four general models that might account for the high rate of comorbidity between substance use and severe mental heath problems. These models include the *common factor* model, the *secondary substance abuse* model, the *secondary psychopathology* model and the *bidirectional* model. These models are summarised in Figure 1.1. For a more in-depth review, see Mueser, Drake and Wallach (1998), and Phillips and Johnson (2001). For disorder-specific reviews, see Blanchard et al. (2000) on schizophrenia, Kushner, Abrams and Borchardt (2000) on anxiety disorders, Strakowski et al. (2000) on bipolar disorder, Swendsen and Merikangas (2000) on depression and Trull et al. (2000) on borderline personality disorder.

Common factor models propose that one or more factors independently increase the risk of both mental health and substance use problems. That is, there are shared vulnerabilities to both disorders. Three potential common factors have been the focus of some research—familial (genetic) factors, ASPD and common neurobiological dysfunction—although many other factors are possible. If genetic factors, ASPD or some other factor was found

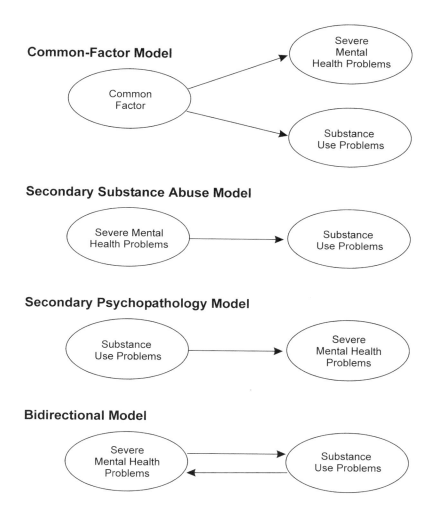

Figure 1.1 Models of comorbidity
From Mueser et al. (2003)

independently to increase the risk of both mental health and substance use problems, this would support the common factor model.

Secondary substance abuse models posit that high rates of comorbidity are the consequence of primary mental health problems leading to substance use problems. Within this general model, three different models have been suggested: *psychosocial risk factor* models (that is, clients use substances to "feel better"; this includes the self-medication, the alleviation of dysphoria and the multiple risk factor models), the *supersensitivity model* (that is, psychological vulnerability to mental health problems results in sensitivity to small amounts of alcohol and drugs, leading to substance use problems) and *iatrogenic vulnerability to substance abuse.*

The secondary psychopathology model of comorbidity is the exact opposite of secondary substance abuse models. Secondary psychopathology models posit that substance use problems lead to or trigger a long-term psychiatric disturbance that would not otherwise have developed.

The bidirectional models propose that severe mental health and substance use problems interact to trigger and maintain each other. For example, substance use problems trigger severe mental health problems in a vulnerable individual. The severe mental health problems are then subsequently maintained by continued substance use due to socially learned cognitive factors such as beliefs, expectancies and motives for substance use (Mueser, Drake & Wallach, 1998).

The available research evidence suggests that there are many possible explanations for why clients with severe mental health problems are so vulnerable to substance use problems. No single model can explain this, and it is likely that multiple models contribute to the coexistence of these two problems, both within and across clients. Thus, in summary, different theories have been proposed to address the high rates of coexistence of severe mental health and substance use problems. Two models have the greatest empirical support: the supersensitivity model (that is, biological vulnerability to mental health problems lowers the threshold for experiencing negative consequences from relatively small quantities of substances) and the ASPD common factor model (that is, ASPD independently increases the risk of developing a severe mental health problem and a substance use problem). However, it is important to note that common social and personal factors (for example, socio-economic factors and deprivation) may also increase the likelihood of ASPD, thereby, in turn, increasing the likelihood of the development of coexisting mental health and substance use problems. The self-medication model (that is, high comorbidity is due to clients' attempts to treat their own symptoms with substances) does not appear to explain the high rate of substance misuse in clients with severe mental health problems, although there does appear to be an association between dysphoria and increased rates of substance use problems.

So remember,

- the prevalence of substance abuse/dependence is higher in clients with severe mental health problems than in the general population
- alcohol is typically the most commonly misused substance, followed by cannabis and cocaine/crack, although drug misuse may be more common in some urban areas
- diagnostic groups do not tend to differ in their preference for one type of substance over another; availability is the most important determinant of which substances are used problematically
- higher rates of substance abuse tend to be found in clients who are male, young, poorly educated and single
- substance use problems are associated with a wide range of negative outcomes, including relapses and rehospitalisations, violence, suicide, interpersonal problems, legal repercussions, health consequences and higher treatment costs
- two of the models proposed to address the high rate of coexistence of severe mental health and substance use problems have the greatest empirical support: the supersensitivity model and the common-factor model; the self-medication model does not have great support.

OBSTACLES TO TREATMENT AND BEHAVIOUR CHANGE

When clinicians attempt to engage and offer treatment to clients with severe mental health problems who use alcohol/drugs problematically, they often encounter a number of obstacles to change. Some of these may be due to motivation, cognitive deficits and social factors that are directly related to experiencing severe mental health problems (Bellack & Gearon, 1998; Drake et al., 2001). In working with this population, it is important to take these factors into consideration.

Motivation

People in the general population who use substances problematically often experience fluctuating motivation to change. However, among those with severe mental health problems, motivation is often confounded by a number of additional factors. These include low self-efficacy, primary negative symptoms of severe mental health problems, such as loss of motivation, energy and drive, apathy and difficulty in experiencing interest or pleasure, and secondary negative symptoms, such as depression and the side effects of medication. Such factors serve generally to reduce motivation among people with severe mental health problems; however, the presence of substance use problems often exacerbates this. Clients may minimise problems related to substance use and focus solely on the perceived positive benefits associated with using substances in the absence of other positive, powerful reinforcers. Thus, motivation often waxes and wanes.

Cognitive

Cognitive functioning is important in making and sustaining changes in behaviour, particularly substance use. People with severe mental health problems, notably schizophrenia, experience significant cognitive impairment (Bellack & Gearon, 1998), some of which may be due in part to the side effects of medication. Specific deficits in the areas of attention, memory, complex cognitive processes and ability for self-reflection are likely to impair utilisation of the standard cognitive and behavioural skills to change alcohol/drug use (Bellack & DiClemente, 1999; Bellack & Gearon, 1998).

Social

The experience of severe mental health problems is often associated with significant feelings of loss. People often lose a social role, and they can be excluded from the normative routes of gaining pleasure and social contact due to the associated stigma of mental health problems. Poor skills and confidence in social situations, school and vocational failure, poverty, lack of adult role responsibilities, lack of structured and meaningful daily activities, and living in neighbourhoods with high rates of drug availability and deviant subgroups may increase exposure to substance-using social networks (Dusenbury, Botvin & James-Ortiz, 1989; Pandina et al., 1990), and substance use may facilitate social interactions with peers (Drake, Brunette & Mueser, 1998; Salyers & Mueser, 2001). The combined effect of severe mental health problems and problematic substance use on interpersonal conflict and financial problems often renders these clients highly vulnerable socially to exploitation by drug dealers and involvement in illegal behaviours (Mueser et al., 2001).

All of these factors can present as obstacles to engaging clients in treatment and behaviour change. However, awareness of these factors can signal the specific treatment needs of this population and guide the treatment-planning process.

TREATMENT NEEDS

The C-BIT approach is based on the principles of integrated treatment (Drake et al., 2001; Graham et al., 2003; Mueser, Drake & Noordsy, 1998a; Mueser et al., 2003), which are driven by the specific treatment needs of people with severe mental health problems who use alcohol/drugs problematically. These include the following principles.

Integration of Mental Health and Substance Misuse Treatments

Treatment programmes that fully integrate the treatment of substance use problems into mental health treatment can overcome many of the disadvantages of traditional sequential or parallel approaches to the treatment of this client group. First, organisational and administrative lapses are effectively eliminated with integrated treatment because limited coordination between different service providers is required: in the main, both mental health and substance misuse services are provided by the same team/clinician. Second, clinical problems related to treating one problem first and the other disorder second are avoided with integrated treatment, as both problems are viewed as "primary" and are targeted for concurrent treatment. Third, conflict between the different philosophical perspectives of mental health and substance misuse professionals on treating combined problems is minimised when the clinicians work side-by-side, and, preferably, for the same agency. In addition, an integrated approach to the treatment of this client group enables the dynamics and interrelationships between the problems the clients present with to be identified, explored and addressed in a systematic and holistic manner.

Assertive Outreach

An *assertive* approach to treatment recognises that clinicians cannot passively wait for clients to demonstrate the initiative and motivation to seek out treatment for their substance use or mental health problems on their own. However, it is important to recognise and be aware that an assertive approach can at times be experienced by clients and their families as intrusive. Thus, although clinicians must make every effort possible to engage reluctant clients actively in treatment, this needs to be done in a sensitive and collaborative way, connecting with clients in their natural environments and providing practical assistance with immediate goals defined by clients (such as housing, medical care, crisis management and obtaining legal aid). Hence, assertive outreach becomes a means of developing trust and a working alliance between the clinician and the client, not only improving medication adherence and monitoring but also enhancing quality of life and the recovery process.

Collaborative Relationship Between the Client and the Clinician

Integrated treatment is based on a collaborative relationship, where the client works in collaboration with the clinician to tackle the problems he/she is experiencing. A positive working alliance becomes a way of engaging clients in the treatment process and providing support for change.

Stage-Wise Approach to Treatment

It is often tempting to run ahead and set idealistic goals of detoxification and abstinence for this client group. However, these goals are often not based on the current engagement and motivation of the client, and thus attempts to implement such interventions result in perceptions of "failure", frustration and disengagement. Thus, a key principle of integrated treatment is to set realistic goals and interventions that are matched to the phase of engagement and stage motivation.

Comprehensive Services

Individuals with severe mental health problems who problematically use alcohol/drugs typically have a wide range of needs, such as finding work or other meaningful activity; improving the quality of family and social relationships; developing a capacity for independent living, leisure and recreation; and developing skills for managing anxiety, depression and other negative moods. Integrated treatment programmes need to be *comprehensive* because the recovery process occurs longitudinally in the context of making many life changes. In addition, even before clients have acknowledged the problems associated with their substance use or have developed motivation to reduce alcohol and drug use, they can make progress by improving their skills and supports. These improvements can increase clients' hopefulness about making positive changes and facilitate their subsequent efforts to change their destructive involvement with substances.

Optimism About the Long-Term Effects of Treatment

Research suggests that integrated-treatment programmes do not produce dramatic changes in most clients over short periods of time; rather, clients gradually improve over time, with approximately 10–20 per cent achieving stable remission of their substance use problems per year. As clinicians, we can at times become disheartened when clients make significant strides forward and successfully change their substance use, only to slip back. However, reflection on how many times we have tried to change a given behaviour/habit and found ourselves slipping back gives some idea of how difficult behaviour change is. Bellack and Gearon (1998) summarise the consensus view on a long-term and optimistic treatment approach quite aptly. They suggest, "There is also general agreement that treatment must be conceptualized as an ongoing process in which motivation to reduce substance use waxes and wanes. They need the ongoing support provided by programs that extend over time and are tolerant of patients dropping in and out, sometimes trying to quit and sometimes not, abstaining for a while only to relapse'' (page 750).

Optimal Prescribing of Medication for Both Mental Health and Substance Use Problems

Reasons for using substances or substance-related beliefs can often be associated with the negative effects of medication, psychiatric symptoms and withdrawal effects. Optimal prescribing of medication often stabilises psychiatric symptoms and reduces withdrawal effects, and can reduce cravings and urges to use substances (Day, Georgiou & Chrome, 2003).

So remember,

- potential obstacles to engage clients in treatment and changing their substance-using behaviours include fluctuating motivation, cognitive deficits and social factors
- the treatment of people with severe mental health problems who use alcohol/drugs problematically needs to include integration, assertive approaches, collaboration and stage-wise interventions. It must address a range of needs over the long term, and clinicians will need to remain optimistic
- optimal medication may increase engagement and reduce cravings to use alcohol or drugs.

Chapter 2

OVERVIEW OF C-BIT APPROACH

OBJECTIVES

The overall objective of C-BIT is to help clients negotiate and maintain behaviour change related to their problematic drug/alcohol use. In line with this, clinicians using C-BIT encourage clients to develop "healthy" alternatives to drug/alcohol misuse, and to recognise the relationship between substance use and mental well-being.

C-BIT is based on a harm-reduction approach (Heather et al., 1993; Marlatt, 1998). Thus, a positive change in terms of a client's problematic drug/alcohol use could be, for example, a reduction in the amount or types of substances used problematically, or a change in the way the substance is used, or even abstinence. However, abstinence is not seen as the only possible goal. Within C-BIT, problematic drug/alcohol use is seen as a pattern of substance use and related negative consequences that interferes with clients achieving their self-identified goals. It is also a pattern of substance use that negatively affects clients' well-being (that is, spiritual, social, physical, psychological/mental and occupational). It is the aim of C-BIT to help clients achieve their self-identified goals within their spiritual and cultural frame of reference.

The aims of C-BIT are thus threefold. First, it aims collaboratively to identify, challenge and undermine unrealistic beliefs about drugs or alcohol that maintain problematic use, and replace them with more adaptive beliefs that will lead to and strengthen behavioural change. Second, it seeks to facilitate an understanding of the relationship between problem substance use and mental health problems. Third, it teaches specific skills for controlling and self-managing substance use and the early warning signs of psychosis, and for developing social support for an alternative lifestyle.

STRUCTURE

The C-BIT approach to problem substance use among those with severe mental health problems is a structured but flexible treatment approach that consists of the following core components: an assessment phase (*screening and assessment*), four treatment phases (*engagement and building motivation to change; negotiating some behaviour change; early relapse prevention;* and *relapse prevention and relapse management*), and two additional treatment components (*skills building* and *working with families and social network members*) that are designed to be used in parallel with the four treatment phases, where appropriate.

The core components of C-BIT seek to target the substance use problem and its interaction with mental health problems in a stage-wise approach. The two additional components complement the core components and provide guidelines for clinicians to address specifically any skills deficits (management of moods, communication, self-esteem and lifestyle balance) and needs of the social network that may improve the client's ability to make and sustain behaviour change. The additional components are designed to be used alongside each of the four treatment phases, when appropriate.

The four treatment phases in the core component can be moved through sequentially (that is, phase 1 through 4). Progression in this way typically takes about 6 months with a client who is initially not engaged in or working on his/her drug/alcohol use. However, for the majority, the amount of time spent in each treatment phase varies from client to client. It is also possible that a client will have a relapse following a long period of non-problematic use/abstinence, and the clinician will then need to revisit the appropriate earlier phase. Some clients may need to spend as much as 6 months in treatment phase 1 (that is, *engagement and building motivation to change*), whereas other clients may have already thought about changing their drug/alcohol use or have made changes themselves. If this is the case, start at the C-BIT treatment phase most suitable for the client at that particular point (that is, in the first case, *negotiating some behaviour change* and, in the second case, *early relapse prevention/relapse prevention and relapse management*). Typically, with many clients with severe mental health problems who use alcohol/drugs problematically, a long-term and optimistic approach needs to be taken.

Although the C-BIT approach seeks to encourage clients to move through the phases and achieve non-problematic alcohol/drug use, it is important to emphasise that, due to C-BIT's harm-reduction philosophy, it is not necessary with all clients to move through all the phases. The harm-reduction goal set with each client will be one that is realistic and achievable, so that a "successful outcome" can be achieved during any of the four treatment phases and can be defined as the client achieving the harm-reduction goal.

HOW TO KNOW WHEN TO MOVE ON TO THE NEXT PHASE

The four treatment phases in C-BIT (that is, *engagement, negotiating behaviour change, early relapse prevention*, and *relapse prevention/management*) roughly correspond to the four stages in the "stages of treatment" as described by Mueser, Drake and Noordsy (1998) and Mueser et al. (2003) (that is, engagement, persuasion, active treatment and relapse prevention). Table 2.1 provides a guide to determine how engaged in treatment the client is and which C-BIT treatment phase/interventions are most likely to be useful at a given point.

To help you decide when you should move on with your client to the next C-BIT phase/intervention, refer to the C-BIT decisional flow chart (Figure 2.1). Once you have done this, the next step is to develop an individualised treatment plan formally to guide the treatment intervention process.

To work through the decisional flow chart and develop a treatment plan, it will be useful to have a client in mind, as in the following example.

Gerry is a 32-year-old man diagnosed with bipolar affective disorder 3 years ago. He has a history of using cannabis and alcohol since his teens. He initially became unwell following the breakdown of a long-term relationship and increased his cocaine use. He usually adheres to his medication but reduces it at times, as he believes it makes him feel "tired and flat". He works in his family's business but feels that his family are quite critical of him and do not acknowledge his efforts. When he feels stressed or anxious in social situations, he sometimes becomes paranoid and experiences grandiose delusions. He uses alcohol and cocaine in a binge pattern, mainly over weekends. He says he feels "great and energetic—the life and soul of the party", and is liked and accepted by others when he is using. He is aware that after a binge he feels tired and low in mood and gets into arguments with his family. Due to these problems, he has had periods of abstinence from cocaine for up to 2 months and says that he needs to stop using. However, at times he believes that a drug-free life is "boring" and thus has lapsed back to using when he has felt "flat" or low in mood.

From this case example, we can see that Gerry has made "some" attempts to change his cocaine use. Thus, according to the decisional flow chart, he would benefit from interventions in C-BIT phase 3 and eventually C-BIT phase 4, focusing on relapse-prevention/management skills for his substance use and mental health problems. However, the example indicates that he is not always adherent to medication. Thus, from the flow chart, we can see that Gerry may also benefit from some further intervention such as medication compliance

Table 2.1 Phases of treatment, definitions and C-BIT interventions (adapted from Mueser, Drake & Noordsy, 1998)

Phase	Definition	Goal	C-BIT intervention
Engagement	Client does not have regular contact with keyworker and does not discuss alcohol/drug use. *"It's up to me if I want to smoke cannabis—and I don't want to talk about it."*	To establish a working alliance with the client and be able to discuss alcohol/drug use and any problems it may be causing.	**Treatment phase 1** *plus* **Skills building and working with families/social network members where appropriate**
Negotiating behaviour change	Client has regular contact with keyworker but does not want to work on reducing problematic alcohol/drug use. *"My alcohol use is not a problem so why should I cut down?"*	To develop the client's awareness of problems associated with alcohol/drug use and build motivation to change.	**Treatment phase 2** *plus* **Skills building and working with families/social network members where appropriate**
Early relapse prevention	Client is motivated to change problematic alcohol/drug use (as indicated by serious attempts at reduction for at least 1 month but less than 6 months). *"Using crack has caused me a lot of problems—so I have to stop using."*	To help client further reduce alcohol/drug use and, if possible, attain abstinence.	**Treatment phase 3** *plus* **Skills building and working with families/social network members where appropriate**
Relapse prevention/ management	Client has not experienced problems related to alcohol/drug use for at least 6 months or is abstinent. *"Since I've cut down I'm not hearing voices—I want to get on with my life."*	To maintain awareness that relapse could happen and to extend recovery to other areas (such as mental health, social, relationships, work).	**Treatment phase 4** *plus* **Skills building and working with families/social network members where appropriate**

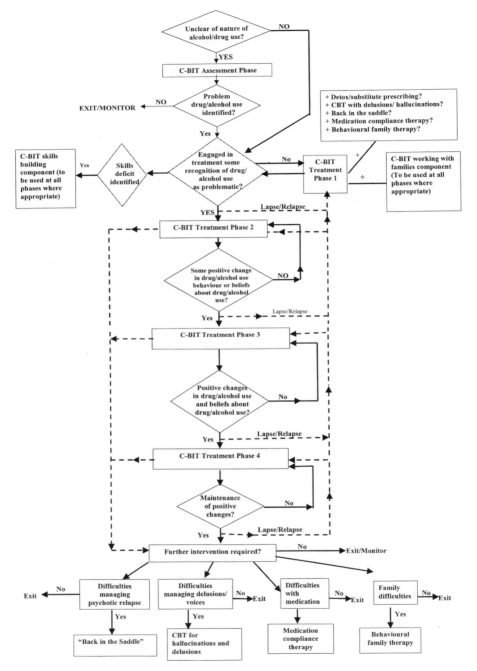

Figure 2.1 Cognitive-behavioural integrated treatment approach (C-BIT) decisional flow chart: How to know when to move on to the next phase

therapy (Kemp & David, 1996; Kemp et al., 1996). Gerry also finds it difficult to cope with certain moods. Therefore, some work could be done with him from the C-BIT skills-building component ''Coping with Different Moods'' (page 122). A number of difficulties within his family are highlighted. It may be that they would find the C-BIT ''Working with Families/Social Network Members'' component (page 215) and ''Behavioural Family Therapy'' (Barrowclough, 2003; Falloon et al., 1996; Sheils & Rolfe, 2000) of help in improving understanding and re-establishing effective communication skills within the family.

Gerry's treatment plan would need to incorporate the above suggestions and would be guided by five main factors:

(1) his ''stage of engagement'' with you in the treatment process (see Table 2.1)
(2) his ''stage of change''
(3) the function of his alcohol/drug use
(4) his alcohol/drug-related beliefs
(5) his goals/staff goals.

To assess formally which stage of engagement with treatment your client is in, you can use the Substance Abuse Treatment Scale (Mueser et al., 2003). In addition, the spiral ''stage of change'' model (Prochaska, DiClemente & Norcross, 1992) will help you to get a sense of your client's readiness to change his/her alcohol/drug use. The model roughly describes the stages of pre-paredness to change (pre-contemplation, contemplation, preparation, action and maintenance) that people go through when attempting to change a given behaviour (see Table 2.2). To help formally assess what stage your client is in with regard to changing his/her alcohol/drug use, you can use the Readiness to Change (treatment version) assessment measure (Heather et al., 1999).

Table 2.2 Stages of behavioural change

Stage	Definition/characteristics
Pre-contemplation	No desire to change, does not see behaviour as problematic May come into treatment because of pressure from others
Contemplation	Is becoming aware of the problem and is considering changing, but has not taken any action in this direction
Preparation	Planning to make changes and take the necessary steps in the near future. May have attempted unsuccessfully to change recently
Action	In the throes of changing factors in lifestyle and environment to help overcome problematic behaviour
Maintenance	Focused on preventing relapse

For example, Gerry's treatment plan would look something like this:

NAME: Gerry

DATE:

REVIEW DATE:

Stage of engage-ment	Stage of change	Function of use	Beliefs	Goals	Areas of inter-vention	By whom
Early relapse prevention	Preparation	To cope with anxiety in social situations and to be accepted by others	Alcohol and cocaine make me feel great and energetic The life and soul of the party	Client goals: Not feel flat and tired on medication Help to cope with stress More support from family Staff goals: (1) Improve medication adherence (2) Anxiety (3) Improve family support and include social network member	(1) Medi-cation (2) Positive beliefs about alcohol and cannabis (3) Man-aging moods (4) Family/ social network	Gerry/ keyworker/ social network member

Compiled by:

TREATMENT SESSIONS

The treatment phases are constructed in such a way to allow clinicians to address some aspect of a client's drug/alcohol use in whatever time available. For example, if a client does not see cannabis use as a problem, but you wish to begin to discuss it, you could spend 10 minutes focused on the section "How to Put Drug/Alcohol Use on the Agenda" (Chapter 5). The next time you see the client, she/he may be more willing to discuss cannabis use openly, and you could spend 20 minutes focused on this section, and so on. The aim of the C-BIT approach is to give clinicians a usable, structured but flexible way of addressing problematic drug/alcohol use with clients.

C-BIT is structured in the sense that it provides a systematic method for clinicians to address their clients' alcohol/drug use. However, it is also flexible, as it allows clinicians to deliver snippets of the treatment in the time available to them and over whatever time period is appropriate for their clients. Within C-BIT, each time you meet with your client, it is not seen as necessary, particularly during the first phase of treatment, to set a formal agenda of things to address during the session. However, it is still important to have an informal "agenda", that is, a clear focus for what you will hope to address during a given meeting with your client, to ensure that the client's substance use is addressed in a collaborative, systematic and structured fashion. In the subsequent phases, when you meet with the client, it is important that an agenda for issues that will be focused on during your meetings be agreed on from the outset. This will typically include any current issues/concerns the client has, a review of his/her past week including alcohol/drug use, a review of the last session/meeting or the tasks the client agreed to do, and any other additional matters that you feel would be helpful to focus on.

At the end of each meeting or treatment session, it is important to summarise the information covered in the session and reinforce/highlight any decisions for change that have been made. This will ensure that motivation is harnessed and a plan is made for the client to take the next step. This could include a brief assessment of the client's motivation to change with the "importance-confidence" ruler (Rollnick et al., 1997). The importance-confidence ruler acts as a rough indicator of whether the client will actually carry out the tasks or changes discussed in the session. That is, if clients rate the changes discussed and agreed on in the session as important and indicate that they feel confident about making the changes, then they are more likely to make change than if they do not.

Chapter 3

OVERVIEW OF C-BIT THEORY AND TECHNIQUES

BRIEF INTRODUCTION TO COGNITIVE THERAPY

Cognitive Therapy for Emotional Disorders

The C-BIT approach to problem substance use among those with severe mental health problems is based on the premises of the cognitive therapy model (Beck, 1976; Salkovskis, 1996), which has been established as an effective treatment of emotional disorders (e.g., Clark & Steer, 1996). Cognitive therapy identifies certain thinking patterns/styles and thoughts as central in the development and maintenance of problems. Fundamentally, the cognitive model posits that thoughts and beliefs affect the way people feel and behave.

An example commonly used to illustrate the cognitive model is as follows. If you were lying upstairs in bed at night, and you heard a loud crashing sound downstairs, and the thought ran through your mind, "It's a man with an axe, come to burgle my house, and he will attack me," you would tend to notice changes in your body (for example, heart racing, sweating and butterflies in your stomach), your mood (that is, anxious and nervous), and behaviour (for example, fight or flight). If, however, you subsequently thought, "It's the cat— He's knocked over a vase downstairs," the bodily changes would start to subside, your mood would become calmer and so would your behaviour.

The key difference between the two emotional responses in the example are "thoughts". In the first instance, the thought, "It's an axe man, come to burgle my house, and he will attack me", is one which will promote anxiety. However, in the latter instance, the thought, "It's the cat—he's knocked over a vase downstairs", holds no threat value and thus leads to a positive change in mood. Padesky and Greenberger (1995) have highlighted the importance of also taking into account the role of environmental factors (such as social, economic, cultural and political) on the impact that thoughts have on mood, biology and behaviour.

Beck (1976) developed the cognitive model from his experiences as a psychiatrist working with people with depression. He found that there were a number of commonalities among the people he saw. Thus, Beck suggested that when people experience troubling and persistent problems with their emotions (that is, depression, anxiety, anger and guilt), these can lead to engagement in certain disruptive behaviours (such as avoidance, social withdrawal and self-harming). These are said to be the result of maladaptive thoughts (that is, negative automatic thoughts) that pop into our heads on a daily basis in given situations. He said that these thoughts are related to underlying beliefs (that is, core beliefs and dysfunctional assumptions/conditional beliefs) that are typically negative, inaccurate and self-defeating. These underlying beliefs are said to lie dormant unless activated by critical life events. Inherent in these thoughts and beliefs are said to be cognitive distortions that contribute to the emotional disturbance. Beck suggested that this maladaptive style of thinking is the result of early life experiences.

Beck and his colleagues (Beck, 1976; Thase & Beck, 1993) have suggested that this maladaptive pattern of thinking needs to be the target of treatment. The therapist's role, within cognitive therapy, is to guide clients to identify and re-evaluate their pattern of thinking, and to generate alternative, more helpful ways of thinking as a way of targeting emotional and behavioural problems (Greenberger & Padesky, 1995; Hawton et al., 2001; Padesky & Greenberger, 1995).

Application of the Cognitive Model to Psychosis

An area of development in cognitive therapy has been the application of cognitive approaches to people with severe mental health problems, particularly psychosis (e.g., Fowler et al., 1995; Kingdon & Turkington, 1994). For example, a cognitive model put forward by Tarrier and Calam (2002) emphasises a stress-vulnerability model. They emphasise vulnerability characteristics in a person's background (such as social deprivation and biological predisposition), rather than early life experiences, as contributing to specific individual predispositions to developing emotional or psychotic disorders. They suggest that proximal factors, such as stressors (for example substance use and family conflict) increase the risk of destabilisation (that is, loss of emotional homeostasis/balance) and activation of these underlying vulnerability characteristics. The experience of psychosis and the associated experiences are said to be mediated by beliefs. That is, if the psychosis and related experiences are perceived as a traumatic event, it is said to disturb the equilibrium of a person's life.

Cognitive Therapy for Problematic Substance Use

In the same vein, cognitive therapy has been extended to the treatment of substance abuse. It suggests that an important difference between individuals who use drugs or alcohol problematically and those who do not is the beliefs held about the substance (Beck et al., 1993). For example, the belief of a problem drinker may be, "Without a drink I can't relax." For such a person, these alcohol-related beliefs are often held rigidly, tend to be overgeneralised and are typically "all or nothing" in nature. In contrast, someone who drinks alcohol socially may think more flexibly about alcohol ("I often find drinking with friends relaxing"). Within the cognitive model for substance abuse (Beck et al., 1993; Liese & Franz, 1996), cognitions at a number of levels are seen as pivotal in the development and maintenance of problem drug and alcohol use. Some of these cognitions are general core beliefs ("I am inadequate") and dysfunctional assumptions/conditional beliefs ("If I try to please people, they will think well of me"). Other beliefs and automatic thoughts specific to substance use are called substance-related beliefs ("If I have a drink, it will take away my depression") (Beck et al., 1993; Liese & Franz, 1996).

People are often unaware of the relationship between thinking and feeling. However, mood, behaviour and thoughts are inextricably connected and contribute to cravings for alcohol or drugs. Thoughts such as "I can't cope without a drink", "I'll feel good if I use some crack" and "Smoking cannabis will make the voices stop" are positive substance-related beliefs that encourage continued use of the substance in a problematic pattern. Such substance-related beliefs, although often not 100 per cent true, actually increase cravings to use. These beliefs that encourage alcohol and drug use are mediated or triggered by mood states, situations, people, money or mental health symptoms that have become positively associated with alcohol or drug use. If a client has made a decision to stop using or to cut down, these thoughts will pop into his/her head more frequently, thus intensifying cravings and urges to use. Note the situation, mood, thought and behaviour (drug use) connection in the following case example:

Robert had been at home for much of the week in his flat alone, feeling a bit bored and fed up. Today was his benefit "pay day", and he felt that he wanted to do something to cheer himself up. Thoughts of buying a small amount of cannabis kept popping into his head, but he pushed them aside because he had made a decision to stop smoking, which he had found made him feel paranoid. Robert went to collect his money and walked back past his friend's flat where he used to smoke. Robert started to remember the "good times" he used to have there, and before long was ringing his friend's doorbell. His friend was just about to smoke and offered Robert some. Initially, he refused, but then the thought popped into his head, "I've been really good and not had any for months so I should be OK if I just have one." The following day Robert felt quite disappointed in himself that he had used, but couldn't understand how it happened.

This case example illustrates the connection between Robert's mood (bored and fed up), situations/environment (having money, walking near his friend's house where he used to use), thoughts (wanting to cheer himself up), cravings (desire and urge to use) and behaviour (using cannabis). With continued use of the substance, a network of idiosyncratic substance-related beliefs develop and are activated by particular situations or internal states ("activating stimuli/high-risk situations"). Once activated, these beliefs serve to intensity cravings and urges to use the substance and provide permission to use ("I've been really good and not had any for months, so I should be OK if I just have one"). Problematic patterns of alcohol/drug use are thus maintained by a number of cognitive distortions in these beliefs. These distortions minimise the anticipated and actual negative consequences of use by keeping the person focused exclusively on the positive benefits of use (for example, "Crack isn't the problem—the problem is I don't have enough money. When I use I feel good"). In addition, such cognitive distortions provide justification for continued use ("The only way I can cope with this is to have a drink"). If you notice, one of Robert's thoughts actually gives him permission to use again ("I've been really good and not had any for months, so I should be OK if I just have one").

Substance-related beliefs may develop through environmental and cultural exposure to drug and alcohol use. Early life experiences and core beliefs/ dysfunctional assumptions may serve to increase the individual's vulnerability to substance use problems, particularly if the person is exposed to substance-using environments, and positive beliefs about substance use become more accessible and salient (Liese & Franz, 1996). Cognitive therapy for problem drug or alcohol use thus seeks to target the distortions inherent within these positive substance-related beliefs. The treatment goal thus becomes an attempt collaboratively to generate with the problem substance user alternative and more flexible and realistic ways of thinking about the substance and the impact it is having, and to develop alternative coping strategies.

Cognitive-Behavioural Integrated Treatment (C-BIT)

C-BIT is based on the premise that the cognitive model and treatment approach also apply to people with severe mental health problems who use drugs or alcohol problematically (Figure 3.1) (Graham, 1998, 2003). For those who have a severe mental health problem and misuse drugs or alcohol, the beliefs they hold about the substances they use are sometimes linked to their experience of severe mental health problems. These beliefs may help the person to feel he/she can self-manage or regulate both the symptoms and the experience of having a severe mental health problem (for example, a client may think, "I feel flat on my medication—cocaine makes me feel live, kicking and buzzing"). Thus, drugs and alcohol may become a coping

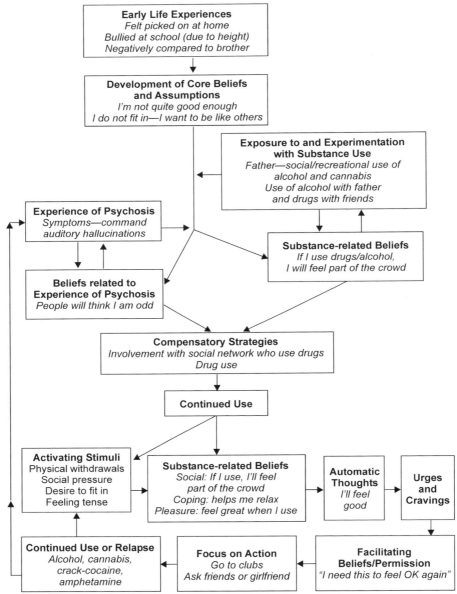

Jake's case conceptualisation based on the cognitive-developmental model of concurrent psychosis and problem substance use

Figure 3.1 Cognitive developmental model of problem substance use and concurrent psychosis

strategy, a means of increasing feelings of pleasure and aid socialisation (Graham, 1998, 2003).

The stress and trauma of a person experiencing psychosis and the associated experiences may well disturb the equilibrium of that person's life, as suggested previously. Thus, alcohol/drug use and the social networks associated with use are often an attempt to restore the balance. Such reasons for using substances and the positive expectations of use are often quite important in an individual's mind, and thus may often be reinforced by continued use. Even though at times there may be negative consequences related to drug or alcohol use, such as debts or increased feelings of paranoia, the positive and more immediate effects often outweigh the long-term negative effects. The distortions in logical reasoning minimise the negative consequences of use and focus attention on its positive benefits. Thus, the positive beliefs held about the effectiveness of substance use generally remain unchallenged. The result is often ambivalence about change or a lack of desire to change. Attempts to encourage or tell the client to stop using will be met with resistance unless these positive substance-related beliefs are directly targeted and modified, and the person is able to recognise the negative impact of substance use on his/her life.

Motivational, Social and Behavioural Elements

The C-BIT approach also includes motivational, social and behavioural elements. The use of motivational, social and behavioural elements within the approach is to facilitate this cognitive process, that is, a shift in beliefs held about the substance. The motivational element serves to initiate the change process, to shift the focus and increase awareness of the impact of the negative aspects of problem substance use that the individual may have disregarded, ignored, minimised or simply traded for positive expectancies about the substance. Motivational interviewing (Miller & Rollnick, 1991) is an approach shown to build motivation and commitment to change. The use of techniques from this approach facilitates the engagement of individuals who initially present as ambivalent or not desirous of change. They help the individual begin to focus on the problems associated with his/her drug or alcohol use and the cognitive distortions that maintain his/her problematic substance use.

Drug and alcohol use are highly social activities. Within the field of addictive behaviours and the cognitive model for substance abuse, social factors are seen as important in the aetiology, onset, and maintenance and change of substance use behaviours. The use of alcohol and drugs typically occurs in social situations and often has ramifications for social relationships and social functioning. As substance use increases in severity, an individual's energy, activities, social networks and relationships increasingly revolve around the person's substance use. Often clients with severe mental health and substance use problems describe their social networks as consisting almost exclusively of drinking and drug-using peers (Drake, Bebout & Roach, 1993). These social groups become ones in which a more favoured identity and social acceptance can be readily found, whereas, in "conventional society", there is less acceptance of apparently odd or bizarre behaviours that can often be related to psychosis. However, if such people are to make significant changes in drinking or drug-use behaviour, they need to reduce their contact with, and reliance on, drinking and drug-using peers, particularly in the early stages of the change process (Trumbetta et al., 1999). Attention therefore needs to be paid to the development of a replacement "healthy" network which attempts to fulfil the positive functions of a social network without encouraging the harmful use of substances (Drake, Bebout & Roach, 1993).

There are a number of approaches to the treatment of addiction problems that involve families and concerned others in the treatment process. Examples include network therapy (Galanter, 1993; Galanter & Kleber, 1999), the community reinforcement approach (Meyers, Dominguez & Smith, 1996; Sisson & Azrin, 1989) and social behaviour and network therapy (Copello et al., 2002). The approaches have more recently been applied to people with coexisting severe mental health and substance use problems in the form of behavioural family therapy (Barrowclough, 2003; Mueser & Fox, 2002). Such techniques within a cognitive approach for the drug or alcohol user with severe mental health problems provide social support for the new way of thinking about the substance and behaviour change, and challenge the old thinking that maintained problematic use.

The behavioural elements included within C-BIT are relapse prevention and skills building. These are essential cognitive-behavioural approaches that provide a person who has begun a behavioural change process with alternative adaptive coping skills that will consolidate the change process. These approaches assist in not only preventing but also managing any potential relapses to problematic drug or alcohol use and/or acute psychosis. Relapse-prevention techniques and skills building are particularly important for the problem substance user who also experiences severe mental health problems. These strategies aim to empower the individual to self-manage the interaction between the symptoms of mental health problems and substance use that may precipitate a relapse to not only problem substance use but also acute mental health problems.

COGNITIVE THERAPY TECHNIQUES IN C-BIT

C-BIT utilises the standard techniques of cognitive therapy for emotional disorders, with some adaptations to meet the needs of those clients who experience a severe mental health problem and use substances problematically. The fundamental aim of these techniques is to help clients to recognise the role of positive substance-related beliefs in maintaining problematic patterns of substance use and poor mental health, and to develop alternative, more accurate and balanced beliefs that promote positive behaviour change.

Treatment Style

The style of C-BIT is similar to that used in other applications of cognitive therapy (e.g., Beck, 1976; Padesky & Greenberger, 1995; Salkovskis, 1996). The C-BIT approach is based on a *collaborative relationship* with clients, where the client is working in a partnership with the clinician to tackle the problems he/ she is experiencing. The approach is non-judgemental toward clients and the difficulties they are experiencing; it embraces a relationship which is built on *empathy, warmth, trust and positive regard* (Rogers, 1991). The style of C-BIT is non-confrontational. It seeks to encourage clinicians to adopt a motivational/ educational role in which they use *Socratic questioning* and *guided discovery* to encourage their clients to re-evaluate the beliefs they hold and consider alternative ways of thinking about their alcohol/drug use and coping with their difficulties. Socratic questioning and guided discovery is a fundamental style within cognitive approaches (Padesky, 1993). ''Rather than directly pointing out information that contradicts a client's negative beliefs, a cognitive therapist asks a series of questions to help the client discover alternative meanings'' (Padesky & Greenberger, 1995). It has been suggested that direct confrontation or persuasion will result in resistance to change, whereas a motivational style that guides the client in discovering alternative ways of thinking about his/her problems will result in positive change (Miller & Rollnick, 1991). A technique used within cognitive therapy and C-BIT that illustrates well the Socratic questioning and guided discovery style of eliciting information from clients is the ''three-question technique'', described more fully on page 32.

Case Formulation

In cognitive therapy, an individualised case formulation or conceptualisation is based on the empirically grounded cognitive model and is seen as key in making sense of the client's difficulties. The case formulation provides a systematic framework for understanding the problems a client presents with. It helps the clinician to answer such questions as how the problems developed and are maintained, what is the relationship between the various problems the client has, and what is the most appropriate intervention (Beck et al., 1993; Liese & Franz, 1996; Persons, 1989). Once an assessment has been carried out, the information is used to guide the development of a case formulation. The process of developing a case formulation is covered in detail on page 47 and should be done in collaboration with the client. This ensures that there is a shared understanding between client and clinician that increases the likelihood of a treatment plan's being developed that matches the client's stage of engagement in treatment and stage of change.

Identifying Thoughts/Beliefs

You may be wondering how you can go about eliciting and identifying your client's problematic thoughts and beliefs. Three techniques are described below to identify "hot thoughts" through Socratic questioning, thought diaries, and drug and alcohol diaries.

Identify "Hot Thoughts"

Some cognitive therapists refer to these thoughts as "hot thoughts" (Greenberger & Padesky, 1995). The typical question asked to elicit these key cognitions is, "Just before you last used/felt that emotion, what went through your mind? Is this the thought that typically goes through your mind?" In addition, when wanting to identify positive substance-related beliefs, you can ask clients what they like about the substance, how they feel the substance helps them, and what they believe are the benefits of using the substance. Asking clients about the benefits of using substances can often be quite an important part of the engagement process, and will help you to understand their reasons for use and the factors that may block their considering change.

Thought Diaries

Thought diaries have been typically used in cognitive therapy to identify current patterns of unhelpful automatic thoughts (see C-BIT Skills-Building Component, page 123). Thought diaries are helpful as they provide a functional analysis of the factors that trigger and maintain problematic thoughts/behaviours/moods. The diary allows the client to record situational and contextual antecedents (that is, where the person was and what he/she was doing when the problematic feelings/behaviour arose), mood (that is, the feelings the person had in that situation), and automatic thoughts (that is, the thoughts that went through the person's mind just before he/she felt that way) (see Appendix 6.2) (Greenberger & Padesky, 1995). Reviewing thought diaries with your client will provide a helpful insight into triggers and maintaining factors, typically thoughts and thinking patterns. These factors will emerge from the patterns or themes of recorded incidents.

Drug and Alcohol Diaries

Drug and alcohol diaries are based on the same principle as standard thought diaries, but the focus is on providing a functional analysis of substance-using behaviour. The diary encourages the client to record the situational and contextual antecedents (that is, day, date, time, where the person was and what was happening), thoughts and feelings (that is, the thoughts and feelings that were present just before the substance was used), behaviour (that is, how much substance was used and money spent) and consequences (that is, how the person thought and felt after using) (see Appendices 0.2 and 0.3) associated with alcohol/drug use. Keeping such a diary allows your client to become aware of the factors that maintain problematic patterns of drug and alcohol use, particularly the key role of positive drug/alcohol-related thoughts and beliefs. Including an opportunity for the client to record how much was spent on the substance allows a chance for reflection on the considerable amount of money spent on this one activity. In addition, the section focused on consequences is useful when helping a client re-evaluate the evidence for positive substance-related beliefs, particularly long-term consequences (see section "strategies to increase awareness of problematic links between mental health and substance use", page 84).

Modifying and Re-evaluating Thoughts/Beliefs

The first step in helping clients re-evaluate their positive substance-related beliefs is to identify cognitive distortions inherent within these beliefs that encourage problematic patterns of use. Once you and your client have identified his/her cognitive distortions, you can begin to help him/her re-evaluate and modify the positive reasons for using and the reasons your client gave against making changes in his/her drug/alcohol use. You will need to acknowledge and emphasise to your client that although drug/alcohol use may meet his/her *immediate short-term* needs it does not always satisfy these needs in the *long-term*. Strategies to help you and your client identify cognitive distortions, and re-evaluate and modify thoughts/beliefs are described in the following sections.

Identifying Cognitive Distortions

You will notice that your client may hold quite positive beliefs about the benefits of using drugs/alcohol, as identified in the comments made about the substance and in the "advantages" column of his/her "advantages–disadvantages analysis" (see page 56). For example, "Without a drink I can't relax", "Cannabis stops my voices", "Everyone I know uses". Inherent within these beliefs are "cognitive distortions" or "thinking errors". These distortions are basically errors in logical reasoning and allow the client to convince or give him/herself permission that it is OK to continue using. We all engage in them at one time or another. With your client, you will need to take a closer look at the "advantages" column in the "advantages–disadvantages analysis" and the *Cons* column in the "decisional balance" (see page 59). Go through each of the reasons the client gave for using/reasons against change, in turn, and identify any "distortions" in these beliefs. If you look closely with your client at the evidence he/she uses to support these beliefs, you may find that the beliefs are *not 100 per cent true all of the time* and that they help your client talk him/herself into using again.

Some examples of common cognitive distortions/thinking errors of people who use drugs/alcohol problematically are listed in the box below.

Minimisation
"I can handle one drink or a little crack."
"Just one won't hurt."

Rationalisation
"I deserve to use this once."

All or nothing thinking
"I've gone past the point of no return, so I may as well continue."
"My voices won't stop unless I smoke cannabis or have a drink."

Overgeneralisation
"Everyone I know uses."

The "Three-Question Technique"

A technique that you will find helpful to assist your client in re-evaluating and modifying the positive reasons for use is the "three-question technique". This technique is based on the notion of Socratic questioning, whereby a series of questions is asked by the clinician to guide a discussion with the client. The client is encouraged by the questions to consider alternative perspectives. Thus, the aim is not to change the client's mind but rather to guide him/her to discover an alternative perspective that reflects, in a balanced way, the evidence (Padesky, 1993). The three questions typically used to guide the discussion are as follows:

(1) What is the evidence for that belief?
(2) Are there times when that is not the case?
(3) If there are times when that is not the case, what are the implications?

For example, if the belief is that "cannabis stops my voices", we may have the following dialogue:

Therapist: *What is the evidence for that belief?*
Shaun: *Whenever I smoke, my voices stop.*
Therapist: *Are there times when that is not the case?*
Shaun: *No well, actually . . . after I smoke two or three joints, then the next day I feel a bit anxious and paranoid and the voices seem worse.*

Therapist: *If there are times when that is not the case, then what are the implications?*

Shaun: *I guess after one or two joints, they do seem to stop for a while, but if I smoke any more, it makes the voices seem worse.*

Therapist: *So, from what you have said, telling yourself, "Whenever I smoke, my voices stop", isn't actually 100 per cent true. A more accurate picture of the way cannabis affects you seems to be, "After one or two joints the voices seem to stop for a while, but if I smoke any more it makes the voices seem worse."*

The clinician's aim here was to help Shaun re-evaluate his initial belief, which was all or nothing and an overgeneralisation. The resultant modified belief is more realistic and is based on the available evidence. Another example of the three-question technique is illustrated below. In this case, the initial belief prevents the client from contemplating change.

For example, the initial belief is, "There is no point in trying to change—I've tried before and failed."

What is the evidence for that belief?

Andrew said that he had tried to stop using cannabis before but had returned to using after one week. He said he usually didn't have much "will-power" to change things, and he gave an example of trying to stop smoking cigarettes for the past year and not being able to.

Have there been times when that has not been the case?

Andrew said that he had been able to cut down his cannabis use when he had to pay off a few debts. He had also stopped smoking cigarettes for two months after he had made a New Year's resolution.

If there are times when that is not the case, what are the implications?

Andrew was eventually able to modify his belief to: "I have been able to make some changes in the past, but will-power isn't enough. This time I have a better chance of success as I have some support and a plan."

In this case, the clinician has helped the client consider evidence that does not support his initial belief. The modified belief helps Andrew to see himself as able to make changes.

Evidence "For" and "Against" in Thought Diaries

Another helpful exercise that encourages clients to re-evaluate their thoughts and beliefs, on a daily basis, is for them to write down in a thought diary the evidence for and against the thoughts, and develop a resultant alternative thought/belief.

If your clients practise re-evaluating unhelpful automatic thoughts, it will encourage flexibility in thinking and open the way to producing new, helpful beliefs about the ability to cope without the use of substances such as: *"I can do this—alcohol actually increases my anxiety; I'll do some relaxation instead. I've done it before without having a drink.''* Helpful thoughts will not be automatic to begin with. They need to be practised, rehearsed and repeated regularly in order to become incorporated into someone's belief system. Such strategies for incorporating new thoughts are described in more detail throughout Part Two of this book, and they are outlined in the following table:

Situation	Moods	Automatic thoughts	Evidence that supports the automatic thought	Evidence that does not support the automatic thought	Alternative/balanced thought
Where were you? What were you doing? Who were you with?	*What did you feel? Rate each mood (0–100%).*	*What was going through your mind just before you felt this way? Which was the most important/worrying thought?*			*Rate how much you believe the alternative thought (0–100%).*
In a meeting at work	*Anxious 90%*	*I need a drink to cope with this. I won't be able to stay in this room. I'm going to make a fool of myself.*	*Everyone else knows more than me. I don't know what I am talking about. I'll go bright red and shaky.*	*Some people here are novices. I have practised my talk. My boss has faith in me.*	*It will be difficult, but I can get through this presentation without making a fool of myself or having a drink. Having a drink may make me do something silly (60%).*

Behavioural Experiments

A behavioural experiment is a practical opportunity for your clients to test out and re-evaluate their thoughts and beliefs in real-life situations (Greenberger & Padesky, 1995). A behavioural experiment also allows your client to discover what will really happen in that situation, which is often not the same as what he/she thinks will happen. To help your client plan and carry out a behavioural experiment, you will find the steps outlined below helpful. By now, you and your client will be aware of what his/her unhelpful thought is, and this will be the thought that you can test out.

For example, fear of being unable to sleep/relax without smoking cannabis in the evening.

Write down the thought to be tested on the Behavioural Experiment Worksheet (Appendix 2.1).

With your client, identify a series of small steps he/she can take to begin to test out this thought. *For example, a first step may be, "Do not smoke cannabis during the day."*

- Get your client to identify what he/she predicts will happen and write this down on his/her worksheet.
- Identify any potential obstacles that may prevent him/her from carrying out the behavioural experiment and strategies to overcome these obstacles.
- Once your client has carried out the experiment, he/she should record the outcome on his/her worksheet.
- To ensure that he/she is really able to test out his/her anxiety provoking thought, identify with your client a number of experiments he/she could try.
- Ask your client to identify what he/she has learned from these experiments and write it down under "lesson learned/take-home message".

Tom's Behavioural Experiment

Thought to be tested *"I'm worried that I won't be able to sleep/relax without smoking cannabis in the evening."*

Experiment	Prediction	Potential obstacles	Strategies to overcome obstacles	Outcome of experiment
Experiment 1 *Do not smoke cannabis during the day.*	*I will feel restless throughout the day.*	*I will get tense and then I will want to have a spliff.*	*Go for a walk if I start to feel tense.*	*I did feel a bit tense, but it passed when I went for a walk and got busy.*
Experiment 2 *Do not smoke cannabis in the evening.*	*I will not be able to fall asleep.*	*My friends may visit me and offer me some cannabis.*	*Go and visit my friend who does not use drugs and spend the evening with him.*	*I did smoke one spliff that evening but it was less than I usually smoke and I did eventually fall asleep.*

Lesson learned/take-home message
"I did feel tense to start with—but when I smoked a lot less than I usually do, I was able to fall asleep, even though it did take a while."

Adaptations of Cognitive Therapy Techniques for People with Serious Mental Health Problems

A number of obstacles have been identified in the treatment of people with severe mental health problems who misuse alcohol and drugs that have been highlighted previously. Two of these obstacles are cognitive deficits and motivation (Bellack & Gearon, 1998; Drake et al., 2001). In the attempt to address these difficulties, C-BIT provides a flexible, albeit structured, approach to treatment. Treatment is not time-limited, sessions are initially quite informal and practical in focus, the length of sessions is determined by the needs of the client, small amounts of information are covered in meetings/ sessions and the style is repetitive over a long-term period. C-BIT seeks to encourage clinicians to present information in a number of ways (verbal, written and practical learning tasks such as behavioural experiments) and to provide frequent summaries of any key learning points during meetings/ sessions with a skills-building focus.

PART TWO

COGNITIVE-BEHAVIOURAL INTEGRATED TREATMENT (C-BIT)

C-BIT CORE COMPONENTS

Chapter 4

ASSESSMENT PHASE: SCREENING AND ASSESSMENT

AIMS

Screening and assessment has three main aims:

(1) To assess the types of substances used and the pattern of use and to determine whether there are problems related to drug/alcohol use which pose a risk to mental health and well-being.
(2) To act as a guide to planning the most appropriate treatment approach and treatment goals.
(3) To engage clients in discussing their substance use and increasing their awareness of the problems caused by their pattern of use.

Outlined within the assessment phase are details of how to assess problematic drug/alcohol use among those with mental health problems. The assessment phase includes a semi-structured clinical interview, screening tools and guidelines on case formulation and how to use the outcome of assessments in treatment planning. The assessment outlined within this phase is not intended to serve as a stand-alone assessment, but rather one which should form part of a fuller assessment process. The C-BIT assessment phase is a specialist assessment. Therefore, its focus is primarily on the assessment of substance use and its impact, and certain areas covered in a more general clinical assessment will not be covered here.

For the semi-structured clinical interview described below, it is recommended that clinicians as far as possible follow the structure outlined. However, it may be that clients are initially unwilling to engage and talk openly about their alcohol and drug use. In such cases, it may be more appropriate initially to go to C-BIT treatment phase 1 and attempt to engage them, and then at a later stage carry out the assessment described below. In other cases, clients may be willing to talk in a limited way about their drug or alcohol use. In such cases, it may be difficult to stick to the structure of the interview. Thus, it would be appropriate to follow the client's lead and gather as much information as possible on that occasion. However, in doing this, it is recommended that you focus on a particular area of the client's substance use, such as current pattern of use, and then at another time collect more detail. In the C-BIT approach, assessment is seen as an ongoing process.

CLINICAL ASSESSMENT OF DRUG/ALCOHOL USE

Helpful resources/references: Beck et al. (1993); Glass, Farrell & Hajek (1991).

As with all assessments, it is important to start the assessment process by building rapport with the client. A strategy that will be helpful is to ask clients about how things are for them at present. This will also give you some ideas about their current functioning. Then you would proceed through the other areas as outlined below. Some examples of the types of questions that can be used are also listed.

(1) *Current functioning.* Information should initially be gathered about current mood, sleeping patterns, appetite/eating patterns, concentration, general motivation and level of interest, daily activities/employment, social support, physical health, suicidal ideation/self-harm behaviours and medication.
(2) *For each substance, ask the client about typical (such as past week) use and current use (previous day).*

   Pattern of use
   • What substances does he/she use?
   • How much does he/she use (cost, quantity and units of alcohol)?
   • Financial cost (per day/per week)? How does he/she fund his/her substance use?
   • How often does he/she use the substance during the week and during a given day? (What time does he/she first use in the morning and how is it spaced throughout the day?)
   • Route of use (smoked, oral, injected, snorted, etc.)? (Has he/she ever injected/shared injecting equipment?)

- Triggers for use or cravings (such as moods, psychotic symptoms or social settings)?
- Moderating factors? (What factors seem to make his/her substance use generally worse/better?)
- How long has he/she used in this pattern? Any recent changes (such as increases/decreases, change of route of administration)?
- Social networks? (Whom does he/she use with and what proportion of the people he/she currently spends time with use substances? How often does he/she use alone?)

Effects of use/other problems
- Withdrawal symptoms experienced when he/she does not have the substance? (For example, first thing in the morning, or if he/she were unable to get hold of the substance, after at least several days of continued use, how would he/she feel?)
- Assess whether client experiences or has experienced any problems resulting from or related to his/her substance use in the following domains:
    mental health/psychotic symptoms
    financial matters/debts
    social/relationships
    physical/health
    housing
    legal/forensic matters
    occupational matters
    child care
    getting aggressive/argumentative.
- Has there been a narrowing of the person's usual repertoire of behaviours, activities or types of substances used?

(3) *Reasons for using and beliefs about substance use.*
- Ask the client what his/her reasons are for using the substance(s) (for example, pleasure, social/cultural and coping). What are some of the things he/she enjoys about using and how has he/she found using substances helpful?
- To help identify beliefs about alcohol/drug use, ask: "What usually goes through your mind just before you use?"
- What are the attitudes of key people in the client's family/social network to drug/alcohol use?

(4) *Take a drug/alcohol history.*
- Developmental history: brief outline of developmental milestones, childhood experiences, family atmosphere, psychosexual experiences, education and occupational/work history.

- Family history: brief outline of parents and siblings, including age, occupation, relationship with client, and family history of substance use and/or mental health problems.
- Age of first use of each substance and how substance use progressed over time.
- When did he/she think that his/her alcohol/drug use became problematic and what was the nature of such problems?
- Periods of abstinence or any changes in use (ask about the most recent period of abstinence and whether he/she has had a period of abstinence; then ask what helped him/her to stop and what helped him/her to remain abstinent).
- Periods of treatment for drug/alcohol use (What types of treatment did he/she find helpful?).

(5) *Assess the relationship between substance use and mental health.* Assess whether the mental health problems/symptoms exist in the absence or presence of substance use.
- If the mental health problem/symptoms are current, determine whether the client has recently used a substance; is the mental health problem due to an acute toxic reaction or is the client experiencing withdrawal effects from the substance?
- When did he/she first experience the mental health problem/ symptoms? Was he/she using substances at that time?
- Does the mental health problem or symptoms occur only during or after recent use of the substance?
- Are there times when the mental health problem/symptoms have improved/worsened? What has helped or made it worse?
- When he/she is using the substance, are the mental health problem/ symptoms worsened? How?
- If he/she has been abstinent from the substance for a few weeks, has he/she continued to experience the mental health problem/symptoms or have these difficulties subsided?
- Is this person's reasons for using substances related to his/her mental health problems/symptoms or his/her experience of taking medication?

(6) *Motivation to change and goals.*
- Does the client see his/her substance use as a problem and want to change or not?
- What does the client see as his/her treatment goal?

ASSESSMENT AND SCREENING TOOLS

In addition to the clinical interview outlined above, it is recommended that some standardised assessment and screening tools be used as and when appropriate. The following assessment and screening tools have been found to be helpful and easy to administer. The tools most appropriate for the client should be used. The assessment and screening tool(s) selected for a given client should be chosen to provide further information/clarify the client's drug/alcohol use. As far as possible and appropriate, it would be useful to carry out a urine analysis and blood test to provide some degree of objective assessment.

Alcohol Screening Measures

Alcohol Use Identification Test (AUDIT) (Saunders et al., 1993)
Michigan Alcohol Screening Test (MAST) (Pokorny et al., 1972)
Blood screen (liver function test).

Drug Screening Measures

Severity of Dependence Scale (SDS) (Gossop et al., 1995)
Drug Abuse Screening Test (DAST) (Skinner, 1982)
Urine analysis.

Assessment of Readiness to Change

Readiness to Change (Treatment Version) Measure (Heather et al., 1999).

Assessment of Stage of Engagement with Treatment

Substance Abuse Treatment Scale (Drake, Mueser & McHugo, 1996).

Assessment of Motivation to Change

Importance-confidence ruler (Appendix 0.1) (Rollnick, Butler & Stott, 1997).

Assessment of Daily Pattern of Substance Use

Drug diary (Appendix 0.2)
Alcohol diary (Appendix 0.3).

Below is outlined information gathered during the assessment of a 23-year-old man. This was his second admission on an acute psychiatric inpatient unit. He had been experiencing auditory hallucinations "voices" telling him to "burn" his neighbour's flat and had taken some steps to act on them. During his intake assessment, he mentioned that he was using drugs and alcohol prior to his admission, but said that he was not willing to discuss it further. However, a few months later, while talking with his primary nurse, he expressed concern about the effect his substance use may have had on him.

Recent Alcohol and Drug Use

Jake's most recent drug and alcohol use was 3 months before, just prior to his hospital admission. At that time, he used cannabis, ecstasy, LSD, alcohol and occasionally crack cocaine. He said he had used ecstasy and LSD on only one occasion, his birthday 3 months before. He described using cannabis on a regular basis, but said he could not recall exactly how much he was using or the cost, but felt it was about £30 per week. He reported using alcohol on a daily basis. This included two to three cans of extra-strong lager (8–12 units of alcohol). He said he would start to drink during the afternoon and into the evening. Sometimes he would drink with friends and sometimes alone. He paid for his drugs and alcohol with benefits or loans from friends or family. He said that he felt the need to drink each day and would crave alcohol every morning. Jake used crack cocaine whenever he had money or could get some on credit from dealers. However, if he started using, he would have what he called a "mad binge" and use up to £60 worth over one or two days.

Jake said that he liked how "good and hyper" he felt when he used drugs and alcohol. It was "something he just likes to do", and it was something "that everybody does". He said he liked some of the hallucinations he experienced through using substances, especially cannabis and LSD. He said that he was a bit worried, as he had noticed that the day after using drugs/alcohol they made "the voices worse and more intense". However, he found that if he continued to use, he would again experience the pleasurable feelings outlined above. The other negative aspects of his substance use, he said, were financial cost, "making him feel sick", "things being distorted and feeling angry, tired and unable to sleep". He said that "everyone" in his social network used substances.

History of Use

Jake has two brothers. He is the middle child. His mum and dad are still together, and he said that he got on "fine" with them, especially his mum. Jake described his mum as very caring but as someone who got "very nervous and wound up about the smallest things". He said that his dad liked a drink and sometimes smoked cannabis. He remembered that when he was a child his mum and dad would, on occasion, row if his dad came home drunk. He got on well with his younger brother as a child, but said he felt picked on by, and was unfavourably compared to, his older brother, who was quite bright, tall and good-looking. Jake said he did reasonably well academically at school and passed five GCSEs, although he was verbally bullied daily and continually teased by the other boys due to his short height. He said that he just never felt "quite good enough" or that he fitted in.

He said that he first used alcohol at 13 years old, when his dad would let him have the "odd alcopop". He first used drugs at the age of 15/16 years with his mates. At that time, he would only use occasionally at weekends. Jake said that he got very interested in dance music when he was 18/19 years and wanted to become a DJ, and so he started hanging around with "clubbers and DJs". He said that he started to use substances more frequently, including amphetamine and ecstasy in dance club settings. He said he wanted to be "part of the crowd". Jake said that his drinking and cannabis quickly increased when he found that cannabis and alcohol helped to "calm his nerves and help him chill out". He said that approximately 2 years before he started to get "pressure and hassle" from his parents to get a "proper job", and so he decided to move out and live with his girlfriend. She occasionally used crack cocaine, and so he decided to try it, as she kept offering him some. He said that he "loved how hyper" it made him feel, and began using it whenever he could. His drug and alcohol use then seemed to increase and became more problematic about 12 months ago, as he was spending all his money on drugs/alcohol, and this was causing arguments in his relationship. He reported that prior to his increased use the voices he was experiencing became more intense, but that he found it harder to ignore them when using or the day after he had used.

He said that he would like to remain abstinent from crack, LSD and speed, but would like to use cannabis and alcohol on an occasional basis.

Mental Health

Jake felt that his mental health problems began over a year ago. At that time, he started to hear the voice of a man. Due to how upset he got as a result of the voices, he was admitted to hospital and on discharge was not experiencing any voices. A few months after his discharge, he recommenced crack use, as, he said, his friends "kept offering him". He does not believe that his drug use became problematic until about 12 months ago. During that time, he said, the voices became much more intense and commanding. The voices were telling him to burn his next door neighbour's flat, as his neighbour was "evil". When asked about this incident, he said he "felt bad" that he had tried to set fire to his neighbour's flat, but that "it was all over now". He thinks that medication has helped him feel better, and he is now less likely to hear the voice. He does think that 12 months ago his mental health problems were made worse by his substance use. His mother is very worried that he will go back to using drugs and alcohol when he is discharged. Jake's father thinks that Jake will be OK if he keeps his cannabis and alcohol use to recreational use.

Physical Health

Jake was quite worried about the amount of weight he had lost when using drugs previously and was quite keen to put on some weight.

Jake's Goals/Plan

Jake's plan is to abstain from crack, LSD and amphetamine. He believes that his substance use makes his psychiatric symptoms worse and that medication has helped him. He is keen not to end up in hospital again. However, he wants to continue to use cannabis and alcohol on an occasional basis. Jake does not appear to have an identified coping strategy or plan to achieve this.

Motivation

Jake's stage of change was "contemplation", and his stage of engagement with treatment was "early persuasion".

Has a Substance Use Problem Been Identified?

Once you have gathered sufficient information during the assessment, you will be able to have some idea of whether a client's drug/alcohol use is problematic. There are a number of factors that will indicate whether drug/alcohol use has become problematic. *Problematic drug/alcohol use can be indicated by any of the following:*

- Self-identified: the client sees his/her drug/alcohol use as causing problems due to its impact on areas of daily living/social functioning (such as legal matters, housing, financial matters, family, social life, work activities or relationships), and mental and physical health.
- Objectively identified: that is, the client's family/friends/professionals involved are concerned about the impact of drug/alcohol use on areas of the client's life. For example, daily living/social functioning (such as legal matters, housing, financial matters, family, social life, work activities, relationships), and mental and physical health.
- The client has difficulty with attempts to control/reduce/stop his/her drug/alcohol use.
- The client shows signs of "substance abuse/substance dependence" (as indicated by a diagnosis or scores on the assessment tools).
- Physical signs: for example, physical signs of withdrawal, physical changes/deterioration, noticeable change in presentation/behaviour, or liver function test revealing damage/deterioration.

If problematic drug/alcohol use has been identified, you will need to proceed with a case formulation and treatment planning. If not, you will not need to take immediate action but should continue to monitor.

CASE FORMULATION

Helpful references/resources: Beck et al. (1993).

A case formulation is a helpful framework to help us make sense of the information gathered during the assessment of the client's current problems. It also helps us to understand how these problems developed and are maintained. It will also serve as a guide to treatment planning. From the details gathered during the assessment, you should be able to develop a case formulation.

To help you to develop a formulation of the client's drug/alcohol use, you will need to generate hypotheses about the following:

(1) What are the factors that maintain these current problems?
(2) How did these problems develop?
(3) What is the relationship between the various problems this client has (particularly drug/alcohol use and mental health problems)?

It might be useful at this stage to refer to the cognitive-developmental model of problem substance use and psychosis (see Figure 3.1), and to use the case formulation worksheet (Appendix 0.4) as a template/guide.

To start the process of developing a formulation, let us begin by trying to answer the three key questions: *What are the factors that maintain these current problems? How did these problems develop? What is the relationship between the various problems this client has (particularly drug/alcohol use and mental health problems)?*

What are the factors that maintain these current problems?

- What are the client's main problems at present?
- What factors (such as situations, moods, psychotic symptoms, withdrawal symptoms or social beliefs about the substance) trigger his/her drug/alcohol use?
- What factors maintain his/her use in a problematic pattern? (What are the client's reasons for using? What are the effects/problems associated with the client's use? What proportion of the client's social network use alcohol/drugs? How does the client talk him/herself into using drugs/alcohol?).
- What beliefs does this person hold about his/her use?
- What positive or negative influences are there towards drug/alcohol use in the social network?

How did these problems develop?

- What key early experiences might have shaped the client's view of him/herself, the world and other people?
- What core/central beliefs does the client hold about him/herself?
- What are the client's conditional beliefs/rules?
- What might have contributed to the client's using substances in the first place?
- What beliefs does the client hold about drugs/alcohol, and how are these beliefs related to core/conditional beliefs?
- What triggered problematic drug/alcohol use?

What is the relationship between the various problems this client has (particularly drug/alcohol use and mental health problems)?

- What is the relationship between the client's substance use and severe mental health problems/treatment?
- What are the links/overlaps in the beliefs this person holds about his/her drug use and mental health problems/treatment?

Let us go back to our case example.

Jake's Case Formulation (see Figure 3.1)

What Are the Factors That Maintain Jake's Current Problems?

Jake had been admitted to hospital, as he had acted on a command hallucination. His problematic drug and alcohol use appeared to exacerbate his mental health difficulties. His substance use also made him feel less able to resist the command hallucinations. Jake's use of alcohol prior to his admission was triggered by physical withdrawal from alcohol, and his use of drugs by a desire to fit in and social pressure from friends to use. Jake holds a number of positive beliefs about drug/alcohol use and the effect substance use will have on him. These beliefs appear to be one of the key factors in maintaining a problematic pattern of use and give him permission to continue using ("It's just something everyone does", "Everyone I know uses", "It helps me to relax and the positive effects are 'wicked'"). Although he is aware of some of the negative effects of using (for example, that substance use makes his psychiatric symptoms worse and financial cost).

From the assessment, it appears that Jake continues to use drugs and alcohol because the immediate pleasurable effects outweigh the long-term negative ones. Another key factor that maintains Jake's drug/alcohol use was his current social network and his desire to "fit in". This means that he would remain vulnerable to lapsing back into a pattern of problematic use, as he says that his friends encourage him to use and the majority of his friends are drug/alcohol users. Moreover, his family disagree about what his goals should be.

How Did Jake's Problems Develop?

From the information gathered in the assessment, we can see that Jake has believed and felt for some time that he was "not quite good enough and that he did not fit in", particularly at school and in comparison to his older brother. However, in an initial attempt to cope with this belief and such feelings, he used drugs and alcohol to "feel a part of the crowd". Jake described a period of problematic drug and alcohol use prior to his recent hospital admission. However, since the age of 18/19 years, Jake's pattern of drug and alcohol use had increased. Jake became more involved in drug/alcohol use when his lifestyle changed, and he began to spend more time in settings where drugs were used and with people who used.

What is the Relationship Between the Various Problems Jake Has (Particularly Drug/Alcohol Use and Mental Health Problems)?

Jake's mental health problems appear to have been present prior to the period of problematic drug and alcohol use. However, his use of substances seems to exacerbate his symptoms and make him feel less able to "control" the voices and therefore more likely to act on them.

Feedback Results of Assessment and Case Formulation

It is important to feedback to the client a summary of the information gathered during the assessment. Where appropriate, this should include the following:

- problems associated with drug/alcohol use (that is, mental health, physical health, financial, legal, occupational, social and housing)
- harmful/hazardous/dependent patterns/levels of use
- any impact on severe mental health and its treatment
- results from blood tests or urine analysis
- case formulation: to help the client begin to understand how his/her problems developed and are maintained. This will also help him/her to begin to think about how he/she can make changes.

TREATMENT PLANNING

By now you will probably already have some ideas about what treatment strategies might be helpful to the client. Some important factors to take into consideration when planning treatment and deciding on the most appropriate intervention are as follows:

- the stage of change the client is in
- the client's stage of engagement with treatment
- the client's self-identified goals and concerns
- short- and long-term treatment needs
- the client's overall needs as recorded in the care plan.

Let us return to our case example.

Jake's Treatment Plan

(1) *Build on Jake's motivation to change (C-BIT treatment phase 2).*
- *Provide psychoeducational information about drugs and alcohol and their impact on mental health and medication to Jake and his family.*
- *Re-evaluate Jake's positive beliefs about the effects/benefits of drug and alcohol use.*
- *Engage Jake in identifying life/personal goals and daily activities of interest.*

(2) *Encourage medication adherence.*
(3) *Develop a relapse-prevention plan (C-BIT treatment phases 3 and 4).*
   - *Identify alternative structured daily activities that help Jake feel good about himself (C-BIT: skills building), and that he can begin to engage in on the ward and when discharged.*
   - *Encourage Jake to monitor early warning signs of psychosis and substance use.*
   - *Develop strategies to cope with "voices" (CBT for delusions and hallucinations).*
(4) *Include family and a social network member in relapse prevention.*
(5) *Provide family with family intervention if appropriate (behavioural family therapy/C-BIT working with families/social network members component).*

C-BIT CORE COMPONENTS

Chapter 5

TREATMENT PHASE 1: ENGAGEMENT AND BUILDING MOTIVATION TO CHANGE

AIM/GOAL

Use an assertive motivational approach to establish a working alliance; that is, a relationship where, together, you can begin to discuss with the client drug/alcohol use, and get the client to identify and become aware of any problems it may be causing.

STRATEGIES TO INCREASE ENGAGEMENT

Some helpful references: Hemming, Morgan and O'Halloran (1999), Mueser, Drake and Noordsy (1998a).

If you are familiar with the principles of assertive community treatment (e.g., Hemming, Morgan & O'Halloran, 1999; Stein & Test, 1980), you will find that the following concepts are known to you. You have probably identified some strategies of your own that have helped you increase and improve engagement with your clients. Listed below are some strategies that have been found to be helpful in building a trusting working relationship with clients who have severe mental health problems as well as a problem with drugs/alcohol. You can use these strategies with your client. They fall into the categories of *assertive outreach, motivational* and *attitudes approaches*.

Assertive Outreach Approach

Practical Assistance

Offer practical assistance with everyday tasks without focusing initially on the drug/alcohol use in an attempt to develop a collaborative working alliance. For example, help the client secure appropriate benefits or housing, provide transportation where appropriate, assist the client to seek help for any physical health needs he/she may have and identify work, hobbies and daytime activities.

Crisis Intervention

Your client may present in a crisis (mental, physical or financial) which is related to his/her drug/alcohol use. By responding relatively quickly, offering practical assistance if appropriate and empathising with his/her situation, you can begin to engage the client, as he/she will start to see your role as a helpful one. However, it is important that crisis intervention is done within clearly identified boundaries, so that the client is not continually "bailed out" and does not have to face some of the negative consequences of his/her problematic drug/alcohol use.

Symptom Stability and Medication Issues

Your client may say that he/she uses drugs/alcohol as a way of coping with his/her psychotic symptoms or the effects of medication. By helping the client to achieve as much stabilisation of any distressing psychiatric/psychotic symptoms as possible at this stage, you are indirectly addressing his/her drug/alcohol use. That is, you are modifying his/her reasons for using the substance as a coping strategy. Stabilisation of your client's symptoms will be increased by encouraging adherence to medication and the development of coping strategies to manage psychotic symptoms (that is, delusions and hallucinations).

   If the client has already identified some adaptive strategies to manage his/her psychotic symptoms, it is helpful to build on these. *These might include distraction techniques (such as listening to a Walkman/radio), ignoring voices or telling them to go away.*

   If the client continues to have difficulties coping with his/her psychotic symptoms a more in-depth, structured approach might be needed; *for example, cognitive-behaviour therapy with delusions and hallucinations (e.g., Birchwood & Tarrier, 1994; Fowler, Garety & Kuipers, 1995; Kingdon & Turkington, 1994).*

   Your client may need some help with taking his/her medication regularly; that is, *may need to be given medication daily or use a Medi-Pac. If the client's concern is about difficulties with side effects, it may be necessary to review the type and dosage of medication.*

If your client has particular problems with medication, some more intensive input focused on this may be appropriate at this stage. *This might include educational information about his/her mental health problem and the benefits and side effects, as well as the type and dosage, of medication.*

If the client continues to have difficulties adhering to medication, a more in-depth approach might be needed: *for example, medication compliance therapy (Kemp et al., 1996).*

So remember, to improve engagement,

- be practical in the help you offer
- offer some crisis intervention
- work toward symptom stability/medication adherence.

Initial Motivational Approach

"Motivational Hooks"

Your client will have particular things that he/she wants in life. These can be personal or life goals. It is possible that problematic drug/alcohol use has prevented attainment of these goals or is incompatible with them. Therefore, goals can be thought of as "motivational hooks". Examples of ***"motivational hooks"*** are getting a job, learning to drive, going on a holiday, starting a relationship, living independently, making friends, going out socially, having more disposable income, not being in debt, not being admitted into a psychiatric hospital and appropriate reduction of medication. Identifying and using a "motivational hook" can be a way of encouraging your client to change his/her drug/alcohol use as a means of getting something that he/she wants.

It is important to identify these "motivational hooks" with your client. The goals your client has identified should be focused on throughout treatment, as they will serve as motivators for the client to engage in the treatment process and eventually modify his/her drug/alcohol use behaviour. To assist your client in identifying and planning toward his/her goal, you will find the following exercise on page 54 helpful.

So remember to fish for,

- "Motivational hooks".

Exercise: *Goal setting and problem solving. To assist with this exercise, use the* *Climbing Mountains: Goal Setting and Problem Solving Worksheet (Appendix* *1.1)*

(1) With your client, identify one of the client's main long-term goals.
(2) Write down where the client is now.
(3) Identify a series of steps that will help the client to achieve this goal.
(4) Identify what he/she could do to achieve this goal.
(5) Identify any obstacles that might prevent him/her from achieving each of these steps and identify strategies to overcome these obstacles.

Clinician's Attitudes

To work successfully with this client group and not become discouraged and despondent when clients successfully make changes and then relapse, it is necessary to take a step back, to readjust our attitudes and goal posts. There is a need to take into account a number of factors that will influence how treatment progresses and what is seen as a "successful" result. These include *the client's stage of engagement in treatment, the harm-reduction philosophy, optimism and a long-term perspective.*

Stage of Engagement in Treatment

Your client's motivation will fluctuate over time and depend on when he/she last used the substance, the client's financial situation, health, etc. For example, the day after using drugs in a binge pattern, the client may tell you that he/she has made a decision "never to use again", because he/she feels so bad. However, the next time you see the client, he/she may be feeling much better, may have "forgotten" how bad he/she felt a few days before and may no longer be interested in discussing how to change his/her drug use. It is important to be aware that motivation will fluctuate and to be consistent, accepting and non-judgemental in your approach, even when the client's motivation wanes. Remind yourself of the stage of engagement with treatment the client is in and what your treatment aim/goal is.

Harm-Reduction Philosophy

At this stage, your client will not yet perceive his/her drug/alcohol use as problematic. Thus, it is important to identify with the client goals that are realistic and easily achievable; that is, a range of goals that limit the harm or damage the client's drug/alcohol use has on his/her life, rather than goals focused just on abstinence from substances.

Optimism and a Long-Term Perspective

Your client probably uses alcohol/drugs for very good reasons in his/her own mind and has strong beliefs about the effectiveness of these substances. In the client's mind and experience, drug/alcohol use is helpful. Therefore, to consider changing drug/alcohol use will mean a major lifestyle change. For any one of us, making a lifestyle change is a big step that takes quite a long time. Therefore, with your client, you will need to remain optimistic that in the long term your client will in some way modify his/her drug/alcohol use behaviour.

So remember to,

- be mindful of the stage your client is in
- set reasonable and achievable goals
- be optimistic; "Rome wasn't built in a day".

HOW TO PUT DRUG/ALCOHOL USE ON THE AGENDA

Helpful references: Beck et al. (1993), Graham (1998), Greenberger and Padesky (1995), Liese and Franz (1996), "Preparing People for Change", ch. 6 in Miller and Rollnick (1991), Motivational Enhancement Therapy Manual by Miller et al. (1995), Rollnick and Miller (1995).

When people become involved in problematic drug/alcohol use, their attention becomes skewed and they focus primarily on the positive aspects of substance use. The strategies outlined below seek to initiate the change process, to shift the focus and increase awareness of the impact of the negative aspects of problem substance use that the individual may have disregarded, ignored, minimised or simply traded for the positive benefits of the substance. Some clients may be aware of both the positive and negative aspects of drug/alcohol use, but may seem to be *ambivalent* about change or not desirous of change. *Ambivalence is said to be the dilemma of change; on the one hand, a person wants to change, but on the other hand, he/she does not. The result is that the client presents with conflicting and fluctuating motivation (Miller & Rollnick, 1991).* Therefore, your aim needs to be, initially, to help the client talk about the positive aspects of substance use, but then to help the individual begin to shift the focus to the problems associated with drug or alcohol use and the cognitive distortions that maintain problematic substance use.

Identify the Role of Drug/Alcohol Use in Everyday Life

Begin by discussing with your client what he/she sees as the positive aspects of his/her drug/alcohol use. Use reflective listening so that the client feels more able to be open and honest. *For example, you could ask: "What's positive about drinking for you?"; "What do you enjoy about crack use?"; "When you use, how do you find it helps you?"*

Exercise: Help your client to complete a questionnaire that helps quickly to identify his/her reasons for using alcohol/drugs (alcohol/drug use motives—see Appendix 1.2). (Cooper et al., 1992; Mueser et al., 1995).

Identify Some Current Concerns/Problems and Unwanted Consequences of Substance Use

Ask your client open-ended questions about any current concerns or problems he/she may have to determine whether any of these concerns or problems are related to the consequences of problematic substance use. Your aim is to raise the client's awareness of the negative aspects of his/her drug/alcohol use and elicit the client's concern. *For example, you could ask, directly, "What sorts of difficulties or problems has your alcohol use caused you?", or ask, indirectly, "You seem to be getting into debt recently—what do you think has changed. What sorts of things are you spending more money on now?"; "You've mentioned that you've not been feeling so well—how do you think your cannabis use might be contributing?"*

Once you have an idea of the concerns your client has regarding his/her drug/alcohol use, you can ask the client to summarise the main concern he/she has. This then becomes the client's *"self-motivational statement of concern"*. It is important quickly to follow up this statement by asking the client about his/her intent to change. This then becomes the client's *"self-motivational statement of intent to change"*. *For example, you could ask what the client thinks might need to change to help reduce the level of concern.*

It is now helpful to write down what the client has identified as the positive aspects of alcohol/drug use and his/her concerns, so that your client can see written down in his/her own words the two sides (positive and negative) of his/her substance use. You can do this by completing with the client an advantages and disadvantages analysis (Appendix 1.2), using the following exercise:

Exercise: To identify the advantages and disadvantages of substance use in the short term and the long term.

(1) With the client (you/the client), jot down on the advantages and disadvantages worksheet the positive reasons for using the substance in the "Ads" column and the negative aspects of using in the "Disads" column (use the client's own words).
(2) Try to get the client to think of these in the short term and then in the longer term. (To find out advantages and disadvantages in the long term, you can ask, for example, "If you keep using alcohol as you are, what problems might this cause 6 months or 12 months down the road"?)
(3) Record self-motivational statements. Ask the client to summarise what his/her main concern is (concern) and what he/she thinks might need to change to help reduce the level of concern (intent to change).

Ray has used a variety of different drugs, including cannabis, LSD and crack, on a recreational basis for the past few years. Over the past year, his crack use has escalated. As a result, on the day he gets paid, he spends most of his money paying off the crack dealers. When he has run out of money or he has arguments with his family about his crack use, he asks his keyworker to give him a loan and says that he wants to stop using. However, when he has money and is using, he says he enjoys using and does not feel he needs to stop.

Therapist: *Ray, over the past year, you seem to be running out of money quickly—what do you think has changed?*
Ray: *Nothing much has changed.*
Therapist: *What sorts of things are you spending more money on now that you weren't a year ago?*
Ray: *Well, I'm using a bit more crack now—and once I start using I find it hard to stop and then I have no money for other things I need.*
Therapist: *So, your crack use can end up costing you quite a bit of money once you start using. What happens if you don't have the money to pay for it?*
Ray: *The dealers can get a bit rough and demanding, and then I have to borrow money off my family. This causes arguments, as they know I need it to pay off the dealers.*
Therapist: *What do you think are the problems your crack use might cause if you keep using like this or 6 or 12 months down the road?*
Ray: *I worry that my health, especially this chesty cough, will get worse, I won't have money to buy the things I want, and that my family won't want to know me and I'll lose them.*
Therapist: *Let's write down these disadvantages to crack use, before we forget them. It sounds as if there are quite a few problems related to your crack use, on the one hand,*

but, on the other, there must be some positive things about it for you. What do you think these are?

Ray: *Of course there are. It gives me such a buzz, I feel light and relaxed, and I've made some friends who also use and that's why it's so hard to give it up.*

Therapist: *Ray, on the one hand, from what you have told me today, I can see why you would enjoy and keep using crack. However, it also sounds as if there is a down side of crack use which has caused you a number of problems that you are concerned about. Particularly, your health, the lack of money and the arguments with your family. It also sounds as if you are worried that these problems will get worse in the longer term if things stay as they are.*

Ray: *Yeah, that's right, but it's so hard to stop once you start.*

ADVANTAGES–DISADVANTAGES ANALYSIS

Name:____*Ray*_____

Date:_____*10th Nov.*_____

Behaviour: ___*Smoking crack-cocaine*_____

	Ads (FOR)	DisAds (AGAINST)
SHORT TERM	• *Enjoy the buzz it gives me* • *Makes me feel relaxed and light* • *Made new friends*	• *Can end up spending all my money on it* • *Dealers can be a bit rough if I can't pay them* • *Family don't like me smoking...causes arguments*
LONG TERM	• *?Enjoy the buzz*	• *Health will get worse* • *Won't be able to buy anything else for myself* • *Will lose my family*

Self-motivational statements

Concern: *My crack use is putting me in a lot of debt and causing problems with my family.*

Intent to change: *I think I need to think about cutting down before it really gets out of hand.*

Figure 5.1 Ray's completed advantages–disadvantages worksheet

---

So remember, to put alcohol/drugs on the agenda,

• find out why your client uses
• get your client to identify any problems it causes or any concerns he/she may have.

BUILDING ON MOTIVATION FOR CHANGE

Now that your client has spoken with you about the positive side to his/her drug/alcohol use and has also written down the advantages and disadvantages of continued use, the client should be growing aware of the negative aspects of his/her substance use. To move your client further forward so that he/she can begin to think of taking steps to change, you will need to do two things. First, start talking to your client about what can be gained from changing his/her drug/alcohol use. Second, ask the client what would be the down side if he/she were to change. This will give you and the client some idea of his/her "decisional balance"; that is, the part of your client that wants to change versus the factors that prevent the client from making changes (ambivalence). You can do this in the following exercise, using the Decision Balance Sheet (Appendix 1.3):

Exercise: *To identify the pros and cons of change in the short term and long term:*

(1) With the client (you and the client), jot down on the Decision Balance Sheet in the client's own words the reasons for change in the 'PROS' column and the reasons against change in the 'CONS' column.
(2) Try to get the client to think of these in the short term and then in the long term. (To get the client to think of the longer term you can ask: "If you keep using crack as you are now, what problems might this cause six or twelve months down the road?")

Tony has bipolar affective disorder. He drinks heavily with his friends. He used to get drunk with his friends and work mates every weekend and have three or four pints most nights after work. Since he lost his job and developed mental health problems, he drinks heavily on most days. He has tried to stop drinking and found it difficult, but says he would like to stop now.

Therapist: *You mentioned that you have tried to stop before but found it difficult. What do you think made giving up hard in the past?*
Tony: *Well, I've been drinking for a long time and all my mates drink.*
Therapist: *From what you have said, I can understand why it has been hard for you to give up. Do you think that giving up might be too big a step to start with?*
Tony: *What do you mean?*
Therapist: *Well—I was wondering if a first step might be to cut down your drinking, which might help build your confidence, and then stop completely later on?*

Tony: *I guess that sounds easier. I could try to reduce my drinking and see how I get on.*

Therapist: *What do you think are all the reasons why it would be a good idea to reduce?*

Tony: *There are lots—but mainly I wish I had money to buy things I want, like I've wanted a portable radio/stereo for a long time but haven't had enough money, and I could learn how to drive.*

Therapist: *Are there any other reasons for reducing the amount you drink?*

Tony: *It would mean that I would eat a lot better, and when I have been drinking heavily I get really bad hallucinations.*

Therapist: *Let's write this down so that we don't forget. What about in the longer term—6 months down the road/1 year—what do you think are the reasons why it would be a good idea to reduce in the long term?*

Tony: *I could become healthier, and probably I'd look after myself better if I wasn't drinking as much, and perhaps I could find another job.*

Therapist: *Sounds as if there are quite a few strong reasons why you would like to change your drinking, but you have found it hard in the past. What do you think are the reasons against cutting down your drinking?*

Tony: *Basically, all my friends and the people I live with all drink, and, as I said before, I've always enjoyed drinking with my mates, so cutting down would be hard.*

Once you have elicited from your client the pros and cons of change in the short term and long term, you can begin to tip the motivational balance in

DECISION BALANCE SHEET

Name:____Tony_____

Date:_____18th July_____

Behaviour: ___Reduce drinking_____

	'PROS' (FOR)	'CONS' (AGAINST)
SHORT TERM	• *Use money to buy things I want such as a radio/stereo* • *Learn how to drive* • *When I'm drinking I don't eat properly* • *Drinking can make me have hallucinations*	• *The friends I have and the people I live with all drink like I do* • *I have always enjoyed drinking with my mates*
LONG TERM	• *I'll be much healthier* • *I can look after myself better* • *Find a job*	?

Figure 5.2 Tony's completed Decision Balance Sheet

favour of change. This can be done by increasing and building up the client's awareness/focus on the difficulties that drug/alcohol causes, on the one side, versus the positive, immediate but only short-term benefits of use on the other.

How to Tip the Motivational Balance in Favour of Change

You can tip the motivational balance by using the four strategies listed below.

1. Elicit Self-Motivational Statements About Concerns or Difficulties Related to Substance Use and Intent to Change

Self-motivational statements need to come directly from the client. They are statements which begin to demonstrate some degree of recognition of a problem and/or some concern about the problem and/or begin to convey some intent to change. *For example, "My life is much worse now"; "I think I need to think about cutting down my cannabis, as I can't go on like this for much longer."*

To evoke self-motivational statements from your ambivalent client, ask an evocative question. *For example, "What is there about your cannabis use that you or other people may see as a reason for concern?"; "How do you feel about the amount you are drinking?"; "What do you think might happen if you don't make a change?"; "What reasons might there be for making a change in your crack use?"; "What might be the advantages of making a change?"*

When your client produces a self-motivational statement, you should immediately offer reinforcement and support. *For example, "I can see why that would worry you"; "Not having a lot of money left every week after buying your cannabis must be difficult."*

In addition, summarise your client's self-motivational statement and reflect it back to the client. To continue evoking self-motivational statements once the client has started, you can ask "What else?" questions. *For example, "What else worries you?"; "What other reasons are there, apart from the lack of money, why you may need to make a change?"; "What other problems have you had?"; "What do you suppose are the worst things that might happen if you keep on the way you've been going?"*

2. Identify "Distortions" in the Positive Beliefs Your Client Holds About His/Her Drug/Alcohol Use

You will notice that your client may hold quite positive beliefs about the benefits of using drugs/alcohol, as identified in the *Ads* column of his/her Advantages–Disadvantages Analysis. *For example, "Without a drink I can't relax", "Cannabis stops my voices",* or *"Everyone I know uses"*. These beliefs are called ***"cognitive distortions" or "thinking errors"***. They are basically beliefs that are distortions of the truth and allow the client to convince or give him/herself permission to continue using. We all engage in them at one time or another. With your client, you need to take a closer look at the *Ads* column in the Advantages–Disadvantages Analysis and the *CONS* column in the Decision Balance Sheet. With the client, go through each of the reasons the client gave for using/reasons against change, in turn, and identify any "distortions" in these beliefs. If you look closely with your client at the evidence he/she uses to support these beliefs, you may find that the beliefs are **not 100 per cent true all of the time**, and that they help your client talk him/herself into using again.

Some examples of common cognitive distortions/thinking errors of people who use drugs/alcohol problematically are listed below:

- "I can handle one drink or a little crack" (*minimisation*).
- "Just one won't hurt" (*minimisation*).
- "I deserve to use this once" (*rationalisation*).
- "I've gone past the point of no return, so I may as well continue" (*all or nothing thinking*).
- "My voices won't stop unless I smoke cannabis or have a drink" (*all or nothing thinking*).
- "Everyone I know uses" (*overgeneralisation*).

Exercise: Using the above list of commonly used distortions, with your client mark the types of distortions your client uses.

---

3. Modify and Re-evaluate the Positive Reasons for Use

Once you and your client have identified his/her cognitive distortions, you can begin to re-evaluate and modify the positive reasons for using and the reasons your client gave against making changes in his/her drug/alcohol use. You will need to acknowledge and emphasise with your client that although drug/alcohol use may meet his/her *immediate short-term* needs, it does not always satisfy these needs in the *long term*. A technique which you will find helpful to assist your client in re-evaluating and modifying the positive reasons for use is the **"three-question technique"**:

(1) What is the evidence for that belief?
(2) Are there times when that is not the case?
(3) If there are times when that is not the case, what are the implications?

For example, if the belief is, "Cannabis stops my voices", we might have the following dialogue.

(1) **Therapist:** *What is the evidence for that belief?*
    Shaun: *Whenever I smoke my voices stop.*
(2) **Therapist:** *Are there times when that is not the case?*
    Shaun: *No—well, actually, after I smoke two or three joints, then the next day, I feel a bit anxious and paranoid and the voices seem worse.*
(3) **Therapist:** *If there are times when that is not the case, then what are the implications?*
    Shaun: *I guess after one or two joints they do seem to stop for a while, but if I smoke any more it makes the voices seem worse.*
    Therapist: *So, from what you have said, telling yourself, "Whenever I smoke my voices stop", isn't actually 100 per cent true. A more accurate picture of the way cannabis affects you seems to be, "After one or two joints, the voices seem to stop for a while, but if I smoke any more it makes the voices seem worse."*

Note that, in the example, Shaun's initial belief about cannabis is both an all or nothing statement and an overgeneralisation. Thus, by the third question, Shaun has slightly modified his belief about the effectiveness of cannabis to rid him of his voices. Shaun's belief is now much more realistic, accurate and based on facts and the evidence.

Once you have been able to, even slightly, modify the positive belief that maintains your client's problematic drug/alcohol use, you can go back and amend the decisional balance to reflect this. It is important at this stage to summarise and reflect back the modified decisional balance (Figure 5.3).

(4) Provide Educational Information About the Effects of Substance Use and Possible Links to the Problems Identified

You may note, from the client's Advantages–Disadvantages Analysis and Decision Balance Sheet that your client's positive beliefs about the effects of alcohol and drugs are not 100 per cent accurate. Therefore, there is now an important opportunity to share gently with the client some more accurate information/facts about the actual effects of the drugs he/she is using. This will increase your client's awareness of any possible links between his/her substance use and the problems/concerns he/she has identified. *For example, if your client's concern is, "I am feeling so nervous and anxious", and his/her belief is, "Alcohol helps me to relax", you can give your client information about the disinhibitory and depressant effects of alcohol and its ability to cause rebound anxiety. This may help the client become more aware of the actual effects of alcohol, particularly over the long term. That is, although initially appearing to alleviate anxiety, alcohol does this only because it causes the person to become disinhibited, and it depresses the central nervous system. Thus, over time, the body needs more alcohol to create this effect, and when there is no alcohol in the system, greater feelings of anxiety will be experienced, as the body has adapted to functioning with alcohol.*

(MODIFIED) DECISION BALANCE SHEET

Name:_____*Tony*_____

Date:_____*18th July*_____

Behaviour: ___*Reduce drinking*_____

	PROS (FOR)	CONS (AGAINST)
SHORT TERM	• *Use money to buy things I want such as a radio/stereo* • *Learn how to drive* • *When I'm drinking I don't eat properly* • *Drinking can make me have hallucinations*	• *(This was an all-or-nothing statement)...Some of the friends I have and the people I live with drink like I do, but I do know some people who only drink occasionally.* • *(This was an overgeneralisation and an all-or-nothing statement)...I have NOT always enjoyed drinking with my mates. After a two-day binge I feel awful and have no money, and we sometimes end up in fights.*
LONG TERM	• *I'll be much healthier* • *I can look after myself better* • *Find a job*	*?*

Self-motivational statement

Intent to change: *I can see that if I make some changes in my drinking I'm going to have more money in my pocket and feel a lot better.*

Figure 5.3 Tony's modified Decision Balance Sheet

So remember, to build motivation,

- tip the balance in favour of change
- re-evaluate the positive reasons for use.

DEALING WITH RESISTANCE

You may find that the first time you try to talk to your client about his/her drug/alcohol use you hit a ''brick wall''. The client may become quite defensive, and you might find that your client ends up arguing on the side ''for'' continued drug/alcohol use while you are arguing on the side ''against'' his/her use. What you have come up against is *resistance*. Resistance from the client often comes about because you are not matching your approach to the stage the client is in, or you are being too confrontational. *For example, if your client says, "I don't drink too much and I don't have any problems with alcohol", **don't meet your client's resistance head on or by arguing or persuading**.* If you find yourself in this position, acknowledge that you have hit a stalemate and use the following strategies that have been found helpful to work with resistance:

- **Reflect back your client's ambivalence;** that is, reflect back to the client his/her resistant statement and an earlier statement that he/she has made that suggests concern about problems related to his/her use. For example, "You don't think you are drinking too much, but at the same time you are worried about the long-term effect on your health."
- **Move the focus** away from the problematic issue and come back to it at a later stage from a slightly different angle. *For example, "Rather than labelling your drinking as a problem, let's just focus on the positive things you were telling me about your drinking right now and the concerns you have for your health in the long term."*
- **Roll with resistance** rather that fighting or opposing it. *For example, "From what you have said, I can see why you feel the way you do about drinking and don't feel your drinking is too much."*
- **Go back** and use one of the earlier engagement strategies (for example, review the positive things about your client's use and any problems/ concerns he/she may have identified).

IDENTIFYING SOCIAL NETWORKS SUPPORTIVE OF CHANGE

Some helpful references: Drake, Bebout and Roach (1993), Galanter (1993), Galanter and Kleber (1999).

Your aim for this part of the treatment is to:

(1) Identify who is in your client's social network.
(2) Help your client see the importance of having network support for change.
(3) Invite one or more key members of your client's network to become involved in the treatment.
(4) Minimise the influence of network members supportive of continued use of substances.

Your client may hold the belief that *all* the people he/she knows use drugs/ alcohol. This belief may also be one of the reasons that he/she cites for continuing to use problematically. This belief may not actually be 100 per cent true. However, it is possible that over time, since your client has been spending a significant amount of time using alcohol/drugs, he/she has spent increasing amounts of time with other people who also use alcohol/drugs and less time with those who do not. There is accumulating evidence in the substance-use literature supporting the crucial role of social networks in helping people to initiate change in relation to their drug/alcohol use behaviour, maintain change, and prevent or manage relapses.

You can help your client increase social support for change in the following ways:

- You can begin to help your client to re-engage with members of his/her social network who are supportive of change.
- Alternatively, if necessary, you can broaden your client's social network by helping him/her to meet new people who could support his/her efforts to change, either by being willing to engage in alternative activities or by providing emotional and practical support at times of risk for relapse.
- Furthermore, in collaboration with your client, you may identify someone from his/her network who is willing to be involved in the treatment sessions.

How to Identify People in a Social Network

Your efforts should therefore be directed towards helping your client to identify who are the people in his/her social network. The first step in this task can be achieved through the use of a network diagram/map (two examples

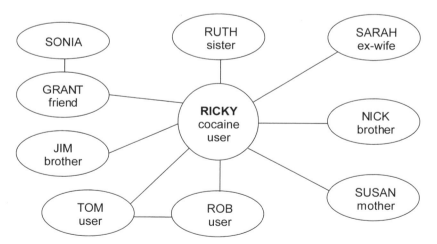

Figure 5.4 Ricky's social network represented diagrammatically

Figure 5.5 Bryan's network diagram

are illustrated in Figures 5.4 and 5.5). Each member of the social network is represented in relation to your client. Sufficient time should be allocated to this task, given that the process of discussion while drawing together the network map is very important. You will find the following steps helpful:

Exercise: *Steps to drawing a social network map:*

(1) Ask your client to think of all the people in his/her social network. Try to include as many people as possible to start with. Do not engage in a detailed discussion about each individual member too soon, as the initial emphasis is on having as many of the network members represented as possible.
(2) Once you have identified a number of people, you could try to discuss issues such as whether the person uses alcohol/drugs; how often your client sees him/her; what the person thinks about your client's use of alcohol/drugs.
(3) Identify those people who may be supportive of change and those people who are supporting or encouraging of the continued use of substances.

By the end of this exercise, if you have carried it out carefully, you will have some knowledge of each one of those people represented in the map and what his/her views/attitudes are towards your client's use of alcohol/drugs.

Ricky (Figure 5.4) is a 25-year-old man using cocaine and suffering from manic depression. You can see that there are a significant number of people represented in Ricky's network. Some of the people, such as Tom and Rob, are drug users themselves and therefore may not be able to support change for Ricky. However, Ricky is close to his brother Jim and his friend Grant, and it may be possible to engage either of them in supporting his efforts to give up his use of cocaine. This can be achieved either by inviting them to the sessions or by making sure that Ricky seeks their support and help between sessions.

Figure 5.5 illustrates the more limited network of Bryan, a young alcohol user with a diagnosis of schizophrenia. Both his parents are very worried about Bryan and have tried to support him in the past, but recently the relationship between them and Bryan has been rather tense. Finally, Bryan's uncle, Robert, has been supportive, but he lives in a different city and visits only infrequently. The work in this case may involve persuading Bryan (provided he sees this as important) to talk to his parents about his need for their support. If appropriate, it may be that you would work with Bryan to expand his network (see page 81).

As a rule, remember that network members need to:

◆ have a positive relationship with your client
◆ be in agreement about his/her aim in relation to substance use
◆ be prepared to be firm but kind, encouraging your client to continue with the treatment
◆ not have an alcohol/drug problem themselves
◆ not be under the age of sixteen
◆ not have any hidden agenda of their own aside from supporting your client in his/her efforts to change.

So remember,

● your client will find it easier to disengage from people who support and encourage the continued use of substances if alternative sources of positive support are available.

FINANCES/MONEY MANAGEMENT

Helpful references: Roberts, Shaner and Eckman (1997)—'Money Management' Session 8.

Your client may be spending a significant proportion of his/her money on drugs/alcohol. However, he/she may be unaware of the role of money in maintaining his/her problematic pattern of substance use. For example, for some clients, the availability of money may trigger cravings for them to use (especially on "pay day"). Alternatively, the lack of money may lead them into a vicious cycle of debt with dealers, whereby spending a significant proportion of their money on drugs/alcohol prevents them from spending money on non-drug/alcohol-related activities or achieving their personal goals. Take, for example, the following case.

Ray gets his benefits on a Tuesday, and by Wednesday he has spent the majority of it on crack-cocaine. Thus, on Thursday, he is broke, and has no food, cigarettes or electricity tokens. He then badgers his keyworker for a loan until his next pay day. The dealer agrees to "trust" (loan) him some crack but wants the money when Ray gets paid on Tuesday. By the time pay day arrives, Ray owes the dealer the majority of his benefits. Thus, a vicious cycle of repaying the dealer on Tuesday and getting drugs on "trust" has started and is hard to break. Eventually, Ray's drug use increases, he is unable to repay the dealer and the dealer takes over his flat or beats him up.

It is difficult for clients to break such vicious cycles and regain control of their finances. Your client may be initially resistant to discussing his/her financial situation with you. However, if he/she is in some financial difficulties or wants to spend money on non-drug-related activities, this is a prime opportunity to raise the subject. Some strategies that have been found to be helpful in improving money management are listed below.

Money-Management Strategies

Identifying Alternatives

Your client probably has a number of things he/she would like to spend his/her money on that drug/alcohol use prevents (such as buying adequate clothing, food, electricity tokens or cigarettes or going out to participate in a non-drug/alcohol-related activity). You will need to help him/her identify these things and to recognise the role of alcohol/drugs in preventing them. You can do this by asking some open-ended questions. *For example, you could ask: "What things have you wanted to buy/do this week but were unable to because of a lack of money?"; "Have you been able to pay your bills this week—do you have any outstanding?"; "Is there anything else you would like to do that the lack of money prevents?"; "What would you say you spend the majority of your money on?"; "Could the amount you are spending on crack be preventing you from doing some of the things you want to do?"; "If you keep spending this amount of money on alcohol, what problems do you think you might have in six months' time?"*

Whatever your client's response is, he/she will benefit from having his/her response summarised and reflected back. *For example, "So, Ray, you have not been able to buy as much food and cigarettes as you would have liked during the past week, and your flat has been quite cold. You also sound a bit worried about how you will pay off your gas bill. It sounds as if you spent more on crack than you wanted to this week, and so you've not been able to do quite a few things that you have wanted to, including visiting your daughter."*

Budgeting Skills

If your client is finding it hard to manage on the money he/she gets paid because he/she is spending a significant portion on drugs/alcohol, he/she may benefit from some help with budgeting and spending money on a weekly basis. This would include identifying with your client all weekly, fortnightly and monthly money coming in and all outgoing expenses, based on how he/she spent his/her money in the previous week. You can then draw up a budget of outgoings that would allow him/her to have a better financial balance, by doing the following exercise with the Budgeting Worksheet (Appendix 1.4). Your client might be initially resistant to this idea, but it may be helpful to compare it to going to see a financial adviser to help optimise your money.

Exercise: *Budgeting Worksheet*

Incoming money	Outgoings	
Weekly and monthly £_____	Electricity	£_____
	Gas	£_____
	Council tax	£_____
	Rent	£_____
	Food	£_____
	Clothes/toiletries	£_____
	Spending money	£_____
	Travel	£_____
	Cigarettes	£_____
	Activities	£_____
	Other (?drugs/alcohol)	£_____
	Total	£_____

You might also suggest to your client that during the early stages of budgeting his/her money it might be helpful to go along with someone who will support him/her to cash the money and buy or pay for the necessities. This might be you as a keyworker, a family member or a friend who is supportive of the client not using drugs/alcohol. Your client might be initially resistant to this idea; therefore, you will need to reinforce its importance as a way of helping him/her to optimise the money he/she gets (that is, reduce his/her debt and increase his/her ability to do the things that he/she wants). This budgeting exercise will need to be repeated on a weekly basis a few days prior to the client's being paid. An incentive each week should be identified. That is, the client budgets for at least one thing he/she would like to do or to spend money on, so that he/she can have a sense of achievement each week.

Use of Bank Accounts

Some clients have found that they are better able to budget their finances if their benefits are paid directly into their bank account and bills are directly debited from this account. Your client may not have a bank, building society or post office account, and may need some help from you to determine whether this option is feasible. He/she may not want to have his/her money paid directly into an account. However, your client could be encouraged to open an account to save toward a small item that he/she is interested in buying; this item will act as an incentive/motivator for him/her to reduce the money spent on drugs/alcohol.

Weekly Payments

The majority of clients on benefits get paid on a fortnightly basis. Some clients who have problems with alcohol/drugs have found that they get into less debt and are better able to handle their finances if they are paid on a weekly basis. This is an option you could discuss with your client and the Department of Social Security (DSS).

Appointeeship

For some clients, the ability to budget on a weekly basis is too difficult, as they will spend the majority of their money on the day they are paid, particularly if their lifestyle and drug/alcohol use have become chaotic. Therefore, you may need to take a much more assertive approach. This may involve encouraging them to enter into a voluntary agreement (an "appointee-ship") that allows you, as their designated keyworker, or a family member to assist in managing their benefits to ensure that basic needs are taken care of. You will need to discuss this with the DSS for further information and guidelines.

So remember, to improve your client's money management, you can,

- identify alternative ways he/she can spend money
- set up a budget plan
- help him/her open a bank account
- arrange for weekly payments
- agree on an appointeeship.

TREATMENT PHASE 1—PULLING IT ALL TOGETHER

Harnessing Motivation for Change

(1) Emphasise the importance and achievability of life goals.

(2) Summarise and whenever possible make links between current concerns/problems and substance use. Emphasise the role of beliefs about drug/alcohol use and social networks in maintaining problematic substance use.

(3) Breaking the vicious circle: build on importance and confidence to modify drug/alcohol use behaviour and remind the client to use his/her self-motivational statements concerning change.

C-BIT CORE COMPONENTS

Chapter 6

TREATMENT PHASE 2: NEGOTIATING SOME BEHAVIOUR CHANGE

AIMS

(1) Achieve some positive change in alcohol/drug using by negotiating achievable harm-reduction goals.
(2) Target alcohol/drug-related beliefs to increase clients' awareness of the problematic links between their mental health and substance use.

IDENTIFYING AND SETTING ACHIEVABLE HARM-REDUCTION GOALS

Following C-BIT treatment phase 1, your client is now engaged with you and has some recognition and awareness of the problems that his/her alcohol/drug use is causing. This treatment phase will help you work with your client to negotiate and achieve some change in his/her alcohol/drug-using behaviours. However, complete abstinence at this stage for your client is probably unrealistic and not necessary. You will find that your client will be more willing to think about change and succeed if changing alcohol/drug-use behaviour feels achievable. A more achievable philosophy for change is *harm reduction*. The idea behind this is that there are several levels at which change can occur that would reduce the overall harm a behaviour is causing the individual, even if the person does not become abstinent.

For example, if Joey is injecting heroin and sharing injecting equipment, some of the hierarchical levels of change that he could begin to adopt are the following:

- *Obtain clean needles.*
- *Not share injecting equipment.*
- *Stop injecting heroin and smoke it instead.*
- *Be prescribed a substitute for heroin such as methadone.*
- *Reduce the amount he is using.*

Thus, with your client, you will need to identify harm-reduction goals. The goal-setting and problem-solving strategy set out in the following case example has been found to be useful in helping clients identify and achieve such harm-reduction goals:

Ricky, 28 years old, has schizophrenia. He uses ecstasy and cocaine on an occasional, recreational basis at the weekends within the gay club culture. He is aware that he typically becomes depressed and, at times, paranoid and does not function too well during the week after he has used these drugs. However, he says that he feels a "normal" part of the gay scene when he uses and is more accepted by his partner. He also says he has a "good time" when he is using, and finds having a mental illness demoralising. Ricky says that he wants "just to get on with his life" (that is, get a job). At first, Ricky did not see his use of drugs as a problem and did not really want to change his pattern of use. However, he began to realise that it affected his ability to function during the week after he had used. To enable him to set achievable harm-reduction goals, the following goal-setting and problem-solving exercise was done (following the five steps outlined above).

(1) Identify long-term goal in terms of Ricky's alcohol/drug-use behaviour or general goals. *Ricky had identified his long-term goal as getting on with his life and getting a job. By re-evaluating his positive beliefs about drug use (C-BIT treatment phase 1, page 62), Ricky was able to begin to see that using on weekends affected his ability to function properly during the week and that this would, in turn, affect his ability to work.*
(2) Write down where Ricky is now in terms of his alcohol/drug-use behaviour. *Ricky reported that he was using two ecstasy tablets and £50 worth of cocaine on two nights during the weekend.*
(3) Identify Ricky's harm-reduction steps, that is, the areas where he could make some changes to his alcohol/drug-using behaviour that would have a positive impact on his life. *Ricky identified five steps to achieve his goal:*
   (i) *Cut down drug use by going clubbing only on one night of the weekend.*
   (ii) *When clubbing, use later on in the night to reduce further drug use.*
   (iii) *Go clubbing less often (fortnightly/monthly) and try to enjoy it without using drugs.*
   (iv) *Get back into a work routine.*
   (v) *Get a job.*

(4) Identify what Ricky could do to achieve each of these goals.

  (i) *Go clubbing on a Saturday night rather than on a Sunday, in order not to feel as bad on Monday morning. Go out with friends who do not use drugs on a Sunday (for example, cinema, bowling, restaurant).*

  (ii) *Spend more time with friends at the club who don't use.*

  (iii) *Modify and re-evaluate the belief that "everyone at the club is using and I'll feel left out if I don't use", and tell myself, "not everyone is using—I can spend more time with my friends who don't use and still have a good time."*

  (iv) *Do some voluntary work on two days of the week (Wednesday and Thursday).*

  (v) *Look for a part-time job.*

(5) Identify any obstacles that might prevent Ricky from achieving each of these goals and identify strategies to overcome these obstacles.

  Obstacle: I want to achieve my goal immediately.

  Strategy: Tell myself to take one step at a time.

  Obstacle: If I use more drugs or go clubbing on more nights than I planned, I'll feel that I'm a failure.

  Strategy: Tell myself that if I have a slip or a setback, it doesn't mean that I have failed—I can learn from the experience and do things differently next time.

So remember, when setting goals,

- harm-reduction goals are more achievable
- be realistic
- identify any obstacles.

WORKING WITH RESISTANCE TO GOAL SETTING

When trying to set harm-reduction goals with your clients, you might experience some resistance and find that they may still be unwilling to make any positive change in their alcohol/drug use. They may give several reasons for not wanting to make any changes. Thus, before you are able to set and achieve any harm-reduction goals, you will need to address these reasons and negotiate with the clients some behaviour change in relation to alcohol/drug use. The two important things to remember during this phase are to remain *optimistic* and to take a *long-term perspective*. Remind yourself that your clients have probably been using these substances for some time and believe them to be an immediate, effective and enjoyable solution. Therefore, it is unlikely that they will want to give them up straight away; change may also be quite a scary prospect.

Some reasons clients give for not wanting to change are as follows: *"I don't need to change—I enjoy using and it's not really a problem"; "There is no point in trying to change—I've tried before and failed"; "I get bored if I'm not using"; "Everyone I know uses, especially all my friends, so it is hard not to use."*

Some strategies found to be helpful in achieving/negotiating change that you can use with your client are as follows:

- emphasising that any goals set will be realistic and achievable by them
- remaining optimistic and taking a long-term perspective toward achieving change
- reviewing their decisional balance with them and all the factors they listed as reasons "for" change
- setting up behavioural experiments to test out beliefs that prevent them from wanting to change
- using cognitive strategies (such as recognising cognitive distortions, the three-question technique and reviewing evidence for and against beliefs) to re-evaluate and modify beliefs that prevent them from wanting to change.

Strategies to Tackle Common Reasons Given by Clients for Not Wanting to Change Alcohol/Drug Use

Your Client Says: "I Don't Need to Change—I Enjoy Using and It's Not Really a Problem"

Your client may believe that changing his/her alcohol/drug use is not really necessary and see it as an enjoyable activity. If this is the case, go back to the work you did in C-BIT treatment phase 1, Chapter 5, in the section **Building on Motivation For Change,** particularly the *Advantages–Disadvantages Analysis worksheet,* which includes all his/her positive reasons for using and the negative aspects of using. Review this worksheet with your client and also remind him/her of the self-motivational statements made regarding his/her *concern* about continued alcohol/drug use and *intention to change* alcohol/drug use because of these concerns. Gently remind the client of how drug/alcohol use may prevent him/her from achieving a personal goal. At this point, you might find that your client begins to *minimise* the negative aspects of his/her alcohol/drug use. It is important to help the client spot the *distortions* in his/her current thinking which allow him/her to convince him/herself that using as he/she currently is, is OK. To help the client move forward, review his/her *Decision Balance worksheet,* which lists all the reasons for wanting to make changes and collaboratively identify a realistic and achievable harm-reduction goal. For example, take the following case example:

Terry says, "I don't want to stop using cannabis. I enjoy it and I can control it." He has just recently started to use cannabis daily after a long period of abstinence from it. In the "Ads" column of his Advantages–Disadvantages Analysis worksheet, he has put that he enjoys using cannabis, his friends use and he can control his use. In the disadvantages column, he has put that it has caused him paranoia and subsequent hospitalisation in the past, increases racing thoughts and ends up costing him a lot of money. Following a review of his worksheet, he begins to engage in a number of cognitive rationalisations and minimisations that seek to minimise the negative aspect of his use and justify his using again ("I was able to stop before, so I am sure I can stop again if I want to"; "I am not harming anyone" and "It is enjoyable"). He is encouraged to identify the cognitive distortions in his thinking and to focus on his previous self-motivational statement of intent to reduce his cannabis use. He does not see stopping his use as an option at present. However, with some negotiation, he agrees to think about reducing his cannabis use to three or four times a week and to reduce the quantity smoked on each occasion.

Your Client Says: "There Is No Point in Trying to Change—I've Tried Before and Failed"

Your client may believe that there is no point in trying to address his/her alcohol/drug use. The client may have been disheartened by attempts in the past to change his/her alcohol/drug use. At this point, you will need to educate your client about the C-BIT approach and inform him/her of how it may be beneficial for him/her. This will help to engage your client in the treatment approach. The client will begin to see that it may be beneficial to him/her. At this stage, it is very helpful to take a "negotiating position" with your client, especially if he/she does not believe that change is necessary or possible. A negotiating position allows you to collaborate with your client and actively engage him/her in working with you on his/her alcohol/drug use. Also remind your client that changing habits are difficult for all of us, and it takes several attempts before we are successful. Using behavioural experiments (see C-BIT skills-building component on managing anxiety (Chapter 9) for a fuller explanation of how to set up and carry out behavioural experiments) and/or reviewing previous attempts to change are helpful to get him/her to work collaboratively with you. Note the following case example:

Andrew experiences paranoia and anxiety about his flat being broken into. As a result, he is afraid to leave his flat and he hears persecutory voices. He is drinking four cans of strong lager and smoking cannabis each night. He does not believe that his paranoia, voices and anxiety could be linked to his drug and alcohol use. Therefore, after identification of the advantages and disadvantages of his cannabis and alcohol use, it is suggested that perhaps his paranoia, voices and anxiety are exacerbated by the

---

Thought to be tested

"There is no point in trying to change—I've tried before and failed"

Experiment	Prediction	Potential obstacles	Strategies to overcome obstacles	Outcome of experiment
Experiment 1 *Not smoke cannabis for 1 week*	*I'll not be able to go more than one day without it*	*My friends will come round and want me to smoke with them*	*Go out and spend time with family who don't smoke*	*Felt tempted to smoke and had one spliff on 1 day during the week*
Experiment 2 *Cut down to two cans (max three) of alcohol per night for 1 week*	*I might be able to do it for one day but I won't last the week*	*My friends will come round and encourage me to drink more than my limit*	*Go out and spend time with family and only buy two cans per day*	*Stuck to my limit!*

Lesson learned/take-home message

"It wasn't easy but I am able to make changes and I've felt less anxious and paranoid this week. The voices have stopped as well."

Figure 6.1 Andrew's behavioural experiment

substances he uses. However, he continues to believe that they are not linked. Thus, a negotiating position/approach was used; he was asked to try the C-BIT approach for a couple of weeks and see whether it made a difference. A behavioural experiment (modified from Greenberger & Padesky, 1995) was devised to test out in real life the following belief: *"There is no point in trying to change—I've tried before and failed"* (see Figure 6.1) (Appendix 2.1).

The three-question technique (C-BIT treatment phase 1, page 62) was another strategy that was used to re-evaluate and modify the belief that "there is no point in trying to change—I've tried before and failed."

(1) What is the evidence for that belief?
Andrew said that he had tried to stop using cannabis before but had returned to using after 1 week, and generally he didn't have much "will-power" to change things, as he had been trying to stop smoking cigarettes for the past year and not been able to.
(2) Have there been times when that has not been the case?

Andrew said that he had been able to cut down his cannabis use when he had to pay a few debts. He had also stopped smoking cigarettes for 2 months after he had made a New Year's resolution.

(3) If there are times when that is not the case, what are the implications?
Andrew was eventually able to modify his belief to: "I have been able to make some changes in the past, but will-power isn't enough. This time I have a better chance of success, as I have some support and a plan."

Your Client Says: "I Get Bored if I'm Not Using"

Your client will probably be somewhat aware of the problems related to his/her substance use, but his/her day may be consumed with a drug or alcohol-using lifestyle. At this stage, it would be useful to identify and develop with your client some structured daytime activities which are non-drug/alcohol related, and to help remove him/her from his/her typical daily activities and environment and reduce the chances of boredom and unstructured time. The anticipated knock-on effect is that the alternative activity reduces the time, opportunity and motivation to use alcohol/drugs.

IDENTIFYING ACTIVITIES OF INTEREST

Your client may find it difficult to identify any activity that he/she is interested in and may say that he/she is not interested in doing anything else and quite likes his/her life as it is. Some suggestions for identifying alternative activities that your client may be interested in follow below.

Exercise: With your client, brainstorm all the activities he/she is interested in or enjoys. You may also find it helpful to use the Identifying Activities of Interest worksheet (Appendix 2.2)

Some prompts that you can use to help identify activities of interest follow below.

Past Interests/Activities

Prior to his/her experiencing mental health difficulties or in the recent past, your client may have been engaged in activities such as music, art or sport. It might be useful to engage your client in a conversation around this. *For example, while visiting Geoffrey, it was clear that he had been involved in professional boxing and professional dancing in the past. Discussing these activities with him was a useful way of engaging him in conversation, building rapport and finding out what his current interests might be.*

Personal Goals Identified/Things He/She Has Always Wanted to Do

Through C-BIT treatment phase 1, you will have identified with your client some personal life goals that you have been using as "motivational hooks". Now is the time to use those motivational hooks and once again to elicit a self-motivational statement about the client's interest in this activity and achieving his/her goal. You can do this by asking some exploratory and open-ended questions. *For example, "What goals have you wanted to achieve that your alcohol use has prevented you from achieving? What are the things that you have always dreamed of doing but not got around to? If you had the opportunity, what would you spend your day doing?"*

Activities Non-Drug/Alcohol-Using Friends Engage in

With your client, using your social circle map, identify friends within his/her social network who may not be in contact but who do not use alcohol or drugs problematically. With your client, begin to think about what activities these friends engage in that the client also has some interest in. Your client may resist this idea and suggest that his/her friends would not be interested in doing the activity with him/her. However, if this does happen, emphasise that, at this stage, you would like just to brainstorm a whole range of activities, some of which may be practically possible and some which are not practical. Your client may have engaged in activities with these friends in the past. It may be useful to think of what these activities were and put them on the worksheet/list.

List of Leisure, Social/Training or Occupational Activities Available in Your Locality/Team

What you will need to have to hand is a list of activities available within your team, locality or local community that the client could participate in. You can then go through the list with your client and get the client to tick those activities that he/she may be interested in. Get the client to put *three* ticks by those activities that he/she is particularly interested in, *two* ticks by those that he/she is not as interested in but would like to find more information about, and *one* tick by things that are vaguely of interest.

Occupational Therapy Assessment of Interests

It may be that your client has found it very difficult to do this exercise and cannot identify any activities in which he/she is interested. It may therefore be appropriate at this stage to refer the client for an occupational therapy assessment of his/her interests.

ENGAGING THE CLIENT'S INTEREST IN THE ACTIVITY

Now you have identified a range of activities that the client has some degree of interest in, you will need to begin to engage his/her interest in the activity and plan toward his/her actually doing it. Below are listed a number of steps that you may find useful to go through with your client:

(1) Rank activities in order of interest. With your client, pick two activities that he/she has identified as being of particular interest and that are feasible or practically possible.
(2) Find out more information about the activity.
(3) Identify a time in his/her week when he/she could try it out.
(4) Think through the practical issues such as cost, transport, time and whether the client would benefit from having someone accompany him/ her.
(5) Adopt a negotiating position, that is, an attitude of "trying it out". Suggest to the client that he/she attend the first time as a "taster session".

HOW TO BUILD SOCIAL NETWORKS SUPPORTIVE OF CHANGE

Your Client Says: "Everyone I Know Uses, Especially All My Friends, So It Is Hard Not to Use"

There will be cases where your client is mostly in contact with problem users of alcohol/drugs. In these cases, your efforts will need to be directed towards building network support for change, and you will need to take a very active role in order to achieve this aim. You will need to use strategies focused on developing network engagement (that is, engaging those people close to your client who are willing to support his/her efforts to change). Engagement can range from being present at sessions to being prepared to do something with the client as an alternative to substance use or being available at the end of the telephone at a time of crisis. The process of network engagement follows on from the identification of the social network (the client's social network map) that you will have already done with your client (see page 65). Communication skills are very important in this type of work. Outlined below are a number of strategies that you will find helpful in engaging a network member to support your client.

Engaging a Network Member

Probably the simplest scenario involves a case where you can identify at least one potentially supportive person. The focus of the work with your client would be on how to approach this person and ask for his/her support. This can be done in a number of ways, ranging from **a** *direct approach made by the client* **to a** *letter from you inviting the person to the next session.* However, it may be the case that you and your client are able jointly to identify people who could be supportive, but your client has not been in contact with that person for some time or the relationship has become strained, due to the client's alcohol/drug problem. In this case, you may need to help your client to make contact with those people in his/her social network with whom the relationship is strained. There are several ways in which you could do this:

- *Help your client compose a letter to be sent to the particular person in question. You will need to help your client to consider what he/she would like to communicate and then draft the letter with him/her. A possible structure for a letter would include:*
  —Initial paragraph: Acknowledge the lack of contact and communicate the current circumstances that led to the client writing.
  —Middle paragraph: Focus on the main themes to be communicated. It is important to acknowledge past support given by the person and communicate how positive it has been. Help your client state the importance of re-establishing contact and make a specific request—for example, to meet at a specific time, to invite the person to a future session.
  —Final paragraph: Restate the importance of re-establishing contact and finish on a positive note.
  If possible, compose the letter and write it during the session.
- *You or the client telephone the person. If the client is to make the telephone call, it will be important to role-play and rehearse the telephone conversation and ensure the client has the necessary skills to do this.*
- *You and/or the client visit the person. It will be important to role-play to practise what will be said and how to deal with any difficulties that may arise.*

Note the following case example:

Ricky (already introduced on page 67) was keen to ask his friend Grant for support in his efforts to deal with his cocaine problem. Ricky had spent time with Grant in the past but had been spending less time recently, mainly because he was mostly mixing with other cocaine users. Ricky had never spoken to Grant directly about his drug use and therefore was somewhat worried about Grant's reaction. During one of the sessions, the therapist and Ricky used role-play to practise approaching Grant and talking to him about the difficulties with cocaine and requesting support. Ricky was able to discuss his worries and felt able in the coming week to talk to Grant, using the skills developed in the role-play practice. At a later stage, Grant joined the sessions and agreed to start playing pool regularly with Ricky as he had done in the past.

Building a Network from Scratch

Sometimes you may need to build network support from scratch. This is not easy, but always remember that small changes can be very important for your client. One new supportive person can be crucial for someone who has been totally isolated or in contact only with other problem users. Below are outlined five steps to building a new network:

(1) Start by reviewing with your client what person in the past has been supportive. You can use the network diagram to carry out this review. Agree on what is meant by support for change.
(2) Discuss systematically other potential sources of support, including the extended family, the church, colleagues from work, old friends, organisations that offer befriending, voluntary work agencies, day centres and hostels.
(3) In discussion with your client, identify the most realistic place/organisation where new contacts could be made.
(4) Introduce the idea of meeting new people and discuss any anticipated problems. You could use problem-solving techniques to identify and tackle any potential hurdles. In order to aid this process, you can ask your client to think about his/her ideal supportive network of people and then look for gaps by comparing the ideal to the existing network.
(5) Finally, you can carry out social-skill practice and role-play in order to help your client develop the necessary skills to approach new people in order that he/she can develop future continued support for change.

Bryan (discussed on page 68) was somewhat isolated and had little contact with peers. During the sessions, this was identified as a problem. It was difficult to generate support for Bryan from his limited social network. A scheme providing befriending for people was found and contacted by telephone during the session. At the next session, the therapist and Bryan agreed to meet at the centre operating the scheme. Bryan made contact with the scheme and received support from a befriender.

The case examples of Ricky and Bryan illustrate two contrasting scenarios. The first case shows how to help a client develop the necessary skills to approach someone in order to enlist his/her support. The second example illustrates an active attempt by the therapist to introduce a new source of support.

STRATEGIES TO INCREASE AWARENESS OF PROBLEMATIC LINKS BETWEEN MENTAL HEALTH AND SUBSTANCE USE

Your client has probably not made any links between the adverse effects of his/her alcohol/drug use and any of the mental health difficulties he/she experiences. If anything, he/she may see that the only link between his/her mental health and alcohol/drug use is a positive one and therefore will not see any reason to change his/her use. For example, your client's substance-related belief may be that *alcohol helps to reduce his anxiety*, or that *cannabis helps her relax and sleep*. Indeed, he/she may believe that a drug such as *crack-cocaine has a positive effect on mood and does not exacerbate psychotic symptoms*. Although your client may have some evidence to support these positive beliefs about the effects of alcohol/drug use on his/her mental health, this is only a *"snapshot"* of what actually happens when he/she uses alcohol/drugs. These beliefs are actually cognitive distortions (as discussed in C-BIT treatment phase 1, page 61) that allow him/her to convince him/herself that it is OK to keep using. You will need to help your client look at the fuller picture; it is almost like pressing the "fast-forward" button on a video recorder. This will help your client also to look at the effects of drug/alcohol use on his/her mental health and well-being not just immediately, but one hour later, later on in the day, the next day, the rest of the week, and so on.

Thus, an aim at this stage is to provide motivation for change by helping your client to see that problematic alcohol/drug use adversely affects his/her mental health and well-being. Two key strategies that will help your client to begin to see this link are *re-evaluating and modifying beliefs and provision of educational information*.

Re-evaluate and Modify His/Her Positive Beliefs About the Impact of Alcohol/Drug Use on His/Her Mental Health
(C-BIT Treatment Phase 1, page 62)

You will need to identify and look more closely at the positive beliefs about alcohol/drug use which your client holds that are related to his/her mental health/symptoms. Together with your client, you will need to re-evaluate and modify these beliefs to enable him/her to begin to see the adverse links between his/her alcohol/drug use and mental health. That is, at times alcohol/drugs may cause or exacerbate some of the mental health difficulties and symptoms he/she is trying to avoid by using substances. Facilitating your client's awareness of this link will help him/her to improve the self-management of his/her substance use and mental health difficulties.

Identify Positive Beliefs About the Impact of Alcohol/Drug Use on Mental Health

You can do this by reviewing what your client sees as the benefits of alcohol/drug use as recorded in the *"Ads"* column of his/her Advantages–Disadvantages Analysis and picking out those beliefs which are linked to mental health. For example, *"Cannabis stops my voices"*. An alternative strategy is to ask your client directly whether he/she has found a link between his/her alcohol/drug use and mental health. *For example, "When you use alcohol, have you found that it helps you? In what particular ways have you found it to be helpful, especially in relation to your mental health? Have you found that it helps to . . . (prompts: improve your mood/make you feel more relaxed/allow you to manage psychotic symptoms, etc.)?"*

Re-evaluate and Modify These Positive Beliefs

You can do this by initially getting your client to identify the cognitive distortions in these beliefs (see list of cognitive distortions, page 61). Then, using the three-question technique (*"What is the evidence for that belief?"; "Are there times when that is not the case?"; "If there are times when that is not the case, what are the implications?"*), re-evaluate the evidence used to support these beliefs and the evidence that does not support them. Help your client to generate an alternative, more realistic belief about the impact of his/her alcohol/drug use on his/her mental health. *For example, **Daniel believes that alcohol alleviates his stress and anxiety**.* The cognitive distortions in this belief are overgeneralisation and all-or-nothing thinking style.

Therapist: *Daniel, you've said that you have found that alcohol alleviates your stress and anxiety. What evidence do you have to support that belief?*
Daniel: *After I drink, I feel relaxed and the tension that I had been feeling goes away.*
Therapist: *Are there times when that is not the case?*
Daniel: *No, it always helps to reduce my stress and anxiety.*
Therapist: *Daniel, tell me about a recent time when you had a drink. You mentioned that you had a drink last night. Tell me about last night—for about how long did you feel relief of your tension, anxiety and stress following your drinking session?*
Daniel: *Well, I felt relief for most of the evening and then I fell asleep.*
Therapist: *How did you feel in the morning?*
Daniel: *I actually felt guilty because I was disappointed in myself for drinking and felt that I had let you down again.*
Therapist: *Daniel, it sounds as if you didn't feel very relaxed in the morning.*
Daniel: *No, I didn't. I felt quite anxious and edgy and a bit depressed that I had failed again.*
Therapist: *So, from what you are saying, it sounds as if there are times when after a drinking session you feel some relief for a few hours, but then you can actually end up feeling quite anxious and edgy. I'm wondering if there are times when alcohol doesn't*

alleviate your tension and stress but actually can set it off. Then, what are the implications?

Daniel: *Probably it's fairer to say that alcohol alleviates my stress and anxiety for a short while, but then it becomes a vicious circle and I feel worse the next day. Then I am more likely to feel depressed and feel like ending it all and to call the team in a crisis.*

Provide Educational Information

Effects of Alcohol/Drug Use on Mental Health

At this stage, it is helpful to provide your client with relevant information about the substances he/she uses and the specific effects of these substances on mental health and symptoms. Your client may be willing to take this information away and read through it by him/herself. Revisit this with your client the next time you see him/her, and check what he/she understood from the information and whether the client would benefit from further discussion with you. This will serve to provide the client with more accurate information and facts about the actual effects that the drugs he/she is using will have on his/her mental health, and help the client to re-evaluate any distortions in his/her residual substance-related beliefs.

Effects of Alcohol/Drug Use on Medication

Your client may not know much about the medication he/she takes. Thus, providing him/her with psychoeducation about his/her medication and its links with the substances used will help the client to become aware of the contraindications, risks and reduced effectiveness of his/her medication to ameliorate his/her symptoms. Your client may find it useful to talk this through with you or his/her psychiatrist; other clients may feel that they are able to speak more freely and respond better to a discussion with the pharmacist. Encourage an open discussion about medication so that your client can begin to see that alcohol/drug use will have an impact on the medication he/she is taking and its effectiveness against his/her mental health difficulties.

So remember, to make links between substance use and mental health,

- take a closer look at positive beliefs about using
- give information about the impact of using on medication and mental health.

TREATMENT PHASE 2—PULLING IT ALL TOGETHER

Harnessing Motivation to Change

- Elicit self-motivational statements concerning taking active steps toward change.
- Make links between poorer mental health/greater psychotic symptoms and substance use. Emphasise the role of substance-related beliefs in maintaining these difficulties and the importance of generating alternative, more realistic views of substance use.
- Breaking the vicious circle: identify achievable harm-reduction goals, problem-solve any difficulties that may arise and goal-set or establish a contract for change.
- Review any concerns about medication.

C-BIT CORE COMPONENTS

Chapter 7

TREATMENT PHASE 3: EARLY RELAPSE PREVENTION

AIMS

(1) Identify activating stimuli and beliefs that trigger desire to use and keep the client in a vicious cycle of problematic use.
(2) Help client generate a relapse-prevention plan of alternative coping strategies and beliefs, and strengthen commitment to change.

FORMULATING PROBLEMS: COGNITIVE MODEL OF SUBSTANCE USE

Some useful references: Beck et al. (1993), Liese and Franz (1996), Marlatt and Barrett (1994), Marlatt and Gordon (1985).

By this stage, your client will be aware of some of the difficulties associated with his/her drug or alcohol use and will have begun to re-evaluate some of his/her distorted positive substance-related beliefs. He/she will also have identified a goal to change his/her substance use and have made some positive change in alcohol/drug-using behaviour. However, the client may feel that his/her alcohol/drug use is out of his/her control, may find him/herself slipping back to using and may feel unable to identify the chain of events that led to using.

During this treatment phase, you can help your client to map out the chain of events that lead to his/her using alcohol/drugs problematically and the interrelationships between these events, using the cognitive model of problem substance use (Beck et al., 1993; Liese & Franz, 1996) (Figure 7.1).

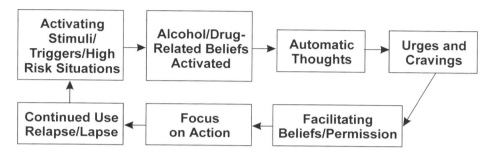

Figure 7.1 Cognitive model of problem substance use (modified from Beck et al., 1993; Liese & Franz, 1996)

You will need initially to explain the link between thoughts, feelings and behaviour by the cognitive model. This will enable your client to begin to see the links between his/her thoughts, feelings and subsequent behaviour (that is, alcohol/drug use). Within the cognitive model of substance use, the chain of "events", as illustrated in Figure 7.1, is said to contribute to a *lapse* (return on one or two occasions to previous alcohol/drug-using behaviour) or *relapse* (complete return to previous alcohol/drug-using behaviour) after a period of change/abstinence.

Activating Stimuli/Triggers/High-Risk Stimulus

These are idiosyncratic cues that trigger drug/alcohol beliefs. They may be internal cues (for example, feelings, images and physical sensations) or external cues (for example, people, places and things).

Drug/Alcohol-Related Beliefs Activated

These beliefs are the positive beliefs that clients hold about the alcohol/drugs they use. As mentioned previously, these beliefs are often cognitive distortions, and they paint a quite favourable and unrealistic picture of alcohol/drug use. They trigger cravings and urges to use and thus maintain problematic patterns of drinking/drug use. *For example, "I feel great and energetic when I use cocaine"; "Drinking makes the voices stop."*

Automatic Thoughts

Once clients' drug/alcohol-related beliefs have been activated, automatic thoughts, which are involuntary and brief versions of their drug/alcohol-related beliefs, are said to be triggered. These automatic thoughts can occur not only as thoughts and ideas but also as images. *For example, "Go ahead"; "Why not?"*

Urges and Cravings

These are said to be the sense of desiring/wishing to have a substance or an impulse to seek out and use alcohol/drugs. Urges and cravings are said to increase during withdrawal/or in the absence of using alcohol/drugs. Therefore, if clients are trying to abstain from using, they will experience more intense cravings and urges. The extent of their cravings and urges will also be determined by how much they ruminate on thoughts about using.

Facilitating Beliefs/Permission

You will have already discussed with your client the beliefs or things he/she says to him/herself that give permission to use alcohol/drugs. These facilitating or permission-giving beliefs are said to centre on themes of entitlement, justification and minimisation of the negative aspects of alcohol/drug use. The cognitive *distortions* in these beliefs allow clients to convince themselves that using again is OK. *For example, "I deserve a drink after the day I have had"; "I'll only have one"; "Everyone is using."*

Focus on Action

When clients reach this part of the cycle, they will have already talked themselves into using and will now be thinking about how they can get hold of alcohol/drugs. *For example, "I'll go upstairs and see my friend, who, I know, will have some rocks"; "I'll walk to the off-licence."*

Continued Use or Lapse/Relapse

Once clients have hold of their substance, they are likely to use it. If they had previously decided to change their pattern of use (reduce or abstain) and they have a slip and return to using alcohol/drugs on one or two occasions as they previously were, this is called a *lapse*. However, if, after this slip, they completely return to their previous alcohol/drug-using behaviour, this is called a *relapse*. If clients have a lapse, it is more likely to turn into a relapse if they engage in a particular distorted style of thinking called the *abstinence/rule violation effect*. *For example, "I've blown it"; "I knew I wouldn't be able to stop."* Clients may then feel that they have failed and give themselves permission to keep on using. *For example, "I might as well keep going"; " What's the point in trying?"*

Exercise: *How to elicit your client's chain of events that lead to problematic substance use*

Use the Relapse Cycle of Problem Substance Use worksheet (Appendix 3.1) to map out the chain of events.

(1) Ask the client to describe a recent time when he/she used alcohol/ drugs, particularly after a period of abstinence, or made some positive changes.

(2) To identify activating stimuli, ask about where he/she was, whom he/she was with, how he/she was feeling, what he/she was doing before he/she used. Also ask, "What situations/things (internal and external) usually make you feel like using?"

(3) To identify alcohol/drug beliefs, ask, "What was going through your mind at that time (just before you got the urges/cravings to use)?"

(4) To identify automatic thoughts, ask, "What thoughts popped into your head?"

(5) To identify facilitative/permission beliefs, ask, "What did you say to yourself that convinced you that it was OK to use or gave you permission to use?"

(6) To identify instrumental strategies, ask, "How did you think/decide you would be able to get alcohol/drugs?"

Consider the following case example:

Irene has a long history of heavy drinking. She drinks in a binge pattern and has had a number of periods of abstinence lasting up to about 8 months. After a recent binge, she says she cannot understand why she started drinking again. When Irene is drinking heavily, her life becomes chaotic and she stops taking her medication. Often the result is that she becomes quite paranoid and disinhibited, and hears voices telling her to kill herself. On some occasions, this has led to her going into hospital. She doesn't want to go back to hospital. Therefore, a brief explanation is given of relapse prevention and the cognitive model of substance use. It is suggested that there are strategies that will help her to recognise the chain of events that have led her to drinking binges in the past, and will put her in the driving seat to manage her drinking and psychotic relapses.

Let us try to map out the chain of events that led to her last two binges.

Relapse 1

Activating Stimuli

Therapist: *So, Irene about how long ago was this? Do you remember roughly where you were and if you were with any one?*
Irene: *It was last summer. I was watching the athletics at home on the TV.*
Therapist: *How were you feeling while watching?*
Irene: *Actually, I was feeling quite good.*

Alcohol/Drug Beliefs, Automatic Thoughts, Facilitative/Permission Beliefs

Therapist: *Do you remember what was going through your mind at that time?*
Irene: *I can't really remember.*
Therapist: *That's OK. Can you remember any thoughts that popped into your head at that time, or what you may have said to yourself that convinced you that it was OK to start drinking again?*
Irene: *Oh yes, I remember saying to myself, "I can handle it. I'll just have a few pints."*

Instrumental Strategies

Therapist: *How did you decide you would be able to get some alcohol?*
Irene: *I thought I'd send someone down to the off-licence, and then I couldn't stop drinking and started drinking in the early mornings.*

Relapse 2

Activating Stimuli

Therapist: *When you started drinking two months ago, can you remember roughly where you were and what was going on?*
Irene: *I wasn't getting any work, and I had just gone back to my ex-boyfriend and I had a holiday arranged.*
Therapist: *How were you feeling about all of this?*
Irene: *Well, I felt disappointed about going back to him, and I began lying in bed thinking about this, and I wasn't sleeping very well.*

Alcohol/Drug Beliefs

Therapist: *Do you remember what was going through your mind at that time?*
Irene: *I thought to myself that alcohol would ease my thinking and that I'd be able to sleep if I had a drink.*

Figure 7.2 Irene's relapse cycle of problem alcohol use

Facilitative/Permission Beliefs

Therapist: *What did you say to yourself that convinced you that it was OK to start drinking again?*
Irene: *That "I needed it—and that I'd have just one."*

Instrumental Strategies

Therapist: *How did you decide you would be able to get some alcohol?*
Irene: *I had lots of money lying around my room, so I thought I could go to the off-licence or send someone.*
Therapist: *What made you stop this time?*
Irene: *Well, I was planning to visit my mother, and I knew she wouldn't want me drinking around her so I stopped.*

Both relapses 1 and 2 were then mapped out on the Relapse Cycle of Problem Substance Use worksheet with Irene (see Figure 7.2).

RELAPSE PREVENTION: HELPING YOUR CLIENTS MANAGE THEIR SUBSTANCE USE

Once you have identified with your client the chain of events that contribute to his/her problematic pattern of alcohol/drug use, you will find that this chain of events forms the basis for the development of a relapse-prevention plan; that is, a plan that identifies alternative ways of coping with the chain of events that typically lead to problematic alcohol/drug use. *Relapse prevention is a plan of action that enables your client to self-manage his/her substance use by replacing his/her alcohol/drug-related beliefs with more realistic and accurate beliefs about alcohol/drugs (control beliefs), and by learning new coping skills and making lifestyle changes.* A relapse-prevention plan should address the cognitive, behavioural and social factors that have maintained your client's problematic use of alcohol/drugs. With your client, you will now need to look at mapping out an alternative route that takes him/her away from the cycle of problematic alcohol/drug use, using the cognitive model of control: Relapse-Prevention Plan worksheet (Figure 7.3) (Appendix 3.2).

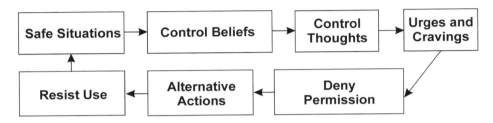

Figure 7.3 Cognitive model of control: relapse-prevention plan (adapted from Liese & Franz, 1996)

RELAPSE PREVENTION: INCLUDING SOCIAL NETWORK MEMBER(S)

It is important that in your attempts to manage and prevent relapse you include, wherever possible, members of the social network of those experiencing the substance-related difficulties. This will ensure two things:

- That your client has shared his/her decision to make a positive change in his/her alcohol/drug use with someone else. This will provide an additional incentive to maintain the changes achieved.
- That your client can receive support from someone whom he/she knows well, and will find supportive to prevent/better to manage relapses to problematic substance use.

An important goal when other people are involved in addition to your client is to promote a shared understanding of the relapse process with all those involved. This will allow you to discuss possible strategies that will help avoid relapse, with a particular emphasis on social support and positive support for change. Your ultimate aim is *to develop a relapse-management plan that involves the person with the problem and those interested in providing positive support for change.* You will therefore need to encourage your client to think of ways of using those involved to support the client's attempts to avoid relapse. This type of support will therefore remain available to the person as part of his/her natural social environment over the long term.

It is highly likely that supportive others are not familiar with the ideas related to lapses/relapses back to problematic drug/alcohol use. Therefore, it is fundamental that you spend time describing and explaining both the ideas and concepts that are part of relapse prevention to those who will be involved in providing support. The explanations you give should include the following:

- It is important to acknowledge that temptation to use more substances when you are trying to abstain or reduce is common in those attempting to change behaviour. For example, if a supportive network member views a relapse/lapse to substance use as a failure or an act of "weakness" on the part of the person with the problem, he/she may withdraw support when the client needs his/her help the most. If, however, the lapse/relapse to problematic drug/alcohol use is understood as a part of the journey towards improvement, network members will be more inclined to continue to offer support.
- You will need to discuss key concepts already described in other parts of this manual, including "activating stimuli/high-risk situations", "lapses" or "slips" and "relapse". Once these concepts are clear, you will have conveyed the message that lapses and relapses can be prevented. Foster a positive orientation towards the person with the substance-related problem and minimise attitudes that may foster a feeling of failure or criticism if the client does indeed lapse/relapse.

In cases where no other person is present in the session, you can still work out a relapse-management plan that involves other people (other people that are supportive but not present at the session, self-help groups, etc.). The emphasis is on social support in the management of lapses/relapses.

Developing a Relapse-Prevention Plan for Substance Use

The relapse-prevention plan of each client is different because the chain of events and beliefs held about alcohol and drug use is unique to each individual. However, there are some general areas that will need to be addressed and included in your client's relapse plan.

In using a cognitive model of control, the Relapse-Prevention Plan worksheet (Appendix 3.2), you will find the following exercise helpful in developing a relapse-prevention plan with your client to help him/her break the cycle of problem substance use:

Exercise: Developing a relapse-prevention plan for substance use

(1) With your client and social network member, identify the key events in your client's relapse cycle that he/she feels have significantly contributed to his/her past relapses. Focus on finding alternative ways of coping with these events first.

(2) Discuss the role the social network member and other social supports can play in the relapse-prevention plan. Agree an overall policy of how to respond to activating stimuli and lapses/relapse, and allocate specific tasks and roles to those involved if feasible.

(3) Identify any warning signs that your client is returning to a pattern of using alcohol/drugs problematically that you, he/she or a social network member can detect.

(4) Generate alternative ways of coping with the client's "activating stimuli" (that is, "safe situations"). Depending on your client's particular activating stimuli, you may need to focus on:
- skills training in coping with different moods and situations that may act as activating stimuli and trigger the urge to use alcohol/drugs (see C-BIT skills-building component—Chapter 10, "Coping with Different Moods")
- building social networks supportive of positive change (see C-BIT treatment phase 2, Chapter 6, section "How to Build Social Networks Supportive of Change")
- coping with pressure from friends/others in his/her network who use drugs/alcohol problematically (see page 188, C-BIT skills-building component—Alcohol/Drug-Refusal Skills)
- identifying alternative pleasurable/rewarding activities (see C-BIT treatment phase 2, Chapter 6, section, "Identifying Activities of Interest")

(5) Generate a set of control beliefs with your client, that is, more realistic, alternative beliefs to previously held positive alcohol/drug-related beliefs (see C-BIT treatment phase 1, Chapter 5, section "Building on Motivation for Change" and treatment phase 2, for help to re-evaluate and modify substance-related beliefs).

(6) Discuss strategies to cope with cravings and urges to use (see below for strategies).

(7) Make a link between mental health and substance use (see below for strategies).

It is important to get your client to rehearse his/her relapse-prevention plan on a regular basis to ensure that he/she is able to use it when the need arises. Your client will also benefit from carrying a summary of his/her relapse-prevention plan on a flashcard that he/she can quickly refer to. For example, let us return to the case example of Irene.

To break her cycle of problematic drinking, Irene decided that the key events she needed to address that had significantly contributed to her past relapses were her "activating stimuli", "facilitating beliefs" and "alcohol-related beliefs". Thus, these three factors in her relapse chain were focused on. Alternative ways of coping with her activating stimuli were identified by brainstorming and by identifying strategies she had used successfully in the past during periods when she was not drinking.

Identifying New Beliefs

Irene's facilitating/permission and alcohol-related beliefs were looked at and re-evaluated by the three-question technique. They were then modified to generate more accurate and realistic beliefs about alcohol.

Therapist: *When you last had a relapse to drinking heavily, you told yourself, "I can handle it". As we discussed, this belief seems to convince you that it is OK to start drinking again. I am just wondering what evidence you have to support this belief, "I can handle it"?*

Irene: *Very little, but at the time I really do feel that I can handle my drinking and am in control. However, soon my drinking is out of control and I'm drinking in the mornings.*

Therapist: *If it is true that your drinking does quickly get out of control, what are the implications?*

Irene: *I tell myself I can handle alcohol, but this is a falsehood. I can't handle it—once I get a taste for it, I am beaten.*

Therapist: *That sounds like a more realistic way of viewing your drinking.*

Irene: *It would be a helpful thing to tell myself in the future when I begin to get urges and cravings to drink.*

Therapist: *That sounds like a good idea. Let's write that down on your relapse-prevention plan, so that you can remember your new belief about alcohol when you get cravings to drink again.*

Therapist: *From what you said earlier, one of the other things you believe about alcohol that triggers cravings to drink is, "Alcohol eases my way of thinking and helps me to sleep." What evidence do you have to support that belief?*

Irene: *I just seem to become less bothered and worried about everything after a few drinks, and then I tend to fall asleep.*

Therapist: *What is your thinking like and how do you feel when you wake up?*

Irene: *I feel quite rough first thing in the morning after a drinking session. I tend to find it hard to think straight, and I feel a bit panicky until I have another drink.*

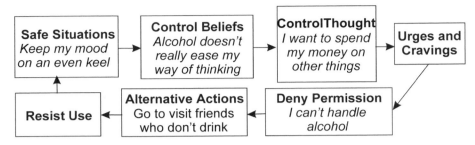

Figure 7.4 Irene's diagrammatic relapse-prevention plan

Therapist: *So, alcohol does seem to help your thinking initially, but then you feel quite rough the next day. If this is true, what are the implications for how you think about alcohol?*
Irene: *I guess I tend to forget about all the bad stuff about drinking and focus on those initial good feelings.*
Therapist: *What do you think is your message in a bottle?*
Irene: *Alcohol eases my way of thinking by helping me to sleep, but in the morning I feel panicky and nervous and find it hard to think rationally.*

Irene's relapse-prevention plan summary **(see also Figure 7.4)**

Social network support: *Bob, Karen, brother, AA meetings and sponsor, keyworker, mental health team.*
Activating stimuli: *high/low moods.*
Safe situations: *how I can keep my mood on an even keel:*
(1) *Make simple plans.*
(2) *Take each day as it comes.*
(3) *Take medication regularly.*
(4) *Spend time with friends Bob and Karen, who don't drink.*
(5) *Go to AA meetings and get a sponsor.*
(6) *Talk through the things that worry me with my friends, brother or mental health team.*
Alcohol-related belief: *"Alcohol eases my way of thinking and helps me to sleep."*
New control beliefs: *"Alcohol eases my way of thinking by helping me to sleep, but in the morning I feel panicky and nervous, and find it hard to think rationally."*
Permission belief: *"I can handle it."*
Deny permission belief: *"I tell myself I can handle alcohol, but this is a falsehood—I can't handle it. Once I get a taste for it I am beaten."*

COPING WITH CRAVINGS AND THE ABSTINENCE-VIOLATION EFFECT

Two important additional areas that need to be addressed when developing a relapse-prevention plan will be outlined here. The first is helping your client to identify and put into practice strategies to cope with cravings and urges to use alcohol/drugs in his/her old pattern of problematic use. The second is helping your client survive the "abstinence/rule-violation effect".

Coping with Cravings and Urges to Use

We have already learned that cravings and urges are said to be the sense of desiring/wishing to have a substance or an impulse to seek out and use alcohol/drugs. Urges and cravings are said to increase during withdrawal/or in the absence of using alcohol/drugs. Therefore, if your client is trying to abstain from using, he/she will experience more intense cravings and urges. The extent of his/her cravings and urges will also be determined by how much he/she ruminates on thoughts about using. Two strategies that have been found to be helpful in coping with cravings and urges are listed below.

Strategy 1: Provision of Psychoeducational Information About Cravings

Facts about cravings

- *Cravings are the result of long-term alcohol/drug use and can continue long after alcohol/drug use has stopped.*
- *Cravings can be triggered by people, places, things, feelings, situations or anything else that has been associated with alcohol/drug use in the past.*
- *Cravings tend to be stronger in the initial period after stopping alcohol/drug use, and then they fade away over time.*
- *Cravings will only lose their power if they are* not *reinforced by using alcohol/drugs. Using occasionally will serve only to keep cravings alive.*
- *Each time a person does something other than drink or take drugs in response to a craving, the craving will lose its power. This process is known as extinction.*
- *Abstinence from alcohol/drugs is the best way to ensure the most rapid and complete extinction of cravings.*

Strategy 2: Practical Behavioural and Cognitive Strategies to Cope with Urges/Cravings

Below are listed a number of behavioural, cognitive and imagery strategies that have been found to be helpful in managing cravings and urges to use alcohol/drugs. You will need to identify with your client the strategies he/she has used and found helpful in the past, and add some of the strategies listed below. Your client will benefit from rehearsing each strategy and how he/she could put it in place.

Behavioural

- counting
- avoidance/leaving the situation, particularly during the early phase
- relaxation/deep breathing
- distraction.

Cognitive

- positive talk (for example, "this feeling will pass")
- challenging alcohol/drug-related beliefs (that is, thinking errors).

Imagery

The urges that some clients experience can often be in the form of images. *For example, Irene found that after a period of four months' abstinence from alcohol images started to flash into her mind of her walking to the local off-licence that she used to buy alcohol from. These images started to increase her cravings to drink.* Some strategies that were found to be helpful in managing/transforming these images are listed below. Each of these strategies was then rehearsed and practised in the session.

- *Mastery.* For example, Irene was asked to conjure up this image and then to imagine herself walking past the off-licence instead of going in and buying alcohol. She was then asked to imagine how good she would feel about her achievement.
- *Alternative* (replace the image with an alternative adaptive, "healthy" image). For example, Irene was asked to conjure up this image and then to replace it with an alternative image, such as walking along the beach on her last holiday when she was abstinent.
- *"Fast forward"* (unfreeze the image and move it on in time, a few minutes, hours, days, etc., to enable the client to see that he/she is looking at only a part of the picture, which may in fact be a distortion of the whole picture). For example, Irene was asked to conjure up this image and then to unfreeze it and fast forward (almost as if pressing the fast-forward button on a videorecorder) and envisage the usual consequences of purchasing alcohol from this off-licence. She was asked to describe the immediate, short- and long-term consequences in quite a bit of detail.
- *"Surfing the urge"* (transform the image from one that feels overwhelming (a wave crashing over you) to an image of successfully overcoming the urge/craving by riding/surfing the urge as a surfer would surf a wave.

Go through the coping strategies described above with your client and jointly identify those that he/she can put in place when experiencing cravings and urges. It will also be helpful to practise them with your client, using recent incidents when he/she experienced cravings and urges. Your client will also find it useful if you summarise on the reverse side of his/her relapse-prevention plan summary flashcard a list of the coping strategies he/she will use against cravings and urges in any future incidents.

Coping with the Abstinence/Rule-Violation Effect

Often people will feel very bad about themselves if they have a lapse and see it as the end of the world or their attempts at abstinence. As mentioned earlier, the *abstinence violation* effect is said to be your client's reaction if he/she had made a decision to stop using, and then used. Alternatively, a *rule violation* effect is said to be your client's reaction if he/she had decided to change his/her pattern of use (for example, to cut down or to stop injecting drugs) and then had a "slip" and used. If the client returns to using alcohol/drugs on one or two occasions as he/she previously was, this is called a *lapse*. However, if following this "slip" the client completely returns to the previous alcohol/drug-using behaviour this is called a *relapse*. If your client has a lapse, it is said to be more likely to turn into a relapse if he/she engages in particular distorted styles of thinking and feeling about him/herself called the *abstinence/rule violation effect*. For example, *"I've blown it"; "I knew I wouldn't be able to stop."* The client may then give him/herself permission to keep on using by thinking, *for example, "I've messed up already so I might as well keep going."*

The main strategy to help your client cope with the abstinence/rule violation effect is *to re-evaluate and modify the thinking errors* that contribute to this effect. The aim is, firstly, for your client to identify the distortions in his/her thinking (such as minimisation, all or nothing, overgeneralisation), and secondly, for you to help him/her to generate a more helpful, less catastrophic and more realistic way of viewing the situation (for example, a slip/mistake rather than a complete failure). *Take, for example, the following list of modified thoughts:*

- *Thinking error:* "I've blown it", **new helpful thought:** "I've just had a slip and I can get back on track."
- *Thinking error:* "I knew I wouldn't be able to stop"; **new helpful thought:** "I have been able to make a change. This is only a slip and I can keep on trying."
- *Thinking error:* "I've messed up already so I might as well keep going"; **new helpful thought:** "I've just made a mistake and I can learn from it and get back on course."

So remember, to help clients manage their alcohol/drug use,

- identify their chain of events maintaining problematic use
- break the chain by identifying an alternative route
- have practical strategies in place to cope with cravings and urges
- remind your clients that a slip (lapse) isn't the same as a relapse!

RELAPSE PREVENTION: FOR SUBSTANCE USE AND ITS LINKS WITH MENTAL HEALTH

By now, you will already have an idea of most of your client's reasons for using alcohol/drugs and the beliefs held about alcohol/drugs and their links with his/her mental health. However, for some clients, the link may not be as clear.

Exercise: To begin to identify the role of mental health in the chain of events maintaining problematic alcohol/drug use, you will find the following strategies helpful:

(1) Discuss with your client a recent episode when he/she experienced mental health problems/psychotic symptoms.
(2) Explore the role of alcohol/drug use within this episode. Find out, at what point he/she began to think about using or actually used alcohol/drugs (before, during or as a consequence of the mental health problems/psychotic symptoms). From this discussion, your aim is to increase your client's awareness of the substance-related beliefs he/she holds which may link substance use to his/her psychosis/mental health and medication.
(3) Elicit from your client the evidence he/she has to support these substance-related beliefs and evidence which challenges these beliefs.
(4) Generate alternative (control) beliefs with your clients that are more realistic and reduce the likelihood of problematic use.

Using open-ended questions and a guided-discovery questioning style, begin to explore your client's beliefs about his/her experience of severe mental health problems; that is, the client's beliefs about the psychotic symptoms experienced and his/her beliefs about the perceived effectiveness of medication to manage these. Together, identify how these beliefs and experiences have affected the coping strategies he/she has developed. This will begin to increase your client's awareness of the functional role (that is, purpose) of drug/alcohol use in his/her life and in relation to his/her mental health.

Let us consider the following case example:

Andrew's flat was broken into a few months ago, and he is worried that it might happen again. He begins to experience paranoia and anxiety about his flat's being broken into. As a result, he is afraid to leave his flat, and he hears persecutory voices telling him that he is no good and voices telling him to attack the people that he thinks broke in. He is drinking four cans of strong lager and smoking cannabis each night. He does not believe that his paranoia, voices and anxiety could be linked to his drug and alcohol use.

Therapist: *Andrew, when was the last time that you felt worried about leaving your flat and/or heard the unpleasant voices?*
Andrew: *This morning when I got up, I wanted to pop to the shops before you got here to get the papers, but I felt so shaky and nervous that I stopped in.*
Therapist: *What were the thoughts going through your mind when you were trying to leave the house?*
Andrew: *I was thinking about the flat being broken into again, and the voices were bad, telling me that I'm no good and that I should get rid of the boys who broke in last time.*
Therapist: *From what you have said, I can understand why you felt worried about leaving your flat. Did anything happen last night that might have unsettled you?*
Andrew: *Nothing that I can think of. I just need to move from this flat and I'll be OK.*
Therapist: *That is something that is being looked into. Until you move, let's see if there is anything that will help you feel less nervous about leaving the flat. Did you have a drink or use any cannabis last night?*
Andrew: *Yes, I drank a little, perhaps three or four cans, and had a couple of spliffs with a friend who came by last night.*
Therapist: *About what time did you stop drinking and smoking?*
Andrew: *Just before I went to bed, but it can't be the drink or smoking that made me feel bad today, as I've drunk and smoked for years and I don't always feel like this. Drinking and smoking with my mates relaxes me, and if I feel bad in the morning, if I have a couple of spliffs I soon feel OK again.*
Therapist: *Andrew, it sounds as if there are times when your drinking and smoking have positive benefits for you. However, have there been times when this has not been the case?*

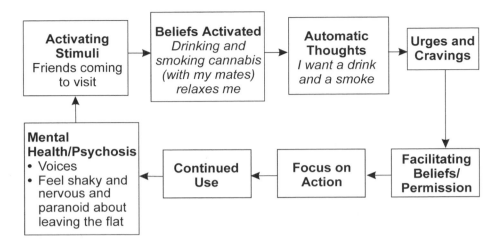

Figure 7.5 Andrew's relapse cycle of problem alcohol/cannabis use and its links with his mental health

Andrew: *Since the burglary when I've got a lot of things on my mind that are worrying me, I tend not to feel so great in the morning if I have drunk or smoked the night before. Also, when I stopped using for a couple of weeks as you suggested, I noticed that the voices stopped and I felt less nervous about leaving the flat.*

Therapist: *So, from what you have said, it sounds as if when you have things on your mind that you are worried about, then smoke/drink in the evening, it makes the voices and nervousness worse. Andrew, if this is the case, then what do you think are the implications for how you use alcohol and cannabis?*

Andrew: *Maybe I need to cut down or not use during those times when I have things on my mind that are worrying me.*

Therapist: *Let's write this down now that we better understand the link between your nervousness about leaving the flat, the voices, and your drinking and smoking in the evening (see Figure 7.5).*

So remember,

- identify the role of alcohol/drug use in poor mental health.

TREATMENT PHASE 3—PULLING IT TOGETHER

Harnessing Change

- Summarise: make links between activating stimuli/high-risk situations and substance-related beliefs and mental health in maintaining problematic substance use.
- Elicit importance-confidence to maintain changes in substance use and self-motivational statements concerning change.
- Breaking the vicious circle: identify relapse-management plan, problem-solve any difficulties that may arise and goal set/contract for change.

C-BIT CORE COMPONENTS

Chapter 8

TREATMENT PHASE 4: RELAPSE PREVENTION/RELAPSE MANAGEMENT

AIMS

(1) Develop a relapse-prevention/relapse-management plan that incorporates psychosis, medication and substance use.
(2) Encourage use of relapse-prevention/relapse-management plan to prevent or manage better relapses to acute psychosis and role of alcohol/drugs.

Relapse Prevention/Relapse Management

Helpful resources/references: Birchwood et al. (1998), Birchwood, Spencer and McGovern (2000), Liese and Franz (1996), Marlatt and Gordon (1985), Weiss, Najavits and Greenfield (1999).

By now, you will have identified with your client the chain of events that have kept him/her in a vicious cycle of using alcohol/drugs in a problematic way. You will have also developed with the client a relapse-prevention plan (that is, an "alternative route") that will help him/her to break out of this problematic cycle of use. With your client, you will have begun to look at the impact that alcohol/drug use has on his/her mental health. To ensure that your client has strategies in place to manage better the use of alcohol/drugs and prevent relapses to psychosis, you will now need to look at building on the relapse-prevention plan you developed in C-BIT treatment phase 3. Your aim now is to develop with your client a more comprehensive relapse-prevention/management plan that incorporates both his/her substance use and psychosis. Some strategies are outlined below that you will find helpful in developing such a relapse-prevention plan, *including social network member(s), identifying a relapse signature, developing a comprehensive relapse-prevention/management plan and using a comprehensive relapse-prevention/management plan.*

INCLUDING SOCIAL NETWORK MEMBER(S) IN RELAPSE PREVENTION

By now, your client will have identified one or more members of his/her social network who are supportive of his/her attempts to change the alcohol/drug use. These people may already be involved in helping the client make the necessary changes in lifestyle. *At this stage, you will need to attempt to involve them in the plan to help the client maintain changes in substance use and manage/prevent risk of relapse to psychosis.* The aim is to ensure that your client can receive support from someone whom he/she knows well and finds supportive in preventing or better managing relapses to problematic substance use or acute psychosis.

An important goal when other people are involved in addition to your client is to promote a shared understanding of the relapse process with all those involved. This will allow you to discuss possible strategies that will help avoid relapse with a particular emphasis on social support and positive support for change. You will therefore need to encourage your client to think of ways of using those involved to support his/her attempts to avoid relapse. This type of support will therefore remain available to the person as part of his/her natural social environment and over the long term.

It is highly likely that supportive others are not familiar with the ideas related to psychotic relapses. Therefore, it is fundamental that you spend time describing and explaining both the ideas and concepts that are part of relapse prevention to those who will be involved in providing support. If supportive others perceive lapse/relapse as a "failure" on the part of the client, they may withdraw support when the client needs their help the most. The explanations you give should include the following:

- Relapses to psychosis may occur, but can be detected by a number of "early warning signs" and prevented or better managed through a relapse-prevention plan.
- It is important to acknowledge that temptation to use more substances when they are trying to abstain or reduce is common in those attempting to change behaviour. Moreover, the client may believe, and on some occasions

may have found, drug/alcohol use to be an effective way of coping with psychotic symptoms or early warning signs. Therefore, he/she may be more tempted to use when experiencing such difficulties. Thus, relapse/ lapse to substance use should not be seen as a "failure" or an act of "weakness" on the part of the person with the problem, but rather as a normal part of the process of changing behaviour.

In cases where no other person is present in the session, you can still work out a relapse-management plan that involves other people (other people that are supportive but not present at the session, self-help groups, etc.). The emphasis is on social support in the management of lapses/relapses.

IDENTIFYING A RELAPSE SIGNATURE TO PSYCHOTIC RELAPSES AND ROLE OF SUBSTANCE USE

For some time, your client will probably have wanted to avoid going into hospital and/or becoming acutely psychotic. However, as with changing his/ her alcohol/drug use, he/she may believe that psychiatric hospital admission and experiencing psychotic symptoms are inevitable, out of his/her control, and feel unable to identify the chain of events that led to such events occurring. During this treatment phase, you can help your client to map out the chain of events that led to his/her becoming unwell and the relationship between these events and his/her alcohol/drug use. The techniques that are described here are similar to the ones you used in C-BIT treatment phase 3 for the client's substance use. You will also find the techniques for psychosis relapse prevention described by Birchwood, Spencer and McGovern (2000), a description which will serve as a useful template.

Rose is a 23-year-old woman diagnosed with schizophrenia. She has been recently admitted to hospital, as she was unwilling to take medication and was behaving aggressively toward her family and people in her local pub. This is her fourth admission in five years. She does not want to be in hospital and at all costs does not want to be readmitted. She says she "just wants to get on with her life". Rose uses a number of different substances but is willing to talk only about her use of alcohol and cannabis. It was therefore agreed with Rose to look at the events that seem to bring her into hospital and the impact her alcohol and cannabis use had on her.

By steps 1–6 outlined in the following exercise, we are able to identify Rose's psychotic relapse signature:

(2) Review with Rose the most recent episode when she experienced a relapse to psychosis or was admitted to hospital.

Exercise: To begin to identify your client's psychotic relapse signature, you will find the following steps helpful:

(1) Introduce the client to examples of early warning signs of psychotic relapse (Appendix 4.1).
(2) Ask your client to review the most recent episode when he/she experienced a relapse to psychosis or was admitted to hospital.
(3) Identify any noticeable changes in perceptions, thoughts, feelings and behaviours, using the examples of early warning signs of psychotic relapse as a prompt.
(4) Identify any particular stressful events or factors that may have triggered these changes. Prompt the client by using open-ended questions about any stressful or unusual events, worries or concerns he/she may have had around that time.
(5) From your discussion, identify the chain of external events and internal events (that is, the relapse signature) that preceded his/her becoming psychotic/being admitted to hospital. Divide events into three stages: early, middle and late.
(6) Find out whether this is the general chain of events leading to his/her becoming unwell. You can do this by asking about another recent occasion and the first time he/she became unwell or was admitted. Repeat steps 2, 3 and 4 for these two episodes to determine whether this is the usual pattern/chain of events (see Table 8.1 on page 115).

Therapist: *Rose, you said that you do not like being in hospital. Can you tell me about what was going on just before you came into hospital this time?*
Rose: *Lots of things. My boyfriend was coming in drunk a lot and picking on me. Nothing I did was right for him. My mum said I was getting sick again, and before I knew it I was forced to come back to hospital.*
Therapist: *When did you come into hospital?*
Rose: *In February.*

(3) Identify any noticeable changes in perceptions, thoughts, feelings and behaviours, using the examples of early warning signs of psychotic relapse as a prompt.

Therapist: *Rose, so how were you feeling at that time?*
Rose: *Well, I was feeling quite fed up and that I'm no good. I was sure that my boyfriend didn't like me.*
Therapist: *Rose, it sounds like you weren't feeling good at all. How did this affect you?*

Rose: *I just started spending time on my own and was thinking a lot.*
Therapist: *What sorts of things were you thinking about?*
Rose: *That bad things always happen to me, and that it's my fault.*
Therapist: *How did this affect you?*
Rose: *I couldn't seem to get to sleep. I couldn't stop the thoughts—they just kept whizzing through my head.*

(4) Identify any particular stressful events or factors that may have triggered these changes. Prompt Rose by using open-ended questions about any stressful or unusual events, worries or concerns she may have had around that time.

Therapist: *Rose, you mentioned that your boyfriend was picking on you. What else was going on just before you were admitted that might have made you feel so bad?*
Rose: *There were quite a few bills to pay, including the rent, and with all the drinking my boyfriend was doing we didn't have enough money left to pay the bills. I guess I started worrying that we would be evicted, but I'm sure my friend Tania, who was in a car crash, had cast a spell on me and that's why I couldn't sleep.*
Therapist: *It sounds as if it was quite a stressful time for you. It must have been difficult to cope with all the things that were on your mind.*

(5) From your discussion, identify the chain of external events and internal events (that is, the relapse signature) that preceded Rose's becoming psychotic and being admitted to hospital.

Therapist: *So, if you had to put in order all the things that were causing you to worry just before you came into hospital, what would you say came first? And then after that, etc.?*
Rose: *I guess it would have been feeling a bit odd and that things weren't going well. I was wondering why bad things always seem to happen to me. I was just feeling edgy all the time.*
Therapist: *What happened after that—and how were you feeling?*
Rose: *I tried to tell my boyfriend that we had to pay the bills, but he kept telling me to leave him alone, and would go out drinking all day with his mates. I felt fed up and frustrated, and started spending a lot of time on my own, wondering why people didn't seem to like me anymore.*
Therapist: *So, what happened after that?*
Rose: *I couldn't get off to sleep and then I was sure that it was because Tania had put a spell on me. I told my boyfriend this, but he told me I was stupid, and I started shouting at him. After that, he just kept arguing all the time, and he would come home off his face every day.*
Therapist: *What happened after that?*
Rose: *Whenever I went out, people would stare at me, and I thought that everyone hates me and blames me for all the bad things that happen. I would hear Tania's voice*

in the background whispering that it was my fault and that I'm a bad person. After that, I could only sleep for about 2 hours each night, and that's when Tania's voice told me that she would never let me rest. I couldn't get any peace, and when my boyfriend wouldn't listen to me I knew he had turned against me. So I would shout at him to get him to understand. Eventually I thought I'd just lock myself in my room away from all the people who hated me.

Therapist: What happened after that?

Rose: Well, I couldn't sleep at all, and the voices kept shouting awful things about me. I didn't move from my bed—I didn't even go to the bathroom to have a wash or anything, I was so frightened. I would scream at the voices, but they wouldn't leave so I locked all the doors and windows of the flat to get peace. The next thing I knew, my mum had called the police and I was in hospital.

Therapist: Let's write down this chain of events that caused you to be so upset, so we don't forget them [see Figure 8.1 on page 120—note that the events are divided into three stages: early, middle and late].

(6) Find out whether this is the general chain of events leading to Rose's becoming unwell. You can do this by asking about another recent occasion and the first time she became unwell or was admitted.

Therapist: Rose, are these stressful situations and feelings similar events to those which happened the last time you came into hospital or the first time you were ever admitted?

Rose: Not really the first time I came in. It was after I lost my temper and beat up my boyfriend and he left me.

Therapist: Was there anything else that was worrying you at that time?

Rose: Well, about 2 months before, in February, I had heard that Tania had been hurt in a car crash. I was sad about this because I had just started to get to know her, and I thought she liked me. I wanted us to be friends. A few weeks later, my mum said she saw someone who looked just like Tania when she went shopping in town, but that the person walked past her without saying hello. I started to wonder if Tania thought it was my fault that she was hurt in the accident. Then I had the scariest dream about Tania—I could feel her presence around me and feel her touching my face.

Therapist: What effect did it have on you when you started thinking like this?

Rose: I felt quite scared, worried and sad, and then I felt angry with my boyfriend because he didn't believe me.

Therapist: So, the first time you came into hospital, it sounds like you had lots of worries about whether your friend blamed you for her being hurt in a car accident, and you found that you could not talk to your boyfriend about it.

Rose: That's right, and then we got into an argument, and I got so angry and I just couldn't stop myself. I didn't mean to hit him that hard. The next-door neighbours heard all the noise and called the police.

Therapist: *Rose, it sounds like it was a difficult time for you and things got out of control. Let's add these events into our chain of events that seem to have led you into hospital (see Table 8.1).*

Exercise: To identify the impact of alcohol/drug use on your client's psychotic relapse signature, you will find the following steps helpful:

(7) Explore the role of alcohol/drug use within the client's relapse signature by identifying the points along the chain of events at which he/she used alcohol/drugs. You can do this by asking the client directly whether he/she used during this episode and at which points he/she used.

(8) Identify the client's pattern of use by asking: *what* he/she used; *amount*: how much he/she used; *frequency*: how often he/she used; *where* did he/she use; *whom* he/she used with.

(9) It is also important to identify the reasons why the client used alcohol/drugs at each point and what were his/her beliefs about using the substance (was it to increase pleasure, to socialise, to cope?).

By following steps 7–9, we were able to identify the role in and impact of alcohol/drug use on Rose's psychotic relapse:

(7) Explore the role of alcohol/drug use within this chain of events, by identifying the points along the chain of events at which Rose was using alcohol/drugs.

(8) Identify her pattern of use.

(9) It is also important to identify the reasons why Rose was using at each point and what her beliefs about using the substance were.

Therapist: *Rose, you mentioned that just prior to this last time you came into hospital, your boyfriend was drinking heavily. How were you drinking or smoking cannabis around that time—were you using every day?*

Rose: *Pretty much every day.*

Therapist: *Let's take drinking [a series of questions/prompts was used to elicit the pattern of use—how much would you drink? What time would you have your first drink and your last? Would you drink throughout the day? Were you drinking alone, with friends or with your boyfriend?].*

Rose: *I can't quite remember how much I was drinking—probably three or four cans of Tennent's Super every day, from the afternoon until I fell asleep. But I've always drunk like that with my mates.*

Therapist: *Rose, if we look at the chain of events that seems to lead you into hospital (see Table 8.1), did your drinking pattern change (increase or decrease) at any point?*
Rose: *Well, probably I was drinking less from the time I started locking myself in the flat.*
Therapist: *Let's take cannabis. Would you be smoking cannabis throughout the day as well? [a series of questions/prompts was used to elicit the pattern of use—how much were you smoking? How many days per week would you smoke? Were you smoking on your own or with others?].*
Rose: *Yeah, I've always smoked through the day about six spliffs, and it doesn't seem to bother me.*
Therapist: *Rose, if we look at the chain of events that seems to lead you into hospital (see Table 8.1), did your pattern of cannabis use change (increase or decrease) at any point?*
Rose: *Well, I guess when the voices started getting louder and I couldn't sleep very well, then I started smoking a bit more.*
Therapist: *What effect was the cannabis and alcohol having on you? How did you think they were helping?*
Rose: *The cannabis was helping me to relax before I went to bed, and then when I couldn't sleep, it was helping me to chill out. I guess with alcohol it's just a habit, and when I'm with my boyfriend and we are drinking, we have more to talk about and I feel less tense.*
Therapist: *When you were drinking and smoking just before you came into hospital this time, do you think it was causing you any problems?*

Exercise: To identify the role of medication adherence in your client's psychotic relapse signature, you will find the following steps helpful:

(10) Explore the role of medication adherence within the relapse signature, by identifying the points along the chain of events at which the client was taking his/her medication as prescribed or not. You can do this by asking the client directly whether he/she was taking his/her medication during this episode and at which points he/she was not.

(11) Identify the client's pattern of medication adherence at each point along the chain by asking: *What* medication was he/she taking; *dosage*: how much was he/she taking; *frequency*: how often was he/she taking it.

(12) It is also important to identify the beliefs the client holds about his/her medication, and the reasons why he/she did or did not take his/her medication at each point in the relapse signature.

Rose: *Not really—except the money it was costing. The drinking was OK, except sometimes by the evening, if I had smoked a lot that day, I'd start to feel a bit paranoid that people, especially my boyfriend, were thinking that Tania's car accident was my fault. Then I'd feel aggressive toward him, and I'd end up arguing or getting into fights with him.*

Therapist: *So, just before you came into hospital this time, you were drinking a bit less, but you were smoking more in an attempt to help you sleep or relax. Let's add this to your chain of events (see Table 8.1).*

By following steps 10–12, we were able to identify the impact of Rose's medication adherence on her psychotic relapse signature:

(10) Explore the role of medication adherence within Rose's relapse signature.

Therapist: *Rose, were you taking any medication just before you came into hospital this time?*

Rose: *I can't remember . . . um. Yes, well, actually I had stopped taking it in January and started taking it again when I couldn't get to sleep.*

(11) Identify Rose's pattern of medication adherence.

Therapist: *So, you were taking it at times and then not at others. At the time when you were taking your medication, can you remember if you were taking the amount you were prescribed?*

Rose: *I was only taking one tablet on the nights I couldn't sleep. I think I am supposed to take two tablets every day.*

(12) It is also important to identify Rose's beliefs about her medication, and the reasons why she took her medication as she did or did not at each point in her relapse signature.

Therapist: *What made you decide to take one tablet less and not to take them regularly?*

Rose: *I felt well. I don't think there is any point in taking them if I am not sick, but sometimes when I couldn't sleep they helped me sleep, so I starting taking them again. But I only took them for a few days, as they stopped working.*

Therapist: *You mentioned that you took only one tablet when you couldn't sleep instead of two. What made you decide to do this?*

Rose: *I don't know. I guess, whenever I take two, I find it too hard to get up, and then I feel tired all day. I also put on lots of weight when I'm taking it regularly.*

Therapist: *Let's make a note of how you think about your medication and how you use it in the period prior to you coming into hospital (see Table 8.1).*

Table 8.1 Rose's psychotic relapse signature and the role of alcohol/cannabis

---

Stopped taking medication

Feeling odd

Thinking I am no good (boyfriend doesn't like me; I'm to blame for car accident)

Bad things always happen to me

Worry and feel frustrated, angry, scared, sad, edgy

Spend a lot of time alone

Difficulty getting off to sleep

Racing thoughts

Arguing with boyfriend

Continued use of alcohol and cannabis (belief: cannabis and alcohol help me relax and cannabis will help me sleep)

Thinking that everyone blames me and is against me

Feeling paranoid

Hear a faint voice

Only sleep for a few hours

Take some of my medication for a few days

Stay in bedroom a lot

Shout at boyfriend

Smoke more cannabis to help me sleep

Feel very paranoid (everyone, especially boyfriend, against me)

Voices get louder

Can't sleep

Lock myself in flat

Small reduction in alcohol use

Smoke more cannabis to help me relax

Screaming at voices

So remember, to identify relapse signatures and role of substance use,

- identify early warning signs of psychotic relapse
- explore the pattern of alcohol/drug use during the relapse signature
- look at the pattern of medication adherence.

DEVELOPING A COMPREHENSIVE RELAPSE-PREVENTION/RELAPSE-MANAGEMENT PLAN

By now, you have identified with your client the chain of events that typically leads up to a psychotic relapse (relapse signature) and the relationship between these events and his/her alcohol/drug use and use of medication. The next step is to develop collaboratively, with your client and his/her social network member(s), *a comprehensive relapse-prevention/relapse-management plan that will help him/her prevent or better manage relapse to acute psychosis and manage the use of alcohol/drugs in the relapse process*. The work you will now do with your client will build on the relapse-prevention plan you have developed with him/her to break the cycle of problematic alcohol/drug use in C-BIT treatment phase 3 and the relapse signature previously identified in this treatment phase.

The plan needs to include a number of practical, simple strategies that the client can use, should he/she begin to relapse, comprising *personal coping strategies, social network support, accessing mental health services and treatment interventions*. The following areas should be addressed within the comprehensive relapse-prevention/management plan: *managing early warning signs and the role of alcohol/drug use, medication adherence and specific skills*.

Managing Early Warning Signs of Psychosis and the Role of Alcohol/Drug Use

The first step in developing a comprehensive relapse-prevention plan is to help your client recognise and monitor early warning signs which serve as early indicators to him/her, you and others that the client's risk of becoming acutely psychotic is increasing. These early warning signs will be the thoughts, feelings and behaviours you have previously identified in the client's relapse signature, including the client's use of alcohol/drugs. It is also possible that some of the early warning signs that occur during the relapse process may also act as activating stimuli for substance use. That is, they activate positive beliefs about drugs/alcohol and trigger or increase urges and cravings to use.

Your client may not be convinced that his/her alcohol/drug use has anything to do with psychotic relapses. He/she may say to you that he/she has "always" used in a particular pattern. However, it will be important to illustrate to your client that at certain times, as when he/she is under stress or experiencing early warning signs, he/she is particularly vulnerable to the negative effects of alcohol/drug use. For example, if John is not sleeping well and is worried about the debts he has, he may use/increase his use of cannabis in an attempt to help him relax and sleep. However, due to the nature of cannabis, continued use or an increase in use at this point would serve only to amplify his concerns and, in turn, exacerbate his sleep disturbance. This would then increase his vulnerability to the onset of psychotic symptoms. An analogy that can be used to illustrate the importance of this point is the "diabetes model". That is, if a person has diabetes and has recently been under a significant amount of stress, he/she may experience an increase in blood-sugar levels. At that time, he/she would be quite vulnerable, and any sugar intake could have quite a negative effect. Even though the person can usually have a small amount of sweet things when his/her blood-sugar level is stable, at this point, due to the current instability in levels, he/she is particularly vulnerable and should completely reduce sugar intake. Thus, the aim of providing educational information to your client regarding the timing of alcohol/drug use within his/her relapse signature is to convey a harm minimisation model. That is, encourage your client to manage his/her substance use when particularly vulnerable and at risk of relapse. This may mean, for example, not using a particular substance if he/she is experiencing early warning signs of relapse to psychosis, reducing use during this period or stopping use until his/her mental health has stabilised.

It is important to break the client's relapse signature down into three stages: early, middle and late. These three stages correspond to the early warning signs that occur in the initial, middle and latter phases just prior to the psychotic relapse. The aim of developing a comprehensive relapse-prevention plan is to help your client put alternative coping strategies in place in each of the three stages. These alternative coping strategies are then used to help the client better manage the early warning signs of psychosis and the activating stimuli of substance use which exacerbate the risk of psychotic relapse.

Medication Adherence

You will have previously identified your client's pattern of medication adherence within his/her relapse signature. To improve medication adherence, it will be important to provide your client with some psychoeducational information about medication and medication adherence. Your client may better respond to this information if it is provided by someone not directly involved (such as a pharmacist). It may also be beneficial to explore with your client the pros (benefits) and cons (costs) of his/her taking medication as prescribed. To promote the optimal use of medication, the aim is to help your client think through a cost–benefit analysis of taking medication that as far as possible minimises the negative aspects of taking medication. For some clients, more in-depth work is needed to address issues around medication, and he/she may benefit from medication compliance therapy (Kemp et al., 1996). It may also be necessary for the client to discuss with his/her consultant psychiatrist his/her concerns about taking medication and negotiate a change in dose or type, to ensure some level of adherence.

Specific Skills

In developing a comprehensive relapse-prevention plan, you will also need to help your client develop any specific skills that will help him/her to be better able to cope. The skills that you will need to develop will vary from client to client and will be determined by a client's needs and existing skills. For some clients, the focus will need to be on teaching new skills; for others, it will be on building on existing skills and coping strategies. Below are listed five additional skills that have been found to be necessary to develop comprehensive relapse-prevention plans. The strategies to teach each of these skills are described in the respective Skills-Building Component:

- communication (see page 164)
- refusing alcohol and drugs (see page 188)
- strengthening alternative activities/networks (see pages 79, 81)
- money management (see pages 213–214)
- mood management (see pages 122–163)
- goal planning and problem solving (see pages 73–79).

USING A COMPREHENSIVE RELAPSE-PREVENTION/ MANAGEMENT PLAN—RELAPSE DRILL

Now that you have collaboratively developed a comprehensive relapse-prevention plan, you will need to help your client use the plan and include the assistance of services and his/her social network member(s). Relapse-prevention plans have been likened to fire drills, because they are plans that are put in place to be preventative and need to be practised even in the absence of any early warning signs. Therefore, to ensure your client uses his/her plan effectively, you will need to ensure the client:

- knows his/her plan
- knows when to use his/her plan
- works together with you, other services and his/her social network member(s) to use the plan
- practises with you the alternative coping methods and control beliefs listed in the plan through role-plays and personalised scenarios
- regularly monitors early warning signs along with those involved
- refines and updates the plan (that is, coping strategies, forms of intervention and supports) as circumstances change.

*Exercise: Developing a comprehensive relapse-prevention/management plan—
relapse drill*

(1) With your client and social network member(s), review the client's relapse signature and break it into three stages: early, middle and late.

(2) Go through each of the early warning signs listed in the relapse signature and identify alternative "healthy" coping responses that can be included in the plan. These should incorporate personal coping strategies, social network support, accessing mental health services and treatment interventions. Also include strategies the client has found helpful in the past. List these on a comprehensive relapse-prevention/management summary in a column entitled "Relapse drill" alongside the "Relapse signature" (see Figure 8.1).

(3) Agree with all involved an overall policy of how to respond to early warning signs/relapse and their roles.

(4) When drug/alcohol use is identified in the relapse signature, you can refer to the client's substance use relapse-prevention plan and include the strategies already identified (safe situations and control/deny permission beliefs) in the "Relapse drill". Encourage the client to differentiate between the types of substances used and to decide whether it is better to abstain or reduce use at key points along the relapse signature.

(5) Include in the "Relapse drill" strategies already identified to increase medication adherence.

(6) Identify any additional skills/coping strategies the client may need to increase the chances of his/her being able to cope with early warning signs.

So remember, to help clients develop a comprehensive relapse-prevention/management plan,

- include a social network member
- develop "healthy" strategies to cope with early warning signs
- monitor early warning signs
- address medication adherence
- look at timing of alcohol/drug use
- develop specific skills
- practise relapse drill!

Support network: Mum, keyworker, Jo

Relapse signature	Relapse drill
Early stage	
Stopped taking medication	*Take medication regularly.* *Remind myself: "The cost of taking meds is putting on a bit of weight and feeling drowsy sometimes. However, the benefits are that I don't get worrying thoughts about Tania, I can sleep and I won't end up in hospital." Keyworker to check I am taking it.*
Feeling odd *Thinking I am no good (boyfriend doesn't like me; I'm to blame for car accident)* *Bad things always happen to me*	*Call mother and keyworker; talk over worries and coping with fears.*
Worry; feel frustrated, angry, scared, sad, edgy *Spend a lot of time alone* *Difficulty getting off to sleep* *Racing thoughts*	*Use relaxation techniques.*
Arguing with boyfriend	*Stay at Mum's if I am arguing a lot with boyfriend.*
Continued use of alcohol and cannabis	*Safe situation: Go out and visit Jo.*
Belief: "cannabis and alcohol help me to relax and cannabis will help me sleep"	*Control belief: "Cannabis and alcohol only help for a little while and then I only feel worse."*
Middle stage	
Thinking that everyone blames me and is against me	*Increase contact with services.*
Feeling paranoid	*Discuss feelings and thoughts.*
Hear a faint voice *Only sleep for a few hours*	*Use distraction (Walkman).*
Take some of my medication for a few days *Stay in bedroom a lot* *Shout at boyfriend*	*Take extra medication as prescribed.* *See my psychiatrist and keyworker.*
Smoke more cannabis to help me sleep	*Safe situation: Stay at Mum's and stop cannabis use. Control belief: "Cannabis is* not *helpful at this stage."*
Late stage	
Feel very paranoid (everyone, especially boyfriend, against me) *Voices get louder* *Can't sleep* *Lock myself in flat* *Small reduction in alcohol use* *Screaming at voices*	*Ring keyworker/emergency contact number. Tel: xxx xxxx* *Ask for respite/hospital.*

Figure 8.1 Rose's comprehensive relapse-prevention/management plan summary

TREATMENT PHASE 4—PULLING IT TOGETHER

Harnessing Change

- Summarise: emphasise importance of monitoring in parallel and relationship between psychotic symptoms, substance use, medication adherence and engaging in alternative ways of thinking, activities and social networks in managing substance use.
- Elicit importance/confidence to maintain changes in substance use and self-motivational statements concerning change.
- Breaking the vicious circle: use relapse-management plan, problem-solve any difficulties that arise and goal set/contract for change.

ADDITIONAL TREATMENT COMPONENTS I—SKILLS BUILDING

Chapter 9

COPING WITH DIFFERENT MOODS: ANXIETY

> **AIM**
>
> To increase understanding of anxiety and learn a variety of techniques to manage it.

Helpful references and resources: Freeman et al. (1997), Greenberger and Padesky (1995).

Managing anxiety is about challenging the thoughts that keep anxiety going. It is not about making anxiety disappear. The methods used take time and practice. To begin with, focusing someone's attention onto his/her anxiety may leave him/her feeling more symptoms. This will be temporary! People may have concerns about their physical health and should be helped to have these concerns checked in conjunction with this work.

THE ROLE OF SUBSTANCES IN CREATING OR MAINTAINING ANXIETY

Using drugs or alcohol can become a strategy to avoid feelings of anxiety when handling difficult situations. People may drink more when they feel anxious in an attempt to reduce the anxiety, but, in fact, heavy drinking increases anxiety. Alcohol actually depresses the activity of the nervous system. This is why alcohol can at first seem to reduce feelings of anxiety. However, the nervous system then needs to work extra hard to counteract the effects of alcohol and regain its correct level of functioning. Thus, when the alcohol level in the body drops, the increased level of activity continues for a while until the body regains its balance, and this results in increased feelings of anxiety. Therefore, withdrawal from alcohol produces a reaction similar to the initial feelings of anxiety that the person was attempting to avoid by drinking. The result is that increasing amounts of alcohol are needed to avoid these feelings and a vicious circle develops. As a person's body becomes more dependent on alcohol, the withdrawal effects become worse. The short-term or long-term effect or "come down" from some drugs, such as cocaine, amphetamines, cannabis and ecstasy, can be anxiety or panic. It is important to note that people's beliefs about the function of substances can maintain both alcohol/drug use and the feeling of anxiety. Thus, as people find that alcohol/ drugs initially decrease their anxiety, they will begin to develop beliefs about the effectiveness of alcohol/drugs to manage their anxiety. For example, *"I believe that cannabis helps me to relax. Cannabis is the only thing that will calm me down. I cannot control this nervous feeling without cannabis." "Alcohol is the only thing that will calm me down."* Thus, each time they feel anxious and use alcohol/drugs, this reinforces the belief that using a substance is a quick and immediate, short-term, effective strategy to handle their anxiety.

STARTING OUT: ASSESSING ANXIETY

Current Anxiety

To begin work, identify with your client the nature of his/her current anxiety. You can do this by asking:

- What are his/her symptoms? *Some common symptoms of anxiety are butterflies in the stomach; feeling hot, sweaty and flushed; heart pounding or racing; palpitations; trembling and shaking; needing the toilet frequently; tightness/pain in the chest; fast, short breathing; dizziness; numb or tingling limbs; blurred vision; difficulty in swallowing; feeling sick; dry mouth; poor concentration/memory; sleep disturbance; irritability; lethargy; and depression.*
- In which situations do they occur?
- How has he/she handled his/her anxiety so far, that is, what does he/she do? *Some common responses to anxiety are avoidance (that is, avoiding the situation or leaving it; using drugs or alcohol), being a perfectionist or controlling events to try to prevent danger.*
- How long has he/she experienced difficulties with anxiety?
- What thoughts go through his/her mind when he/she is feeling anxious? *Some common types of anxiety-provoking thoughts are overestimation of danger,*

underestimation of ability to cope, underestimation of help available and catastrophic thoughts. For example, "I will never be able to cope. I will have a heart attack and die." "If I can't do this simple task, my boss will sack me and I will be homeless and destitute."

- **What type of anxiety does he/she experience?** *There are different types of anxiety: situation specific, generalised and panic. Situation-specific anxiety occurs only in certain situations, such as crowded shops or before presentations. For example, "I can't go to the shops on my own any more." "I am always at work when I feel anxious." Generalised anxiety can occur at any time, even when your client does not feel under pressure or does not have anything in particular to do. For example, "I just wake up feeling dreadful." "Sometimes things aren't a problem; other times they are impossible." "I can never predict if I am going to be able to manage my tasks." Panic is the experience of brief and overwhelming physical symptoms of anxiety.*

From your client's description, you can decide whether his/her anxiety is situation specific or generalised, by asking questions such as:

(1) Are there times of the day when the anxiety is better/worse?
(2) Is there any pattern to the anxiety? (keeping a diary of a week's anxiety may be useful).
(3) Is any one person always associated with anxious times?
(4) Are there any situations where you always/never feel anxious?

If his/her anxiety appears to be situation specific, complete the following behavioural and cognitive components. If it appears to be more generalised, focus on the cognitive strategies.

History

It can be important for people to see how their difficulties with anxiety developed, and it is always useful to identify what is maintaining it. You can explore how a person's anxiety developed by asking him/her the following questions:

- How were you as a child? How were you described? Were you seen as different? for example, nervous, highly strung, overprotected, physically different (that is, pointed out as being taller, larger, wearing glasses, etc.).
- How did family members/other role models deal with stress? Were your role models helpful or unhelpful in learning how to cope with stress and deal with life? (Was anyone else anxious? Did anyone use alcohol to cope or not talk about things?).
- What were the trigger incidents? (that is, any traumatic event/life stress that may have contributed to the onset of anxiety). Look for traumatic conditioning; that is, a stressful experience in a particular situation leading

to excessive fear in similar situations in the future—for example, getting stuck in a lift and then becoming anxious in small spaces.
- What were the life events—discuss what effect a range of life events could have on someone's coping (loss of job, marriage break-up, having a child, leaving school, etc.).

Maintaining Factors

You can identify the factors that maintain your client's anxiety by exploring:
- situations he/she currently avoids due to anxiety
- places and triggers–people, noises, particular environments or tasks, use of alcohol or drugs
- anxiety about feeling anxious (that is, interpreting symptoms as health problems or life-threatening)
- patterns of thinking that involve catastrophic, all-or-nothing, over-generalisation type automatic thoughts
- unhelpful strategies/safety behaviours (that is, behaviours he/she engages in that make him/her feel less anxious)—being very busy, smoking more, using more caffeine/alcohol/drugs
- use of alcohol or certain types of drugs that increase anxiety symptoms
- the wrong help—other people taking over your client's responsibilities and creating dependence.

You should now have an idea of:

- what anxiety feels like for your client
- whether it is generalised or situation specific
- how it may have developed
- how it is being maintained.

STRATEGIES TO MANAGE ANXIETY

Below are listed three main strategies to help your client manage his/her anxiety: *psychoeducational information, cognitive strategies and behavioural strategies*.

Helping Your Client Understand Anxiety

It is important to normalise anxiety, as some people may begin to feel worried and abnormal because they experience anxiety. You can do this by giving them some information about anxiety, as outlined in the box below:

Anxiety is the body's normal response to an emergency situation. It prepares us for "fight or flight"; to fight or run away. The body responds by becoming prepared for action. There is an increase in adrenaline in the body. The result is the following symptoms: breathing rate is increased for more oxygen, muscles are tensed to run or fight, stomach stops digesting, etc. This bodily response preserves life when it is properly activated. It is called the "fight or flight" response.
(**Exercise:** *brainstorm situations where this response could be vital.*)

However, sometimes this bodily response can be triggered in situations that are not emergencies. Some situations will begin to be perceived as a threat, and this will inappropriately activate the bodily response, leading to anxiety. The following model shows how this occurs:

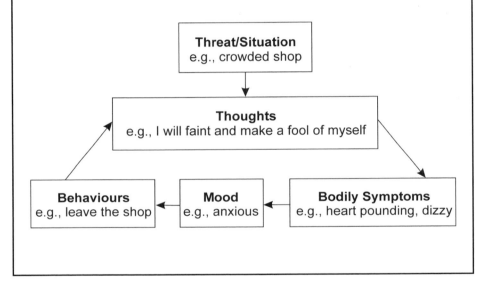

As you can see, thoughts play a very important role. It is how we perceive or interpret the situation that makes us believe it is an emergency and triggers our body's anxiety response.

With your client, you can develop strategies to break this cycle at any point to allow your client to regain control of his/her anxiety. An approach of cognitive and behavioural techniques combined with relaxation skills is often the most successful in the long term. Strategies that have been found to be effective in learning to manage anxiety are described below.

Managing Anxious Thoughts: Cognitive Strategies

> **AIM**
>
> To identify and tackle unhelpful thinking patterns that maintain anxiety.

People hold beliefs about all topics, from politics to child rearing, as a way of making sense of the world. These beliefs are represented in daily life by our automatic thoughts. These are the thoughts that pop into our heads without any effort. The aim of this section is to identify the thoughts that provoke and maintain your client's anxiety ("I can not cope in this situation") and help him/her to replace these with more helpful thoughts ("I have done this before and coped"). Your client will usually believe that his/her way is the only way of interpreting a situation, and that there is little he/she can do about it. You can explain to your client that if he/she learns how to be aware of the thought in his/her head, he/she can re-evaluate it and replace it with a modified, non-anxiety-provoking thought.

The following example will illustrate how thoughts can provoke feelings of anxiety and that it is possible to interpret a situation in a number of ways, creating a number of resultant emotions:

Therapist: *You are walking down the street on a sunny day and you see some people you recognise. Just as you are about to speak to them, they duck into a shop without acknowledging you. What goes through your mind?*
Client: *I've done something to upset them. They don't want to talk to me. No one likes me.*
Therapist: *How would you feel?*
Client: *Upset and anxious.*
Therapist: *Is there another way to think about the way they behaved?*
Client: *I suppose they may have been rushing and not seen me. The sun may have been in their eyes. They may be stressed out.*
Therapist: *How would you feel if you thought this?*
Client: *Fine. Maybe I would call them later to see if they are OK.*

As you can see from this example, the same situation has produced two different sets of feelings because of the different ways of perceiving or interpreting the situation.

Unhelpful Automatic Thoughts

Unhelpful automatic thoughts are specific, involuntary, negative, plausible, distorted, habitual, subjective, idiosyncratic, abbreviated, repetitive and situation specific. They are usually short and direct ("I can't cope"; "People are looking at me and think I look odd"), seem to pop into your head and are negative in content. Because of their content, these negative automatic thoughts can trigger anxiety feelings. In order to help your client manage his/her anxiety, you will need to help him/her re-evaluate and find alternatives to his/her negative automatic thoughts.

For your client to alter a pattern of thinking, he/she needs to do the following.

First, identify unhelpful automatic thoughts

Identify the client's current pattern of unhelpful automatic thoughts. A thought diary that can help with this is shown in the table below (see Appendix 5.2). The diary lists *situation* (antecedent): where the person was and what he/she was doing when the feelings of anxiety arose; *mood*: the feelings the person had in that situation; and *automatic thoughts*: the thoughts that popped into your client's head just before he/she became anxious.

Situation	Mood	Automatic thoughts
Where were you? What were you doing? Who were you with?	*What did you feel? Rate each mood (0–100%).*	*What was going through your mind just before you felt this way? Which was the most important/worrying thought?*
E.g., in a meeting at work	*Anxious 90%*	*I need a drink to cope with this.* *I won't be able to stay in this room.* *I'm going to make a fool of myself.*

If the automatic thoughts that go through your client's mind are "what if . . . ?" questions try to help your client to answer the question by asking him/her, "What is the worst thing that you imagine will happen?" Doing this may be hard for your client, as you will be discussing his/her underlying fears.

Second, re-evaluate and modify unhelpful automatic thoughts

Your client will then need to challenge these automatic thoughts to produce more helpful alternatives. The impact of generating more helpful thoughts in situations that usually make him/her feel anxious is to reduce the extent to which he/she will feel anxious. To help with re-evaluating unhelpful automatic thoughts, use the three-question technique. Ask the following questions:

- *What is the evidence for this thought?*
- *Is this always the case?*

- *Is there another way of thinking about this?*
- *What ways do I have of coping with this situation?*

Another helpful exercise that will encourage your client to re-evaluate his/her anxiety-provoking thoughts is for him/her to write down in the thought diary the evidence for and against the thoughts and an alternative thought, as in the following example:

Situation	Moods	Automatic thoughts	Evidence that supports automatic thought	Evidence that does not support the automatic thought	Alternative/ balanced thought
Where were you? What were you doing? Who were you with?	*What did you feel? Rate each mood (0–100%).*	*What was going through your mind just before you felt this way? Which was the most impor-tant/worrying thought?*			*Rate how much you believe the alternative thought (0–100%).*
E.g., in a meeting at work	*Anxious 90%*	*I need a drink to cope with this. I won't be able to stay in this room. I'm going to make a fool of myself.*	*Everyone else knows more than I do. I don't know what I am talking about. I'll go bright red and shaky.*	*Some people here are novices. I have practised my talk. My boss has faith in me.*	*It will be difficult, but I can get through this presentation without mak-ing a fool of myself or hav-ing a drink (60%).*

If your client practises re-evaluating unhelpful automatic thoughts by the strategies outlined above, this will encourage flexibility in thinking and will open the way to producing new, helpful thoughts such as *"I can do this—I've done it before."* Consider the following example:

Unhelpful thought	Helpful alternative
I'm going to faint.	*I've never fainted before. It's a symptom of anxiety. I can try to relax and breathe slowly.*
I need a drink to cope with this.	*Alcohol actually increases anxiety; I'll do some relaxation instead. I've done it before without having a drink.*
What if I'm sick? I'll make a fool of myself.	*I can prepare myself for the day. I'll have a drink of water. I can do this.*

Helpful thoughts will not be automatic to begin with. They need to be practised and repeated regularly in order to become incorporated into someone's beliefs and to have an impact on his/her anxiety. Keeping a thought diary on the above model can help with recognition of unhelpful thoughts and give practice in challenging them and producing alternatives.

Exercise: Encourage your client to keep a thought diary.

So remember, to be able to help your client reduce his/her anxiety:

- Identify anxiety-provoking automatic thoughts.
- Look for the evidence for and against these anxious thoughts.
- Generate alternative helpful and balanced thoughts.

Behavioural Strategies: Dealing with Avoidance

References/helpful resources: Greenberger and Padesky (1995).

Managing Bodily Symptoms

A simple relaxation technique will begin to help initially to reduce physical symptoms (see Appendix 5.1). Get your client to practise this when he/she is not anxious, so that it will be easily remembered when he/she needs it. This will also help to reduce residual anxiety, making someone less likely to move into a panic attack. As shown diagrammatically below, if residual anxiety is lower, the same amount of situational anxiety will not produce a panic attack.

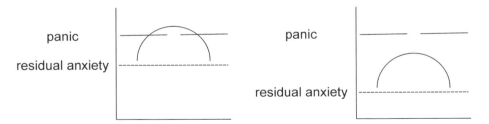

Dealing with Avoidance

The importance of teaching your client some behavioural strategies to cope with his/her anxiety is that it provides him/her with a range of methods to deal with avoidance. Avoidance is said to be one of the main symptoms of anxiety (Greenberger & Padesky, 1995). For example, it is avoidance when your client physically avoids going into a situation he/she finds difficult, or uses alcohol/drugs to avoid feelings or cope with a situation he/she finds difficult, or leaves the situation prematurely. Your client has probably found that, by avoiding the situation, he/she initially experienced a marked reduction in anxiety. However, avoidance actually maintains your client's anxiety, as it prevents him/her from testing whether his/her worst fear will occur. Consider the following case example:

Ray feels anxious about going into town because he believes that he will meet people who saw him when he was acutely psychotic. Thus, he no longer goes into town, or, if he has to go, he drinks, as he feels this helps him to cope with feeling anxious. This avoidance of town and people who might have seen him when he was unwell may initially help him to feel less anxious. However, the more he avoids this situation, the more anxious he becomes about facing it in the future. Avoiding the situation also prevents him from testing whether his anxious thoughts and worst fear ("If I go into town, I will meet people who saw me when I was ill and acting oddly, and they will remember how I used to act and laugh at me") will materialise.

Two methods that have been found to be effective to help your client to deal with his/her avoidance will be described here—behavioural experiments and graded hierarchies. *Using simple relaxation techniques (see Appendix 5.1) in conjunction with these two techniques will assist initially in reducing physical symptoms of anxiety. This will enable your client to begin the process of approaching previously avoided situations.*

Behavioural Experiments

A behavioural experiment is a practical opportunity for your client to test his/her anxious thoughts and worst fear. Your client probably has an image or belief that something catastrophic will happen if he/she goes into the situation. Behavioural experiments allow your client a chance to go into the situation, having planned in advance, and to test his/her anxiety-provoking thoughts and worst fear. A behavioural experiment also allows your client to discover what will really happen in that situation, which is probably not the same as what he/she fears will happen.

To help your client plan and carry out a behavioural experiment, you will find the following steps helpful:

(1) You and your client by now will be aware of what his/her anxiety-provoking (unhelpful) thought is. This will be the thought that you can test out. *For example, fear of being unable to sleep or relax without smoking cannabis in the evening.* However, if you are still unsure, go back to the earlier section which explains how to identify unhelpful automatic thoughts (page 128).

(2) Write down the thought to be tested on the Behavioural Experiment worksheet (Appendix 2.1).
(3) With your client, identify a small step he/she can take to begin to test this thought. *For example, "Do not smoke cannabis during the day."*
(4) Get your client to identify what he/she predicts will happen and write this down on his/her worksheet.
(5) Identify any potential obstacles that may prevent him/her from carrying out the behavioural experiment and strategies to overcome these obstacles.
(6) Once your client has carried out the experiment, he/she should record the outcome on his/her worksheet.
(7) To ensure that he/she is really able to test his/her anxiety-provoking thought, identify with your client a number of experiments he/she could try.
(8) Ask your client to identify what he/she has learned from these experiments and write it down under "lesson learned/take-home message".

Let us take, for example, Tom's behavioural experiment:

Thought to be tested

"I'm worried that I won't be able to sleep or relax without smoking cannabis in the evening."

Experiment	Prediction	Potential obstacles	Strategies to overcome obstacles	Outcome of experiment
Experiment 1 Do not smoke cannabis during the day.	I will feel restless throughout the day.	I will get tense and then I will want to have a spliff.	Go for a walk if I start to feel tense.	I did feel a bit tense, but it passed when I went for a walk and got busy.
Experiment 2 Do not smoke cannabis in the evening.	I will not be able to fall asleep.	My friends may visit me and offer me some cannabis.	Go and visit my friend who does not use drugs and spend the evening with him.	I did smoke one spliff that evening, but it was less than I usually smoke, and I did eventually fall asleep.

Lesson learned/take-home message

"I did feel tense to start with, but when I smoked a lot less than I usually do, I was able to fall asleep even though it did take a while."

Graded Hierarchies

A graded hierarchy is a list in order of intensity of situations that a person is fearful of. That is, it represents the whole range of situations a person experiences anxiety in, from the situation where the most anxiety is experienced at the top, to the situation in which the least anxiety is experienced at the bottom. By exposing him/herself to these situations, your client will begin to recognise that he/she is not as anxious as he/she thought he/she would be. If your client starts from the situation he/she identified that would cause him/her the least anxiety, and gradually works up the hierarchy, he/she will begin to become more confident about tackling situations in which he/she experiences the most anxiety. The following are some steps you will find helpful in developing a graded hierarchy and graded exposure tasks with your client:

(1) Identify the most feared situation and the least feared situation.
(2) Identify the feared situations between these two.
(3) Ask your client to rate how anxious he/she would feel in each situation listed on his/her hierarchy on a scale of 0–100. Write this on the Hierarchy of Feared Situations worksheet (Appendix 5.3).
(4) Identify how your client could expose himself or herself to that feared situation.
(5) Each time he/she exposes him/herself to that situation, get him/her to rate how anxious he/she felt on a scale of 0–100.
(6) Encourage your client to use the simple relaxation techniques (Appendix 5.1) and the strategies he/she has learned to re-evaluate and modify any unhelpful or anxiety-provoking thoughts.
(7) It will also be helpful to role-play with your client, where possible, how he/she will deal with a feared situation on his/her hierarchy.
(8) With your client, regularly review how he/she has progressed up his/her hierarchy and identify any potential obstacles and strategies to overcome these obstacles.
(9) At each stage, encourage your client to identify the "lesson learned/take-home message".

Consider the following case example:

Ray feels anxious about going into town because he believes that he will meet people who saw him when he was acutely psychotic. Thus, he no longer goes into town, or, if he has to go, he drinks, as he feels this helps him to cope with feeling anxious.

   Ray's hierarchy of feared situations and graded exposure is expressed in the following table:

Feared situation	Prediction and anxiety rating (0–100)	Task	Actual anxiety (0–100)	Outcome of task
Go into a small shop in town without having a drink beforehand.	People will stare at me, and I will start to feel faint and have to leave the shop quickly. **Anxiety rating: 10**	Go into a small shop on the outskirts of town when the shops are quiet; do not have a drink before I go.	**Actual anxiety: 5**	I did not have a drink before I went. I did feel nervous, but no one seemed to stare at me. I did not rush out of the shop.
Do not drink before I go to a large shop in town.	I might see someone who recognises me from the past, and they will remember how I was when I was ill. **Anxiety rating: 25**	Go early into a large shop when the shops are quiet and do not have any alcohol in the house so that I can not have a drink before I go.	**Actual anxiety: 15**	I did not see any one who seemed to recognise me. Although I felt nervous to start with, I eventually started to enjoy myself.
Do not drink before I go into town and have a look in a few shops when it is quiet.	I might start to panic, especially if I see someone who recognises me from the past, and I think they remember how I was when I was ill. **Anxiety rating: 40**	Not have any alcohol in the house and go to a shop that I am familiar with. Go when the shops are fairly quiet.	**Actual anxiety: 20**	I felt nervous when I got into town, but once I started looking in the shops I felt not so bad, and no one stared at me.
Do not drink and visit one shop in town when it is fairly busy.	I will start to panic when I see someone who recognises me from the past, and they will remember how I was when I was ill. **Anxiety rating: 60**	Not have any alcohol in the house and go to a shop that I am familiar with.	**Actual anxiety: 50**	I thought I saw someone looking at me. I thought it looked like they remembered me, but they just carried on shopping. I felt nervous but did not panic.
Do not drink and visit a number of shops in town when it is busy.	I will not be able to cope and will definitely panic. *Anxiety rating: 100*	Not have any alcohol in the house and go to shops and buy something special for myself.	**Actual anxiety: 40**	No one stared at me, and toward the end I felt proud of myself for going out.

Lesson learned/take-home message: *"I did feel nervous to start with, but when I actually went into town it wasn't as bad as I thought it would be, and no one seemed to remember how I was before. I did not need a drink to help me cope."*

So remember, to help your clients to stop avoiding situations,

- encourage them to test anxious thoughts
- gradually expose them to feared situations.

ADDITIONAL TREATMENT COMPONENTS I—SKILLS BUILDING

Chapter 10

COPING WITH DIFFERENT MOODS: ANGER AND IMPULSE CONTROL

AIM

To increase understanding of anger and learn a variety of cognitive and behavioural techniques to manage it.

Helpful references/resources: Bellack et al. (1997), Gambrill (1977), Greenberger and Padesky (1995), Novaco (1993), Powell and Taylor (1992).

Anger can be both a positive and a negative emotion. Anger can become a problem when it occurs too frequently, is too intense, lasts too long, leads to aggression or disrupts our relationships. The idea of managing anger is not to remove the emotion completely. The aim is to help your client to manage his/ her reaction to anger-provoking thoughts, so that, rather than an aggressive response, he/she has a more adaptive coping response. Anger can be mistakenly used as a tool to gain power and control in a given situation. Therefore, learning to manage anger needs to be treated as an opportunity to provide your client with alternative methods to feel empowered. Your work will need to be well structured and clear to reduce the likelihood of your client's feeling frustrated. Some people may internalise their anger, and this can result in them feeling helpless, resigned or depressed. These individuals will need to be encouraged to increase their expression of anger feelings in a positive manner. It may be necessary for your client to work on issues such as self-esteem, social skills and assertiveness in conjunction with learning to manage his/her anger. It is also important to consider your client's environment when looking at managing anger. If your client's situation encourages anger/aggressive behaviour, this may make it difficult for him/her to implement new coping strategies learned outside the therapeutic setting. Physical factors such as noise can elevate physiological arousal, activate your client's negative cognitive patterns (Novaco, 1993) and increase the likelihood of angry emotions. Thus, it is important to consider the role such factors may have.

THE ROLE OF DRUGS/ALCOHOL
IN CREATING/MAINTAINING ANGER

Substances such as anabolic steroids actively increase aggression, and this is the desired effect to improve performance in competitive events (such as sports). Alcohol serves to disinhibit people; thus, under the influence of alcohol, they may display/express underlying feelings of anger or aggression felt prior to and during drinking. Alcohol may also exacerbate aggressive feelings. The effects of substances such as LSD, cannabis and magic mushrooms depend upon the person's mood at the time he/she uses them. Use of these drugs can contribute to paranoia and aggression.

Substances may be used as a form of "Dutch courage" to enable a person to express himself or herself, or try new activities. However, as many substances actually impair performance, the result may be a lack of success that, in turn, actually lowers confidence and self-esteem further. For the client, this lack of confidence and success may then increase feelings of anger directed towards either him/herself or others. Substances may provide temporary relief from the internal tensions caused by unexpressed anger. They may allow a person to avoid dealing with the cause of his/her anger by blotting out his/her feelings rather than dealing with them. This is only a temporary strategy, and the underlying issues will still be present as the person sobers up, leading to a further craving to drink and therefore setting up a vicious cycle.

Your client may see anger as an undesirable emotion and will battle against showing it. He/she may use drugs/alcohol to blot out his/her true feelings or to give him/her permission to be angry. That is, he/she can blame the substance for the emotion and not take responsibility for how he/she is feeling. For example, "I only reacted that way because I'd had a drink." Powell and Taylor (1992) describe the emergence of anger immediately after withdrawal from heroin. This anger was maintained for a number of weeks after the detox was complete. Therefore, anger-management strategies may be useful in conjunction with detox from heroin.

THE ROLE OF PSYCHOSIS IN CREATING/MAINTAINING ANGER

People can feel an enormous sense of loss when they receive a diagnosis of psychosis. They have to alter their image of themselves and may feel they have to alter their life ambitions and plans. This sense of loss could lead to an angry reaction while the person adjusts. Experiences within the health service may be perceived as unsatisfactory and lead to anger. The fact that a client can be admitted to hospital under the Mental Health Act could provoke anger, especially if the client does not agree with or understand the reasons for admission. The symptoms experienced while psychotic could create anger. *For example, Clive experiences command hallucinations that people are laughing at him behind his back and that he should "sort them out". Mary experiences distressing symptoms of voices and paranoia that her family can not understand. This leads her to feel misunderstood, frustrated and constantly distracted from the activity she is attempting to concentrate on.*

Clients may feel that a "rational" part of them is always battling against or being angry towards their voices or impulses. While this may feel negative to clients, their anger can be utilised as a helpful strategy to manage psychotic symptoms (for example, telling the voices firmly to go away).

STARTING OUT: ASSESSING ANGER

To begin work, identify with your client the nature of his/her anger. You can do this by assessing the following factors.

Current Anger

- What are his/her symptoms of anger? *Some common symptoms are tight muscles, increased blood pressure, increased heart rate, flushed face, clenched fists, fast breathing, poor concentration, sleep disturbance, irritability, fighting, arguing, shouting, etc.*
- In which situations do these symptoms occur?
- How does the client respond to his/her angry feelings so far; that is, what does he/she do? *Some common responses to anger are physical/verbal aggression, defensiveness, resisting other people, attacking or arguing, or withdrawing to punish others or protect the self.*
- How long has he/she experienced difficulties with anger?
- What thoughts go through his/her mind when angry? *Thought patterns associated with anger often incorporate the idea that our rules or expectations have been violated. This can lead to thinking that other people are threatening or hurtful, or are treating us unfairly. For example, "No one listens to me—that was not my*

fault", "I am going to get even for the way they have treated me", "That was not fair—they should not have done that."

Angry styles of thinking have been defined as follows: catastrophising ("I can't stand it—it's devastating"), demanding/coercing ("He should respect me more"), overgeneralisation ("He never listens to me"), categorical/labels ("His type are all jerks") and misattributions/one-track thinking ("He did that on purpose to upset me"). Gambrill (1977) believes that the negative self-statements made by people who experience anger can reflect the following variety of beliefs:
—necessity for success
—intolerance of mistakes
—unreasonable expectations of others
—necessity of retaliation.

- What type of anger does he/she experience? Anger can range from irritation to rage. How angry your client becomes in a given situation will be influenced by his/her interpretation of the meaning of the event. If your client views the response of someone as a personal affront, he/she will become angrier than if he/she views the response as a general one. If the level of anger displayed appears out of proportion with the situation, this may be due to a build-up of chronic anger from a catalogue of past events where the person feels he/she has been abused. He/she develops a sense of being on guard against being abused again and so reacts in an exaggerated way to any perceived threat.

History

It is important for people to understand how their difficulties with anger have developed and are maintained. You can explore the development of your client's anger by asking:

- How did family members/other role models deal with anger?
- Were your role models helpful or unhelpful in learning how to cope with anger?
- Were people around you argumentative and defensive?
- Is there a history of events where the person feels he/she was abused, leading him/her to feel he/she needs to be on guard for future attack?
- Is there a history of turning anger inwards and not dealing with it, leading to depression and resignation?
- What were the rules or family beliefs that may have contributed to the development of anger?

Maintaining Factors

You can identify the factors that maintain your client's anger by identifying:

- the triggers for feelings of anger: people, noises, particular environments, use of alcohol or drugs, patterns of automatic thinking
- the patterns of thinking the client typically engages in. *For example, does he/she use emotive language (labelling thinking)? Does he/she predict when he/she will have a disagreement and create a self-fulfilling prophecy by entering the situation already feeling angry?*
- how he/she expresses feelings of anger (such as holding them in or aggression) and the responses of others (that is, the consequences)
- whether he/she bears a grudge or ruminates on past perceived affronts.

It would be useful for your client to keep a diary of his/her anger for a few weeks so that he/she can identify thinking patterns and antecedents more clearly (see Appendix 5.4).

You should have an idea of:

- what happens when your client gets angry
- the thoughts that go through his/her mind
- how your client's anger developed
- what factors keep him/her feeling angry.

STRATEGIES TO MANAGE ANGER

Below are listed three strategies to help your client manage his/her anger: *psychoeducational information, cognitive strategies and behavioural strategies.*

Helping Your Client Understand Anger

It is important to normalise anger, as some people can begin to feel frustrated and upset at themselves because of the way they are responding. You can do this by giving them some information about anger, as outlined in the box on the opposite page.

As you can see, thoughts play a very important role. It is how we perceive or interpret the situation that makes us believe it is an emergency and triggers our body's anger response. With your client, you can develop strategies for the client to break this cycle at any point to regain control of his/her anger. A combined approach of cognitive and behavioural techniques with relaxation skills is often most successful in the long term. Strategies that have been found to be effective in learning to manage anger are described below.

Anger is a normal bodily response to an emergency situation. It is part of the "fight or flight" response that prepares us either to fight or run away from danger. The body responds by producing adrenaline, resulting in increased breathing rate for more oxygen, muscles tensed to run or fight and stomach not digesting to send blood to muscles. This bodily "fight or flight" response preserves life when it is activated properly.
(**Exercise:** *Brainstorm with your client where the "fight or flight" response could be vital.*)

However, sometimes this bodily response can be triggered in situations that are not emergencies or threatening to us. Due to our past experiences, some situations may begin to be perceived as threatening, and this will inappropriately activate the bodily response, leading to anger. The following model shows how this occurs:

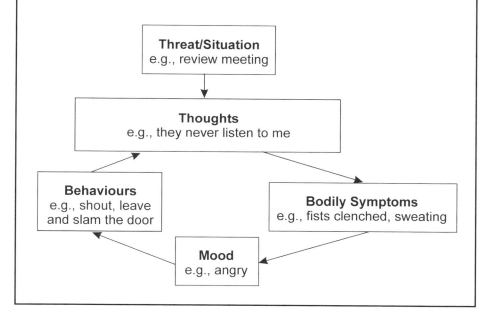

Managing Angry Thoughts: Cognitive Strategies

AIM

To identify and tackle unhelpful thinking patterns that maintain anger.

People hold beliefs about all sorts of topics, from politics to child rearing, as a way of making sense of the world. These beliefs are represented in daily life by our automatic thoughts. These are the thoughts that pop into our heads without any effort. The aim of this section is to identify the thoughts that provoke and maintain your client's anger ("They have done that to annoy me." "They should not have done that") and help him/her to replace these with more helpful thoughts ("I don't need to get wound up. I can handle this"). Your client will usually believe that his/her way is the only way of interpreting a situation and that there is little he/she can do about this. You can explain to your client that if he/she can become aware of the thought in his/her head, he/she can then re-evaluate it and replace it with a modified non-anger-provoking thought.

The following dialogue will illustrate how thoughts can provoke feelings of anger and that it is possible to interpret a situation in a number of ways, creating a number of resultant emotions.

Therapist: *You are sitting on the bus, and someone steps on your foot and knocks your shopping bag over. What goes through your mind?*
Client: *People should be more careful. They did that on purpose. I bet they won't apologise.*
Therapist: *How would you feel?*
Client: *Like shouting at them to be more careful. Quite angry or cross.*
Therapist: *Is there another way to think about how they behaved?*
Client: *I suppose the bus could have been busy or lurched suddenly. I've bumped people before accidentally.*
Therapist: *How would you feel if you thought this?*
Client: *More sympathetic. I might check if they were OK. I wouldn't blame them.*

As can be seen from this example, the same situation has produced two different sets of feelings because of the different ways of perceiving or interpreting the situation.

Unhelpful Automatic Thoughts

Unhelpful automatic thoughts are specific, involuntary, negative, plausible, distorted, habitual, subjective, idiosyncratic, abbreviated, repetitive and situation specific. They are usually short, direct ("You can't do that"), seem to pop into your head and are negative in content. Because of their content, these negative automatic thoughts can trigger anger. In order to help your client manage his/her anger, you will need to help him/her re-evaluate and find alternatives to his/her negative automatic thoughts.

To try to alter his/her pattern of thinking, your client needs to do the following.

Identify unhelpful automatic thoughts

A thought diary can help to identify your client's anger-provoking automatic *thoughts* (see Appendix 5.4). The diary records *situation* (antecedent): where the person was and what the person was doing when the feelings of anger arose; *mood*: the feelings the person has in that situation; *physical signs of tension*; and *automatic* thoughts: the thoughts that popped into a person's head just before the person became angry. Encourage your client to keep a daily thought diary. This will enable you to identify the pattern of thinking that tends to provoke angry feelings. Here is an example.

Situation	Moods	Physical signs of tension	Automatic thoughts
Where were you? What were you doing? Who were you with?	*What did you feel? Rate each mood (0–100%).*		*What was going through your mind just before you felt this way? Which was the most worrying/ important thought?*
E.g., in a meeting at work	*Angry 70%*	*Clenched teeth and fists*	*I need a smoke to calm down. He shouldn't speak to me like that. He always puts me down in front of other people.*

Re-evaluate and modify unhelpful automatic thoughts

Your client must learn to re-evaluate these automatic thoughts to produce more helpful and realistic alternatives. Generating more helpful thoughts in situations that usually make him/her feel angry will help him/her stay in control and not lose his/her temper.

To help your client re-evaluate unhelpful thoughts, use the three-question technique. Ask the following questions:

- *What is the evidence for this thought?*
- *Is this always the case?*
- *Is there another way of thinking about this?*

Also encourage your client to think of other ways that he/she could cope with this situation. Another helpful strategy to encourage your client to re-evaluate his/her anger-provoking thoughts is to write in his/her diary the evidence for and against the thoughts and an alternative thought. An example follows.

Anger diary

Situation	Moods	Physical signs of tension	Automatic thoughts	Evidence that supports identified thought	Evidence that does not support the identified thought	Alternative/balanced thought
E.g., in a meeting with my doctor and keyworker	Angry (80%)	Clenched teeth and fists.	He shouldn't speak to me like that. They're not listening to me. They think they know better than me. I need a joint to calm down.	He didn't answer my question. They dismiss my ideas and smirk at me. Cannabis relaxes me	They've never deliberately upset me before. They are trained to work with this. A joint doesn't always calm me down	I'll listen to their opinions and try to manage without a joint and see how I feel.

So remember, to tackle thinking that triggers anger, you can,

- identify negative automatic thoughts
- re-evaluate anger-provoking thoughts to produce more helpful alternative thoughts in situations where he/she feels angry.

Behavioural Strategies

Managing Bodily Symptoms

As your client becomes angry, his/her posture and bodily tension will alter. A typical angry posture would include clenched fists, hunched shoulders, clenched or grinding teeth, and tense and clenched muscles in the arms and legs. If your client can become aware of his/her bodily response to feeling angry, he/she can use this as a cue to use a relaxation technique or employ another method of reducing the feelings of anger.

Simple relaxation techniques will begin to help to reduce physical symptoms (see Appendix 5.1). Get your client to practise these when he/she is not angry, so that they become second nature and are easily remembered when needed. Some immediate short-term measures to control symptoms are as follows:

- counting from 1 to 10
- taking slow, steady breaths, saying "breathe in—breathe out" to him/herself as he/she breathes.

Taking Time Out

When working with clients who experience problems with anger, it is useful to look at the concept of taking "time out". This is different from leaving a situation prematurely (that is, avoidance), as the client actively chooses to postpone responding to the situation until he/she is better able to deal with it. This would involve:

- explaining what he/she is doing ("I cannot discuss this now—I will speak to you in half an hour")
- utilising cognitive and behavioural techniques to calm down and plan how to deal with the situation
- returning to the situation with a new perspective.

Here is a case example:

Martin feels wound up in a care-plan review. He can feel himself becoming angry. His fists and jaw are clenched; he is breathing more quickly and is feeling like punching someone. Martin is thinking, "He is winding me up on purpose. They never listen to me and think they know what's best for me. He shouldn't be allowed to speak to me like that." Martin could ask to leave the meeting and ask for a 10-minute break. In that 10 minutes, Martin can look at his thinking and generate alternative thoughts ("They don't mean to wind me up. They are trying to help"), and use a simple relaxation technique. He could also visualise himself speaking up in the review and plan what he would need to say and do. After 10 minutes, Martin can return to the review feeling calmer and more able to discuss what has occurred.

It would also be useful to incorporate training in communication skills or assertiveness to provide your client with alternative ways of responding in anger-arousing situations (see Communication Skills section, pages 164–193).

Behavioural Experiments

As discussed in Chapter 9 on managing anxiety, avoidance is a common reaction to feeling strong emotions. If your client does not enter into situations that make him/her feel angry, leaves such situations prematurely, or responds in an aggressive way, he/she will experience a temporary reduction in uncomfortable feelings. However, avoidance in the long term will maintain the problem of experiencing anger. Your client can use behavioural experiments as a practical way to test the anger-provoking automatic thoughts and beliefs that tend to lead to anger. A behavioural experiment allows your client to plan in advance for a situation where he/she expects to feel angry, and to see what really happens in that situation rather than avoid it.

To help your client plan and carry out a behavioural experiment, you will find the following steps helpful:

(1) You and your client will be aware of what his/her anger-provoking (unhelpful) thought is from the thought diary. With your client, select the most typical thought, but start with a thought that does not provoke extreme feelings of anger. This will be the thought you can test. *For example, "If I don't have a drink before confronting my friend about his attitude, I will lose my temper and shout at him."* However, if you are unsure, go back to the earlier section (page 128) that explains how to identify unhelpful automatic thoughts.
(2) Write down the thought to be tested on the Behavioural Experiment worksheet (Appendix 2.1).
(3) With your client, identify a small step he/she can take to begin to test this thought. *For example, do not drink during the day.*
(4) Get your client to identify what he/she predicts will happen and write this down on his/her worksheet.
(5) Identify any potential obstacles that may prevent him/her from carrying out the behavioural experiment and strategies to overcome these obstacles.
(6) Once your client has carried out the experiment, he/she should record the outcome on his/her worksheet.
(7) To ensure that he/she is really able to test his/her anger-provoking thoughts, get your client to identify a number of experiments he/she can try.
(8) Ask your client to identify what he/she has learned from these experiments and write it down under "lesson learned/take-home message".

Consider the example of an experiment on the opposite page.

Problem Solving

Effective problem-solving skills are also vital in helping your client to learn how to manage his/her anger. Sometimes anger will occur as a result of your client's feeling frustrated, overwhelmed, confused or unable to cope with a

Mike's Behavioural Experiment

Thought to be tested

"I am sure that if I don't have a drink before confronting my friend about his attitude, I will lose my temper and shout at him."

Experiment	Prediction	Potential obstacles	Strategies to overcome obstacles	Outcome of experiment
Experiment 1 *Do not drink during the day.*	*I will get wound up waiting to see my friend.*	*I don't know how else to stop getting wound up.*	*Arrange to go out with my partner and keep busy doing sport.*	*I got a bit wound up, but playing tennis soon got rid of the feeling.*
Experiment 2 *Do not drink in the evening.*	*I will lose my temper and shout at my friend.*	*I will meet my friend at the pub and will be tempted to drink alcohol.*	*I will drive to the pub so that I have to have soft drinks, or suggest we meet at another venue.*	*I drove to the pub and had one pint. I got a bit heated but didn't shout.*

Lesson learned/take-home message

"I managed to control my temper without having lots of alcohol."

particular situation. By using effective problem solving, your client will be able to clarify his/her concerns and identify a way forward. A simple problem-solving technique is outlined below:

(1) Clearly define the problem.
(2) Brainstorm to generate possible solutions. At this stage, do not judge any of the ideas, but include them all.
(3) Identify which ideas can be completed alone and which may need assistance from someone else. Specify what help is needed and from whom.
(4) Identify advantages and disadvantages for each solution.
(5) Select the best solution or combination of solutions.
(6) Plan how to carry out the solution.
(7) Implement the plan.

Your client may have used drugs/alcohol as a possible solution to his/her problems in the past. Remember to help your client look at the long-term implications of using drugs/alcohol and the other problems that it may create for him/her, and identify alternative, more effective coping strategies.

So remember, to help your clients better manage anger, you can,

- identify the physical symptoms of anger
- encourage the clients to "take time out"
- use behavioural experiments to test their anger-provoking thoughts
- help them develop effective problem-solving skills.

IMPULSE CONTROL

AIM

To recognise current impulsive behaviour and learn cognitive and behavioural strategies to manage impulses.

Feelings of anger may be maintaining your client's drug/alcohol use, because he/she believes it either helps him/her to express his/her anger or helps him/her to control angry feelings. These beliefs will lead to an impulse to use drugs/alcohol when he/she feels or expects to feel angry. An impulse is a sudden urge to partake in a specific behaviour—for example, to drink, to take drugs or to become angry. An impulse provides immediate gratification and can therefore be perceived by your client as a successful strategy in the short term. However, in the long term, this impulsive behaviour can create additional problems for your client. *Impulse control is about learning to recognise a learned pattern of response to a given situation and choosing to respond in a different way.*

Identify Triggers for Impulsivity and Physical Cues

As your client is about to respond in an angry way, or use alcohol or drugs impulsively, he/she will notice particular physical sensations, such as agitation and muscle tension. If your client can become aware of the physical sensations that occur just prior to behaving in an impulsive way, he/she can use them as cues to use impulse-control strategies. To help your client to recognise the physical cues for impulsivity, get him/her to keep a diary of situations in which he/she behaved impulsively (see Appendix 5.4).

Cognitive and Behavioural Strategies

The following are some cognitive and behavioural strategies to control impulsive use of anger, drugs and alcohol.

- **Counting:** As soon as your client recognises that he/she desires to behave impulsively (for example, become angry, cut him/herself or use drugs/alcohol), get him/her to count from 1 to 10 while taking deep breaths. This will put the brakes on the impulse by breaking the impulsive cognitive pattern. He/she will then be able to think about his/her response to the situation in a more controlled way.
- **Relaxation:** As your client begins to recognise the physical cues that he/she is becoming tense, irritable and agitated, or is about to act in an impulsive way, encourage him/her to utilise a relaxation technique (see Appendix 5.1).
- **Consequences:** Teach your client, before reacting, to weigh up the immediate consequences of his/her action against the long-term consequences. One way to do this is to get your client to see his/her actions as an image on a videotape. Then he/she can fast-forward the "video recorder" and visualise the impact of the behaviour in the long term. He/she would then be in a better position to make a more informed choice about the behaviour.
- **Immediate need versus delayed gratification:** This is another way of looking at the consequences of an impulsive action. Encourage your client to think through whether an impulsive behaviour will have an immediate desired effect but then have negative consequences. If so, he/she can brainstorm another course of action that will make him/her happier in the long run. *For example, Sue has argued with her mother. Her immediate thought is that cannabis will calm her down and stop her from throwing things at her mum. However, she thinks about how paranoid she has felt in the past when she has smoked cannabis after an argument. Sue decides that to respond to how she feels right now would not really help her. Sue's new plan is to have a cup of tea and discuss the argument with her mum later.*
- **Commentary:** As in the counting strategy outlined above, your client can talk him/herself through a situation to slow down his/her thinking processes. This would involve commenting in his/her head on what is happening, and how he/she is feeling. Once his/her thought processes are slowed down, your client can start to make active choices rather than behaving in an impulsive way.
- **Time out:** As described earlier in this section, taking planned time out, utilising alternative coping strategies and then returning to a situation with a new perspective can be very effective in controlling potentially regrettable impulses.
- **Cue-management cards:** People who behave impulsively can find it difficult to think of alternative strategies, at the time when the impulse is

at its greatest. When one is in difficult situations, it is hard to recognise what is happening and clearly plan what to do. Your client may find it helpful to produce a credit card-sized reminder/management card to keep on his/her person as a reminder of his/her trigger situations and chosen strategies. See the following box for an example.

- *If my shoulders hunch up or I clench my teeth, I will use my relaxation technique.*
- *If Barbara is getting on my nerves, I will count to 10 and repeat to myself, "She doesn't mean to."*

So remember, strategies to help your clients control impulsive behaviour include,

- identifying physical cues for impulsivity
- counting, relaxation, weighing up the consequences, self-talk/ commentary, taking time out
- suggesting that they carry a cue-management card.

ADDITIONAL TREATMENT COMPONENTS I—SKILLS BUILDING

Chapter 11

COPING WITH DIFFERENT MOODS: DEPRESSION

> **AIM**
>
> To increase understanding of depression and learn a variety of cognitive and behavioural techniques to manage it.

Helpful references/resources: Fennell (1994), Freeman et al. (1997), Greenberger and Padesky (1995).

There are said to be two main types of depression. Depression can be reactive; that is, it develops as a result of an event (for example, a negative life event such as a death). Alternatively, depression can be endogenous; that is, a person is predisposed to experience depression, and it occurs irrespective of life events. Depression in itself can be so severe that it produces psychotic symptoms, or sometimes a person may become quite depressed in response to experiencing psychosis. Depression can also occur as part of a cyclical illness of mania and depression. Certain situations are known to put people at risk of developing depression. These include childbirth, disrupted childcare following the loss of a parent, childhood sexual abuse, poor parenting and social trauma, such as unemployment.

THE ROLE OF DRUGS/ALCOHOL IN CREATING AND MAINTAINING DEPRESSION

Heroin, alcohol and benzodiazepines all have a depressant effect on the central nervous system. These substances may create a depressed mood in your clients and may also counteract the effect of antidepressant medication. Alcohol is commonly thought of as a stimulant because, in the short term, it can act as a disinhibitor, but it is actually a depressant. Your client may take stimulants (such as cocaine/crack and amphetamines) to increase his/her level of activity and energy in an attempt to overcome depression or the negative symptoms of schizophrenia (these are very similar to depression for a lot of people). However, after a period of cocaine or amphetamine use, some clients may feel quite low in mood, depressed and at times suicidal. Use of stimulants may mask low mood and therefore prevent your client from receiving treatment.

THE ROLE OF PSYCHOSIS IN CREATING/MAINTAINING DEPRESSION

A client can feel an enormous sense of loss when he/she receives a diagnosis of psychosis or experiences psychotic symptoms. He/she has to alter his/her image of him/herself and may feel he/she has to alter life ambitions and plans. This sense of loss could lead to a depressed reaction while the person adjusts. Experiences within the health service may be unsatisfactory and lead to depression because the client experiences a loss of efficacy or confidence to cope or effect change. The symptoms experienced while psychotic could create depression. For example,

- *Freda experiences constant auditory hallucinations with negative content about her ability to cope and achieve, and about her self-image. She feels she will never be able to keep a boyfriend when he finds out that she is ill.*
- *Lenny feels that he does not want to be permanently on medication that creates side effects, and feels that he will no longer be able to achieve his ambition of becoming an architect.*

It is important to help your client to manage his/her moods, and particularly depression, as they can be a maintaining factor for substance use. That is, your client may use drugs/alcohol to manage his/her depression or low mood. Negative thinking and lack of motivation can also act as triggers for drug/ alcohol use. Depression and lack of motivation may reduce your client's ability to participate in therapy for his/her psychosis or attend educational, leisure or vocational activities.

STARTING OUT: ASSESSING DEPRESSION

To begin work, identify with your client the nature of his/her depression. You can do this by asking *how he/she currently feels, how the depression developed in the first place* and *what seems to keep the depression going.*

Current Depression

- What are his/her symptoms? *Some common symptoms are poor sleep, early waking, poor appetite, weight loss, lower mood in the morning, lack of energy, lack of motivation, posture (shoulders hunched, head hanging down, no eye contact and slouched in chair or in bed), isolating self, poor communication (monosyllabic and negative content), sadness, lack of enjoyment, poor concentration and decreased confidence.*
- In which situations do they occur? *Also check whether his/her symptoms of depression tend to occur only during or following a period of drug/alcohol use, as this may indicate that the depression is related to substance use.*
- How has he/she handled his/her depression so far—what does he/she do? *Some common responses to depression are inactivity, anxiety, social isolation/ withdrawal, suicidal ideation/attempts, helplessness, hopelessness, a lack of self-care, attempt to overcome low mood by flurry of activity that cannot be maintained and use of drugs/alcohol.*
- What has he/she found that makes his/her depression better or worse?
- How long has he/she experienced difficulties with depression? What seemed to trigger it in the first place?
- What thoughts go through his/her mind when he/she feels depressed? *Thoughts related to depression are characterised by pessimism and negative self-image. Your client may feel guilt and display low self-esteem. For example, "I can't do it"; "I'm letting everyone down"; "What's the point?"; "This will only get worse."*
- What type of depression does he/she experience? *Depression can range from sadness, characterised by the ability to mask the mood when in company, to severe clinical or psychotic depression. It can be reactive or endogenous. It could be part of a cycle of mania and depression.*

History

It can be important for your client to understand where his/her difficulties with depression have come from and what is maintaining them. Explore a person's history of depression by asking:

- Were there any significant life events (such as death, loss of employment/ role, etc.) or critical incidents that may have triggered the depression?

- Are there any early experiences that may have contributed to particular beliefs that leave the client predisposed to depression (for example, history of child sex abuse or physical abuse)?
- Has your client experienced a significant change in his/her social network?
- Has your client experienced physical health problems, chronic pain or other psychiatric problems?
- Is there a history of turning anger inward and not dealing with it, leading to depression and resignation?

Maintaining Factors

You can identify the factors that maintain your client's depression by asking:

- What is his/her social environment (for example, poverty or isolation)?
- Does your client have a support network (people he/she can turn to or talk to) of friends and family?
- What level of responsibility does he/she hold? (Is this too much or not enough? Has it changed recently?)
- Is he/she using a depressant or a stimulant substance, and what are his/her reasons for use?
- Is he/she withdrawing, becoming isolated and not participating in activity?
- Is his/her thinking typical of someone who feels depressed (that is, negative, distorted or hopeless)?

You should now have an idea of:

- your client's current depression
- how it may have developed
- how it is being maintained.

STRATEGIES TO MANAGE DEPRESSION

Below are listed three strategies to help your client manage his/her depression: *psychoeducational information, behavioural strategies and cognitive strategies:*

Helping Your Client Understand Depression

Depression is one of the most common mental health problems. At some point in their lives, 60–70 per cent of adults experience symptoms of depression that affect their functioning. There is no definite cause identified for depression. It is generally agreed by health professionals that a combination of the following circumstances act together to create depression: genetic vulnerability, social vulnerability (socially disadvantaged or isolated) and psychological vulnerability (history of loss or disrupted childhood). In medical terms, depression can be defined as a lack of the chemicals serotonin or norepinephrine in the brain. Depression may create a variety of cognitive, behavioural, physical and emotional symptoms or changes in your client.

Below is Beck's cognitive model of depression (Fennell, 1994):

Early experiences
(e.g., strong work ethic; mugged when 15 years old)
↓
Formation of dysfunctional assumptions
(e.g., If I work hard, I can improve myself. I am a victim)
↓
Critical incident(s) (e.g., develop psychosis)
↓
Assumptions activated
(e.g., I must do well at everything I undertake)
↓
Negative automatic thoughts (e.g., I'm useless. I can't change things)
↓
Symptoms of depression
(e.g., lack of motivation, loss of appetite, not enjoying activities)
↙   ↙   ↓   ↓   ↓
behavioural   motivational   affective   cognitive   somatic

Depression or low mood is a normal emotion and is particularly relevant as a reaction to negative or traumatic life events such as death or unemployment. Depression only becomes a problem when its severity or frequency is affecting your client's ability to carry out his/her roles and responsibilities, or is affecting his/her quality of life. It is important for your client to realise that there is a range of strategies he/she can implement and have control over that will affect his/her mood. Severe depression does not usually resolve itself without some intervention or effort. Under depression, your client's energy levels and cognitive patterns will conspire against his/her feeling optimistic or capable of effecting change.

Behavioural Strategies

The behavioural strategies that have been found to be beneficial for depression seek to address how people's behaviour is affecting the way they feel. By using weekly activity diaries (see Appendix 5.5), your client can begin to identify patterns in his/her behaviour and the effect these have on mood. Lack of activity and isolation are likely to add to your client's feelings of depression. Therefore, scheduling simple activities for each day and incorporating exercise and company into your client's week will initially help to lift his/her mood. Be sure to make the activities achievable so that your client experiences a sense of achievement. Clients will often minimise achievements, saying things such as, *"That was nothing—anyone can do that. I used to do so much more."* Again, you can help your client to adapt his/her thinking to something more helpful such as, *"Compared to last week, I have achieved a great deal. It doesn't matter what other people can do—that was an achievement for me."* The two behavioural strategies that have been found to be helpful are planning pleasurable activities and behavioural experiments.

Planning Pleasurable Activities

Practical strategies and "trying out" ideas are a good way to start. Get your client to keep diaries so that he/she has evidence of changes in his/her mood that he/she can use to challenge negative thinking about his/her abilities and successes. A useful tool is an activity diary that allows the client to record activity every hour for a week. To start, ask your client to include a pleasure rating between 1 and 10 (1 being no pleasure, 10 being the most pleasure) for each activity. This will help your client to begin to identify his/her activity/ inactivity patterns and to begin to see the effect activity has on his/her mood. *For example, consider the following activity diary:*

Time	Sunday	Monday	Tuesday
9 am	*Lie in with partner (4)*	*In bed (3)*	*In bed (3)*
10 am	*Shower and breakfast (3)*	*In bed (2)*	*In bed (2)*
11 am	*Walk with partner (6)*	*In bed (2)*	*Shower and breakfast (3)*
12 noon	*Walk with partner (5)*	*Watching TV (2)*	*Walk to shop (4)*
1 pm	*Meal at pub (7)*	*Watching TV (2)*	*Wrote letter (2)*
2 pm	*Visited friends with partner (6)*	*Had snack (2)*	*Watching video (5)*
3 pm	*DIY at home with partner (5)*	*Watching TV (1)*	*Had snack (3)*
4 pm	*Watching TV with partner (8)*	*Attempted DIY and failed (1)*	*Watching video (5)*
5 pm	*Preparing snack (3)*	*In bed (1)*	*Tidied up and partner returned (6)*

Once your client has identified his/her activity pattern, you can work towards increasing the number of enjoyable/pleasurable activities in his/her life. To start with, ask your client to identify activities he/she used to enjoy and no longer participates in. You can then encourage your client to include one such activity in his/her day, either every day or every other day. Ask your client once again to keep an activity diary and rate how pleasurable activities were. Review the activity diary on a regular basis to encourage your client to plan and participate in more pleasurable activities on a daily basis.

Effective problem-solving skills are also vital in planning and carrying out activities. Your client may feel unmotivated and unwilling to attempt any activities. To help him/her overcome this, you can teach him/her problem-solving skills and suggest ways to activate him/herself. These could include using the above activity timetable to ascertain a realistic picture of his/her current activity and then planning practical, easily achievable activities for each day. Planning to spend a particular length of time doing an activity tends to provide a greater feeling of achievement than planning to complete a task. Your client will also need to tackle the thoughts that are keeping him/her inactive. One simple problem-solving technique is outlined as follows:

(1) Clearly define the problem.
(2) Brainstorm to generate possible solutions. At this stage, do not judge any of the ideas, but include them all.
(3) Identify which ideas can be completed alone and which may need assistance from someone else. Specify what help is needed and from whom.
(4) Identify advantages and disadvantages for each solution.
(5) Select the best solution or combination of solutions.
(6) Plan how to carry out the solution.
(7) Implement the plan.

Your client may have used drugs/alcohol as a possible solution to his/her problems in the past. Remember to help your client look at the long-term effects of using drugs/alcohol on his/her mood and the other problems that it may create for him/her. *For example, if your client plans to weed the whole garden one afternoon and then does not complete the task, he/she will see him/herself as a failure. If he/she plans to weed for an hour, the quantity of weeding is less important. He/she can reward the effort, not the outcome.*

Behavioural Experiments

Your client can use behavioural experiments as a practical way to test the automatic thoughts and beliefs that he/she has developed that maintain feelings of depression. A behavioural experiment allows your client to plan in advance for a situation where he/she expects to feel depressed and to see what really happens in that situation. To help your client plan and carry out a behavioural experiment, you will find the following steps helpful:

(1) You and your client will be aware of what his/her depressive (unhelpful) thoughts are. Choose the main thought that maintains feelings of depression, as this will be the thought you can test. However, if you are unsure, go to the following cognitive strategies section, which explains how to identify unhelpful automatic thoughts. *For example, "There is no point in trying to go to the day centre because nothing but alcohol helps me feel better."*

(2) Write down the thought to be tested on the Behavioural Experiment worksheet (Appendix 2.1).

(3) With your client, identify a small step he/she can take to begin to test this thought. *For example, do not have a drink before going out for half an hour to the day centre.*

(4) To ensure that he/she is really able to test his/her depression-maintaining thoughts, get your client to identify a number of experiments he/she can try.

(5) Ask your client to identify what he/she has learned from these experiments and what he/she predicts will happen, and write this on his/her worksheet.

(6) Identify any potential obstacles that may prevent him/her from carrying out the behavioural experiment and strategies to overcome these obstacles.

(7) Once your client has carried out the experiment, he/she should record the outcome under "lesson learned/take-home message".

Consider the following experiment:

Sue's Behavioural Experiment

Thought to be tested

"I need to have a drink to feel well enough to get out of bed."

Experiment	Prediction	Potential obstacles	Strategies to overcome obstacles	Outcome of experiment
Experiment 1 *Get out of bed before lunchtime without having a drink.*	*I won't feel well enough to get up. I will need a drink.*	*I won't wake up. I will drink before I get up.*	*Set alarm clock or ask partner to phone me. Make sure there is no drink in the bedroom when I go to sleep.*	*Got up at 11 o'clock after alarm and partner phoning twice. Had first drink at 12 o'clock.*
Experiment 2 *Get up as usual, but have a shower and breakfast before having a drink.*	*I will need to drink as soon as I get up to manage having a shower, etc.*	*Drink in the bedroom. I won't be hungry.*	*Move all of the alcohol out of the bedroom the night before. Shower first and dry hair. Make a light breakfast.*	*Got up at 1 o'clock; enjoyed shower. Couldn't eat much but had a cup of tea and no alcohol until 3 o'clock.*

Lesson learned/take-home message

"I managed to get up and achieve things without having a drink."

Helping Your Client to Use Behavioural Strategies to Cope with Feelings of Depression Rather Than Using Drugs/Alcohol

Even though drugs/alcohol may give what feels like immediate relief from feelings of sadness, low mood and lack of energy, in the long term they do not tackle the problem of depression, and they can create more depressed symptoms. It will be important to provide your client with ongoing psychoeducational information about the impact of substance use on mood. Also encourage your client to try out his/her new skills for managing mood, so that he/she can weigh up the costs versus benefits of using the new skills against drug/alcohol use as a coping strategy.

For example, consider the following case example:

Claire, a 40-year-old woman with a diagnosis of schizophrenia, drinks half a litre of vodka daily. She describes feeling low in mood and confidence, saying, "I am hopeless. Things will never get better. I might as well just stay in bed because I can't do anything useful." She is currently spending most of her day in bed and is not managing basic self-care activities. She goes out twice a week to a day centre if her keyworker takes her.

Claire learns to plan simple activities into each day such as having a shower, styling her hair, doing some food shopping, getting the bus to the day centre, and taking care of her house and garden. She is still using alcohol to motivate herself to carry out her activities. Her cost-benefit analysis might look like this:

Strategy	Benefits	Costs
Alcohol	*Instant "pick me up"* *Gives me confidence* *Drowns out thoughts*	*Hangovers* *Can't do anything without it* *Expensive* *Alcohol can make you feel depressed*
Activity plans	*Feel pleased when I finish a job* *Don't think as much if I am busy* *Look better*	*Don't get that instant buzz*

Lesson learned/take-home message

"In the short term, alcohol makes me feel better. However, in the long term, the activity plans have less costs and make me feel as good as alcohol does."

So remember, to help your clients reduce feelings of depression,

- encourage them to include pleasurable activities into each day
- help them solve problems
- carry out behavioural experiments
- help them weigh up the costs and benefits of substance use.

Managing Depressed Thoughts: Cognitive Strategies

AIM

To identify and tackle unhelpful thinking patterns that maintain depression.

Your client may feel overwhelmed by a multitude of issues that are indistinct and difficult to identify. Get your client to talk through all of the issues he/she feels are affecting him/her and try to sort them into categories such as social isolation, loss, role, etc. This organisation and categorisation can make problems seem more manageable and controllable.

People hold a range of beliefs that help them make sense of the world. These beliefs are represented in daily life by our automatic thoughts. These are the thoughts that pop into our heads without any effort. The aim of this section is to identify the thoughts that maintain depression and to help your client to replace these with more helpful thoughts. Your client will usually believe that his/her way is the only way of interpreting a situation and that there is little he/she can do about this. You can explain to your client that if he/she becomes aware of the thought in his/her head he/she can re-evaluate it and replace it with a modified thought that will not maintain feelings of depression.

The following dialogue will illustrate how thoughts can provoke depression, and that it is possible to interpret a situation in a number of ways, creating a number of resultant emotions.

Therapist: *You wake up, and there is a list of seven things that need to be completed (make the bed, make breakfast, go shopping, go to the post office, etc.). What would go through your mind?*
Client: *I am never going to be able to do all of these things today, I don't have the energy.*
Therapist: *How would you feel?*
Client: *Fed up and overwhelmed.*
Therapist: *You begin working on the tasks and complete five of them. One cannot be completed because it needs someone else's help, and they are unavailable. What would go through your mind?*
Client: *I knew I wouldn't get everything done. I've let everyone down. I've messed up again.*
Therapist: *How would you feel?*
Client: *Very low.*

Therapist: *Is there another way of thinking about what has happened? For example, if you told a friend that you had completed five tasks in a day, what would they think?*
Client: *Probably that I had worked hard and had a successful day. I had done everything that I could.*
Therapist: *Then how would you feel?*
Client: *Pleased with myself.*

As can be seen from the example, the same situation has produced two different sets of feelings because of the different ways of perceiving or interpreting the situation.

It is important to re-evaluate depressive thinking patterns; otherwise, the following vicious cycle can be set up, maintaining the low mood:

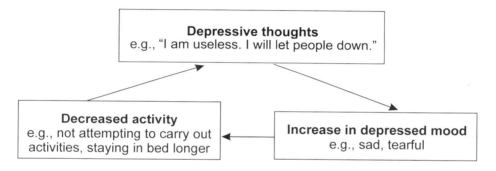

Coping with Unhelpful Automatic Thoughts

Unhelpful automatic thoughts are specific, involuntary, negative, plausible, distorted, habitual, subjective, idiosyncratic, abbreviated, repetitive and situation specific. They are usually short and direct ("Things will never get better"), seem to pop into your head and are negative in content. Because of their content, these negative automatic thoughts can trigger feelings of depression. In order to help your client manage his/her depression, you will need to help him/her re-evaluate and find alternatives to his/her negative automatic thoughts.

To try to alter his/her pattern of thinking, your client needs to do the following:

Identify Unhelpful Automatic Thoughts

A diary that can help with this is shown below. The diary looks at *situation* (antecedent): that is, where your client was and what he/she was doing when the feelings of depression arose/increased; *mood*: that is, the feelings your client had in that situation; and ***automatic thoughts***: that is, the thoughts that popped into your client's head just before he/she became depressed/lower in mood. For example, note the following diary format:

Situation	Moods	Automatic thoughts
Where were you? What were you doing? Who were you with?	*Rate each mood's severity (0–100%).*	*What popped into your head?*
E.g., at the day centre before a group.	*Depressed 85%.*	*I won't say anything useful in the group. This is not going to help. I'll spoil it for other people. I need a drink to cope with this.*

Re-evaluate and Modify Unhelpful Automatic Thoughts

Your client will then need to re-evaluate the evidence that he/she uses to support these automatic thoughts to produce more helpful and realistic alternatives. Generating more helpful thoughts in situations that usually make your client feel depressed will break the cycle of thinking that maintains depression and lift his/her mood.

To help your client to re-evaluate unhelpful thoughts, use the three-question technique:

- What is the evidence for this thought?
- Is this always the case?
- Is there another way of thinking about this?

Another helpful exercise to encourage your client to re-evaluate the thoughts that maintain his/her depression is to record in the thought diary the evidence for and against the thoughts and the alternative thought. *For example, consider the following diary page:*

Situation	Moods	Automatic thoughts	Evidence that supports identified thought	Evidence that does not support the identified thought	Alternative/ balanced thought
Where were you? What were you doing? Who were you with?	*What did you feel? Rate each mood (0–100%).*	*What was going through your mind just before you felt this way? Which was the most impor- tant/worrying thought?*			*Rate how much you believe the alternative thought (0–100%).*
E.g., at the day centre before a group.	*Depressed 85%.*	*I won't say anything useful in the group. This is not going to help. I'll spoil it for other people. I need a drink to cope with this.*	*I'm craving a drink. I can't think of anything to say.*	*I managed to stay for the group last week without drinking. I did speak up and others supported me.*	*I can get through this without drink- ing. I don't need to say a lot to get some benefit from the group (70%).*

So remember, to address the thinking that maintains depression, you can,

- identify negative automatic thoughts
- re-evaluate depressive thinking to produce more helpful alternative thoughts.

ADDITIONAL TREATMENT COMPONENTS I—SKILLS BUILDING

Chapter 12

COMMUNICATION: SOCIAL SKILLS AND ASSERTIVENESS

Communication skills are those skills that allow us to make contact with other people, to make our needs and wishes known and to provide information. Communication can be verbal (that is, out of the mouth) or non-verbal, which includes body language, facial expression, tone, etc. Communication skills also include listening skills, literacy skills and using equipment such as telephones and computers. Specific symptoms of schizophrenia can affect communication, as in delusions, hallucinations, cognitive deficits and negative symptoms:

- *Delusions:* if people believe that the KGB are recording their conversations, they may be reluctant to discuss their true feelings.
- *Hallucinations:* voices may instruct people not to listen or may be distracting.
- *Cognitive deficits:* such deficits result in poor concentration and difficulty in following conversation or the line of argument (deductive reasoning), or memory problems may make effective communication difficult.
- *Negative symptoms:* blunted affect (face does not show emotion), poverty of speech, anhedonia (unable to experience pleasure) and apathy (don't care what happens) also decrease the chances of, and motivation for, effective communication.

To improve your clients' abilities to communicate effectively, you will need to facilitate the development of *social skills and assertion skills.*

SOCIAL SKILLS

> ### AIM
>
> To increase awareness of social skills and learn strategies to improve them.

Helpful references/resources: Bellack et al. (1997), Roberts, Shaner and Eckman (1997).

The term "social skills" includes the concept of being aware of social or cultural norms in conversation and conduct. Without social skills, it is difficult to form and maintain social relationships. Your clients may never have formed social skills, or may have lost them or confidence to use them through the process of developing mental health problems and becoming involved in problematic drug or alcohol use. Your clients' difficulties with social skills may come from one or more of three main sources:

(1) cognitive and emotional difficulties (such as depression, poor concentration, confusion and use of substances that impair functioning)
(2) the way they cope with or adapt to mental health problems (for example, they reject diagnosis, refuse support and thus feel overwhelmed and helpless, and stop activities through lack of confidence)
(3) social disadvantage either before the mental health and substance use problems developed or as a result of them (for example, unemployment, poor education, abuse, disrupted relationships or stigma).

In addition, one theory related to schizophrenia is that clients have increased arousal in the brain and difficulty in screening stimuli (Creek, 1990). Venables (1964) states that to decrease this arousal and remain comfortable clients cut themselves off from social stimuli and therefore from social situations. Thus, clients avoid social sensory input and become isolated, and you will need to be aware that this may decrease clients' motivation to participate in social skills training or to use the skills once they have been learned. Anxiety and depression will also have an impact upon someone's social skills. As these problems with mood are often associated with both severe mental illness and substance use, it is worth assessing whether clients' poor social skills are a result of such moods. A depressed client may appear flat and expressionless, lack initiative and lose interest in friends and activities. People who are anxious may display rapid speech and poorly controlled gestures, and be oversensitive in their reactions. Anxiety can lead to a fear of being the centre of attention, and so clients withdraw in social situations.

The Impact of Drugs/Alcohol on Social Skills

Your clients' difficulties may be exacerbated by their use of alcohol or drugs. This use may have alienated their previous social network, and they may be associating only with other users. This could limit the skills they are using. The effects of alcohol or drug use may be masking the skills they do have. Alcohol or drugs may also be compensating for a lack of skills, in the short term, by providing confidence or reducing symptoms of anxiety and depression. However, the long-term effects of using drugs/alcohol will be a reduction in skills and confidence. Using alcohol or drugs or attempting to stop this use can lead to the need for specific skills in social situations (that is, drug/alcohol-refusal skills).

SOCIAL SKILLS TRAINING FOR MENTAL HEALTH PROBLEMS AND SUBSTANCE USE

The goals of social skills training in substance use are to learn more adaptive ways of meeting the needs that the substance use currently meets and to resist offers to use substances in social situations. The goals of social skills training in mental health are to improve the ability to form and maintain social relationships, with a view to "normalising" life and considering aims such as employment, education and the development of hobbies and interests.

Starting Out: How to Recognise a Social Skills Deficit

Clients with a social skills deficit will often have a history of poor mixing with others and a lack of relationships. They will probably display difficulties in a wide variety of social situations. *The indicators are a failure to communicate with others; peculiarities of appearance, posture and gesture; lack of affect; poor perception of others' needs and low empathy with others. For example, a client may have few friends, be described as odd, make no eye contact, invade others' personal space and be unable to express his/her needs/wishes at a meeting or therapy session.*

History/How Social Skills Deficit Developed

Explore with your clients their pattern of forming (or not forming) relation-ships. Look for strengths or weaknesses in skills. You can assess how social skills deficits developed by asking: *How many role models did they have and how skilled were they? Are there specific situations where deficits occur? Have there been times in their lives when they had more or fewer friends? What was going on for them at these times?* Some more specific questions follow:

- How did your family discuss things when you were little?
- Did you spend time around lots of different people when you were little?

- What friends did you have when you were at school?
- Are there any situations where you do/don't feel able to communicate effectively?

Ask about their patterns of communicating now. It is useful to observe these as well.

- Can you remember the last time that you had an argument or did not get your point across with someone at home?
- When was this?
- Can you describe the situation to me?
- What exactly did you say?
- Is that what usually happens when you talk to that person?

Maintaining Factors

Determine what is maintaining your clients' poor social skills:

- How skilled are their current role models?
- Are there any signs of anxiety or depression?
- Are they using drugs or alcohol in a pattern that creates deficits in social skills?
- Are they isolated and so lack opportunities to practise their skills?
- How do they feel about their mental health problems? Are they ashamed, aware of unusual behaviour, etc.?
- Is their concentration poor? Do they appear overloaded in social situations?

So remember,

- determine whether your client has a social skills deficit
- identify the factors that have helped to create and maintain this deficit.

SOCIAL SKILLS TRAINING

AIM

To identify specific social skills deficits and then practise and improve social skills in these areas.

Social skills training is usually completed in an educational style, with facilitators *modelling the appropriate skills* and *using role-play, video and feedback to practise skills*. This training is ideally suited to group work, as a group provides an immediate social situation for your clients to work in. Within the sessions, opportunities will arise to provide educational information about drug/alcohol use and its impact upon social skills. For example, stimulants decrease concentration and therefore reduce the information gained through observational skills because of lack of attention.

The different social skills can be grouped into eight sets (Creek, 1990), as follows:

- observation skills
- listening skills
- speaking skills
- meshing skills
- expression of attitudes
- social routines
- tactics and strategies
- situation training.

Each set should be tackled separately. When teaching each of the eight social skills listed above, you will need to follow the following five steps:

(1) You need to *set specific targets for the session,* looking at the rationale for using each skill and its relevance to your client's lifestyle.
(2) Next, you will need to *model the skill,* showing how to cope with a situation, not how to master it, as this will be more realistic for your client and easier to emulate.
(3) Get your client to *perform the skill,* using the same or similar dialogue.
(4) *Feedback* should be given immediately, focusing on praise and the skill itself, not the person. Identify any areas that your client needs to correct and practise these in detail. Encourage your client to improvise at this stage, making the responses more personal.
(5) *Set homework tasks* so that your client is integrating his/her new skills into his/her own environment and widening his/her ability by trying them in different situations.

Observation Skills

This set includes *gathering information* about a situation and other people's attitudes and feelings, and recognising the causes of their behaviour. It is also about recognising emotions and observing our own behaviour. An outline of this training set follows:

Observation skills deficit: *Client unable to recognise emotions and respond appropriately.*

Targets for session: *To be able to recognise three specific emotions by looking at body language and expression. Identify ways of responding to these emotions appropriately.*

Rationale: *If you can recognise someone's emotions accurately, you will know whether it is a good time to speak to him/her and will understand his/her response better. For example, if your father is looking angry, it may not be a good time to ask a favour, or the signs of anger may help you to understand why he snaps at you.*

Model: *Use pictures or video, or model specific emotions such as anger, sadness and fear, using facial expression and body language. Ask your client to identify the emotion being modelled.*

Practice: *Ask your client to display the chosen emotions by expression and body language.*

Feedback: *Provide feedback on performance and achievements.*

Discuss: *If you recognise this emotion in someone you are speaking to, what would you normally do? Is this effective? What is that person's response and the outcome of the interaction? Could other people's emotions or your response be altered if either of you has used drugs/alcohol?*

Model: *Demonstrate effective ways to respond to the recognised emotions. For example, you recognise anger and then suggest that you come back in 10 minutes to discuss your request, saying, "Now doesn't seem like a good time—may I come back in 10 minutes to discuss going out on Saturday?"*

Practice: *Get your client to repeat the above dialogue. Then get your client to recognise an emotion and plan a way of dealing with it, using his or her own examples.*

Feedback: *Provide feedback on achievements. Practise further weaker areas.*

Homework: *Get your client to recognise emotions during conversations and practise ways of responding to them.*

Listening Skills

This set includes ***reflecting feelings, questioning and providing listener feedback*** by nodding, eye contact and verbal response (for example, "uh-huh"). *Use of these listening skills during a conversation (that is, attention feedback) demonstrates that a person is paying attention to what is being said and encourages further conversation.*

Listening skill deficit: *Client does not provide attention feedback.*

Targets for session: *To recognise the importance of attention feedback and learn two methods of providing this.*

Rationale: *Someone who can tell that you are paying attention to what he or she is saying will be more likely to continue a conversation and attend to anything that you wish to say.*

Model: *Get your client to talk to you and model someone lacking in attention-feedback skills so that your client can experience the negative aspects of not using attention feedback.*

Discuss: *What could you (the therapist) have done to show you were listening? Discuss with your client whether his/her drug/alcohol use ever affects his/her concentration so that listening would be harder to do?*

Model: *Use attention-feedback strategies identified, such as nodding; saying "uh-huh", "yes", "umm", etc.; and making eye contact while your client talks to you.*

Practice: *Get your client to repeat this exercise, this time with him/her modelling good listening skills.*

Feedback: *Provide feedback on performance and achievements. Practise further areas of need.*

Homework: *Practise using attention-feedback skills and notice response to these skills.*

Speaking Skills

This set covers ***disclosing factual information and feelings*** and the characteristics of speech, such as non-verbal accompaniments and fluency.

Speaking skills deficit: *Client does not speak fluently and uses few non-verbal accompaniments.*

Targets for session: *To recognise the importance of non-verbal accompaniments to speech and learn methods of using these. To improve skills in speaking fluently.*

Rationale: *Non-verbal accompaniments and speaking fluently make conversation more interesting and easier to attend to and make you appear more confident/competent.*

Model: *Speak hesitantly about a chosen topic without using varied tone, inflection, speed and loudness.*

Discuss: *How did it feel to listen to the speech? What would have made it more interesting or easier to listen to? Does use of drugs/alcohol affect your ability to speak clearly and fluently?*

Model: *Use tone, inflection, speed and loudness while speaking fluently about a chosen topic.*

Practice: *Get your client to practise using the above skills. It may be useful to tape-record this. Your client may wish to chose his/her own topic for you either to model or to practise with.*

Feedback: *Use tape and provide feedback on performance and achievements. Practise further areas of need.*

Homework: *Practise speaking fluently by preparing in advance for meeting people. Remember to use non-verbal accompaniments to speech.*

Meshing Skills

This set covers *content* and changing content and timing.

Meshing skills deficit: *Client not skilled at recognising timing cues in conversation.*
Targets for session: *To recognise cues for timing in conversations and use them effectively.*
Rationale: *An awareness of timing cues allows conversation to run smoothly and lets both parties feel listened to.*
Model: *Get your client to talk to you and model someone not aware of timing cues who interrupts speech and does not respond appropriately.*
Discuss: *What happened to the above conversation? Was it successful? How could it have been improved? Preoccupation with thoughts about drugs/alcohol may make you miss timing cues in conversation.*
Model: *Accurately recognise timing cues while your client talks to you. It may help to provide a script to follow.*
Practice: *Swap roles. You read the script to your client, who responds appropriately to timing cues.*
Feedback: *Provide feedback on performance and achievements. Practise further areas of need.*
Homework: *Recognise how other people use timing cues and respond appropriately to them.*

Expression of Attitudes

This set looks at matching another person's style and then choosing a different style to try to influence him or her.

Expression of attitudes skill deficit: *Client does not alter style to achieve different aims.*
Targets for session: *To try out different styles of communicating and see that they have different effects.*
Rationale: *By altering your style of communicating, you can achieve different effects, such as influencing the person listening.*
Model: *Use different styles of saying the same information—attempting to influence, persuade or agree with someone.*
Practice: *Use the same information to practise different styles of communicating and see the different outcomes.*
Feedback: *Provide feedback on performance and achievements. Practise further areas of need.*
Homework: *Practise adapting style of communicating to achieve different results.*

Social Routines

This set includes greetings, farewells, making requests, accessing strangers, offering compliments, praise or sympathy, giving explanations, making apologies, saving face and assertion. See also drug/alcohol-refusal skills, as this is a particularly difficult issue to explain in social settings.

Social routines skills deficit: *Client unable to make requests effectively.*
Targets for session: *To be able to make requests clearly.*
Rationale: *Being skilled at making a request does not mean that you will get what you ask for, but it does mean that the other person will know exactly what you want and how important it is to you, and that person will be more likely to justify his/her reasoning and explain why, if it is not possible for the request to be granted.*
Model: *Make a request specifying exactly what you want and why it is important to you.*
Practice: *Making requests, planning exactly what to request and reasons why the request is being made.*
Feedback: *Provide feedback on performance and achievements. Practise further areas of need.*
Homework: *Plan and make requests in the way learned.*

Tactics and Strategies

This is about **putting together the strategies learned** to produce different behaviour. Typical strategies are as follows:

(1) *making a request and using a persuading style of communicating instead of losing one's temper*
(2) *using active listening skills and recognition of timing to change the topic instead of interrupting and not paying attention*
(3) *recognising others' emotions and disclosing feelings instead of ignoring the emotional content of conversation.*

Situation Training

This training is about **putting the skills learned to use in different situations**. This will involve planning the situations to be encountered and the skills needed in these, and then practising the dialogue in a "safe" environment. You will then need either to help your clients to try out the skills in the new setting or discuss the outcome of this when they have tried it alone. Each client will need to learn a different combination of skills and will want to practise these in unique situations. Use the information and circumstances that they describe to you to make it easier to create the exercises. This will, in turn, also make them relevant to your client.

> **So remember, to improve your clients' social skills,**
>
> - identify the specific skills your clients need
> - discuss why the skill is useful
> - model the use of the skill
> - get your clients to practise with you and in their usual routines
> - provide positive feedback
> - encourage clients to consider how the effects of substances may affect their social skills.

APPLYING SOCIAL SKILLS TO SPECIFIC SITUATIONS

Work-Related Skills

If your client aims to enter or maintain employment, there may be some specific skills he/she needs to practise. These could include:

- interview skills
- asking for feedback about job performance
- responding to criticism
- following verbal instructions
- problem solving.

Interview Skills

Interview skills could include making a good first impression, explaining why you are interested in the job, answering common questions and non-verbal communication. Following the format used in the social skills training section, *brainstorm what these skills involve* and then *practise by modelling and role-play* to improve your client's skills. It may be useful to *discuss strategies to manage anxiety that do not involve using drugs/alcohol*.

Asking for Feedback About Job Performance

This includes asking for feedback on a specific aspect of the work (such as asking the appropriate person for feedback) and awareness of the process of receiving feedback (such as needing an appointment and listening skills). *Brainstorm these questions* with your client and then *practise the specific skills and dialogue by role-play*. Remember to deal with your *client's response to the feedback*. If the feedback is negative, this may trigger urges to use drugs/alcohol, so he/she will need to plan in advance for this.

Responding to Criticism

This includes listening skills, reflecting what has been said, requesting advice on possible improvements and questioning for clarity. Receiving criticism is difficult for everyone; therefore, it may be useful to look at ways to stay calm and to deal with unpleasant emotions, such as anger or distress, without using drugs/alcohol.

Following Verbal Instructions

This includes listening skills, reflecting what has been said and questioning for clarity. Prolonged use of substances and mental health difficulties can both cause cognitive impairment, making following instructions difficult. *Look at strategies for remembering instructions*, such as writing them down, and use graded examples, working from simple instructions to complex ones.

Problem Solving

In a work situation, clients will come across a number of situations in which they will need good problem-solving skills if they are to cope effectively without resorting to alcohol or drugs, or becoming frustrated or despondent. The steps involved in problem solving are as follows:

(1) Define the problem.
(2) Brainstorm to generate possible solutions. Ask your client not to judge any ideas at this stage.
(3) Identify the advantages and disadvantages of each solution.
(4) Select the best solution or combination of solutions.
(5) Plan how to carry out the solution.
(6) Implement the plan.

Use of drugs/alcohol may well be identified as a possible solution. Remember to look at the long-term implications of using this strategy and the other problems that it may create for your client.

Your clients may recognise other issues, such as using the telephone, reading and writing reports/letters, or computer literacy, as issues they need to work on. Many job centres and colleges can provide training in these skills.

> **So remember,**
>
> - if your clients are aiming towards employment, work on specific skills they may need in a work environment.

ASSERTIVENESS

> **AIMS**
>
> (1) To facilitate understanding and recognition of assertive responses and behaviour.
> (2) To teach strategies and skills to increase assertive responses and reduce the use of passive and aggressive responses.

Helpful resources/references: Birchwood, Fowler and Jackson (2000), Roberts, Shaner and Eckman (1997).

Assertiveness is the ability to recognise your own needs and wants, and to communicate your needs, feelings and opinions without violating the rights of others. People can communicate and respond in a range of ways, from *passive* to *aggressive. Assertiveness* is said to be midway on this continuum of ways to respond and communicate. The continuum looks like this:

PASSIVE _____ ASSERTIVE _____ AGGRESSIVE

Passive people are characterised by having difficulty in standing up for themselves, saying "yes" but feeling resentful about this, or not expressing an opinion. They will also appear closed off in their body language (for example, arms folded over body and little eye contact). The typical phrases of a passive person are "perhaps", "maybe", never mind" and "I wonder if you could ... ?"

Aggressive people are characterised by expressing their opinions forcefully in such a way that the rights of others may be violated, not listening to other people and pushing themselves forwards to the detriment of others. They will also tend to be domineering in their use of body language (for example, invading personal space and staring). The typical phrases of an aggressive person include "you should/ought/must" and "it's your fault".

Assertive people are characterised by stating their opinions, needs and preferences in a way that is not punishing or threatening to others, listening to others, taking time to reflect on how they want to respond, and accepting or rejecting requests politely with reasons. They will also use open, relaxed body language (for example, appropriate eye contact and attentive listening). The typical phrases of an assertive person include "I" statements, "we could" and "what do you think?"

In the short term, reacting in a passive or aggressive way may seem to be successful or productive for your clients. However, in the long term, there will be situations that cannot be handled in these ways or in which these strategies will not work. For example, passivity can lead to feelings of frustration and anger in your clients if they begin to feel that others are taking advantage of them. It can also lead to stress for your clients if they take on more than they are able to manage. Aggression could alienate your clients from their social circle and mean that they are not included in activities and decisions.

Effects of Psychosis and Alcohol/Drug Use on Assertiveness

The experience of having a psychotic episode or using drugs or alcohol can result in a change in the way people respond and communicate. They could become more passive or aggressive. A client's personality, experiences and beliefs will determine whether he/she responds and communicates in a passive or aggressive way. As a result of experiencing psychotic symptoms or other mental health difficulties and being admitted to psychiatric hospitals, your clients may feel helpless, inferior or stupid, or feel that others perceive them in this way. Such feelings may contribute to their becoming increasingly passive. For example, they may begin to think, "My opinion does not count." Alternatively, clients may start to respond and communicate in more aggressive ways. For example, they may think, "I am not stupid and I won't be treated that way by anyone." Clients can also feel stigmatised as "mental" or "mad". If they feel unable to challenge this, they could respond passively, whereas others may rebel against such stigmas by becoming aggressive and seek to challenge and distance themselves from treatment services.

It has been suggested that clients often respond to the experience of psychosis in one of two ways: either shut it out and not think about it, or seek to integrate the experience into their perception of themselves and accept it (Birchwood, Fowler & Jackson, 2000). Clients who follow the former path may well display aggression, particularly when mental health services attempt to engage them in treatment for a problem that they do not feel they have. Alternatively, your clients may feel overwhelmed by their mental health diagnosis and perceive that they have lost control of their lives. This could result in their behaving in a passive manner, particularly if they believe that "doctor knows best". Thus, when they are in contact with mental health professionals, they enter into a more passive role and experience difficulty in expressing their feelings. Professionals may also encourage the "doctor knows best" idea to gain cooperation, which could, in the long term, lead to reactive aggression.

In addition to the impact of psychosis on aggression or passivity, the use of alcohol and drugs will often amplify emotions already present in your clients. Thus, it may exaggerate or exacerbate a client's natural tendency towards aggression or passivity. Alcohol or drug use may also become a way of coping with particular experiences, feelings, demands, stressors or conflicts that clients feel unable to cope with. Therefore, particular beliefs about the substance will be developed which reinforce the need to use the substance in such situations. Thus, for example, if clients believe that they cannot cope without the substance, this can lead them to feel helpless if they haven't used and could result in their appearing passive. In such a case, someone may use alcohol to give them the "Dutch courage" to assert his/her views, feelings or needs. Moreover, the effect of some substances (such as steroids and cocaine) may produce aggression.

The Importance of Assertiveness Training

If your clients are to make and maintain positive changes in their alcohol or drug use, they will need to be equipped with assertiveness skills. Such skills and strategies will increase the likelihood of your clients being able to deal with high-risk situations and activating stimuli which trigger the desire to use drugs or alcohol (lack of confidence, stressors, conflicts, demands, feelings, etc.). For example, your clients may have had contact in the past with dealers who are quite pushy and aggressive. In the past, your clients may have behaved in a passive way and used drugs even if they did not have the cash, out of fear of refusing. If your clients can behave assertively in these situations, they will be more likely to maintain changes in their drug or alcohol use because they will feel more in control of their life and be more able to refuse drugs or alcohol if tempted.

So remember, it is important to work on assertiveness with your clients so that they can,

- effectively communicate their needs and treatment goals
- make and maintain changes in their alcohol/drug use
- negotiate effective treatment for their mental health, improve their quality of life and reduce the need for alcohol/drugs
- communicate more effectively with their friends and family, thereby reducing stress and conflict, and improving their social network.

ASSERTIVENESS TRAINING

Starting Out: Assessing Communication Styles

Current Communication Styles

To begin work, explain to your client the continuum of types of responses and communicating styles (that is, passive, assertive and aggressive) and how he/she is characterised. To assist him/her to identify his/her particular style of responding and communicating in situations, you will find the following Communication Styles chart (see Appendix 6.1) useful:

Situation	Response	Style
Where, with whom, what were you doing?	*What did you do?*	*Passive, aggressive, assertive*
With family; they realised I am still using cannabis.	*Shouted "What do you expect when you treat me like this?", walked out, slammed door.*	*Aggressive.*
With keyworker talking about taking medication.	*Agreed to take higher dose of medication that makes me feel unwell.*	*Passive.*

You can use a chart like this to determine whether there is a typical pattern in your client's behaviours and responses. From the example, the client tends to show always a passive response to authority figures and an aggressive response to his family.

History/How Communication Styles Develop

Explore with your client the types of communication styles (behaviours and responses) that he/she has used in the past and how these have developed and changed over time. Discuss whether these strategies have been effective or not (whether they resulted in the desired outcome or not).

Maintaining Factors

Explore what may be keeping your client in this particular pattern of being passive or aggressive. You can do this by asking questions such as:

- Do you respond differently when you are using/not using drugs/alcohol? (For example, does the client respond aggressively only when drunk?)
- What are the consequences of behaving in this way? In the short term, is it an effective strategy?

- Do you know of other ways you could respond in this situation? (Look for lack of skills or confidence.)

So remember,

- identify the type of response that your client is using—is it aggressive, passive or assertive?
- identify how these responses developed and are maintained.

STRATEGIES TO TACKLE LACK OF ASSERTIVENESS

Below are listed a number of *cognitive* and *behavioural* strategies that can be used with your clients to increase their assertiveness skills.

Cognitive Strategies

AIM

To identify and re-evaluate thinking patterns associated with a lack of assertiveness.

To tackle lack of assertion, you will find it important to identify and assist your client to re-evaluate his/her *underlying beliefs* and *automatic thoughts* about his/her abilities, mental health and substance use. Strategies are detailed below.

Automatic Thoughts

Automatic thoughts are specific, involuntary, negative, plausible, distorted, habitual, subjective, idiosyncratic, abbreviated, repetitive and situation specific. They are usually short and direct (for example, "I can't say 'no' to that"), seem to pop into your head and are negative in content. Because of their content, these automatic thoughts can lead to people responding and behaving in a passive or aggressive way.

Encourage your client to use a thought diary (assertiveness) (see Appendix 6.2) over a period of a least a week to record his/her automatic thoughts when in different situations. The thought diary looks at **situation**, that is, where your client was; **automatic thoughts**, that is, the thoughts that popped into your client's head just before he/she responded to the situation; and **style of response**, that is, did they respond passively/aggressively/assertively? *For example, Jane is a 29-year-old woman who has experienced three episodes of psychosis in the last 5 years. She currently uses cannabis problematically and uses alcohol occasionally.*

Jane's Thought Diary (Assertiveness)

Situation	Style of response	Automatic thoughts
Where were you, who were you with, what were you doing?	*Passive, aggressive or assertive.*	*The thoughts and beliefs that popped into your head just before you responded to the situation.*
With family; they realised I am still using cannabis.	*I shouted at them and slammed the door (aggressive).*	*They don't understand what I am going through. It's not my fault. Can't they understand that I can't cope without it?*
With keyworker, talking about medication.	*I went along with what she said (passive).*	*I can't refuse her. She knows more than me. My opinion does not count.*

Re-evaluating Automatic Thoughts

If the automatic thoughts that go through your client's mind are "what if . . . ?" questions, try to help your client to answer the question by asking him/her, "What is the worst thing that you imagined could happen?" Doing this may be hard for your client, as you will be discussing his/her underlying fears. Your client will then need to challenge and re-evaluate the automatic thoughts identified in his/her thought diary, to produce more flexible and realistic alternative ways of thinking. Generating more helpful thoughts in situations where he/she usually responds aggressively or passively will allow him/her to respond in a more assertive way.

To help your clients to be able to re-evaluate their automatic thoughts, teach them to use the three-question technique:

(1) What is the evidence for this thought?
(2) Is this always the case? Are there times when this is not the case?
(3) If there are times when this is not the case, what are the implications? Is there another way of thinking about this?

Another helpful way to encourage your client to re-evaluate the thoughts that provoke a passive or aggressive response is for him/her to record in his/her diary the evidence for and against the thoughts as described above. He/she can then generate an alternative way of thinking that reduces the likelihood of his/her responding in an aggressive or passive way. Consider the following example of a thought diary:

Jane's Re-evaluated Thought Diary (Assertiveness)

Situation	Style of response	Automatic thoughts	Evidence for	Evidence against	Alternative thoughts
Where were you, who were you with, what were you doing?	*Passive, aggressive or assertive.*	*The thoughts and beliefs that popped into your head just before you responded to the situation.*			
With family; they realised I am still using cannabis.	*I shouted at them and slammed the door (aggressive).*	*They don't understand what I am going through. It's not my fault. Can't they under-stand that I can't cope without it?*	*They have never used cannabis.*	*They have been under-standing in the past.*	*They find it difficult to understand why I use cannabis. I can help them to understand me more by talk-ing to them.*
With keyworker, talking about medication.	*I went along with what she said (passive).*	*I can't refuse her. She knows more than me. My opinion does not count.*	*She does know more than me.*	*I know myself better than she knows me.*	*My opinion does count. I can listen to her and then let her know how I feel as well.*

So remember, to tackle a lack of assertiveness, you can,

- use thought diaries to help your clients recognise their thinking patterns
- use the three-question technique and "evidence for and against" to help your clients re-evaluate their thoughts.

Behavioural Strategies

AIMS

(1) To use behavioural experiments to re-evaluate passive/aggressive "thoughts".
(2) To provide skills to behave assertively.

Behavioural Experiments

Behavioural experiments can be used to re-evaluate your client's thinking patterns, that is, confirm or challenge the way he/she is interpreting information.

To help your client plan and carry out a behavioural experiment, you will find the following steps helpful:

(1) By now, you and your client will be aware of what his/her unhelpful thought is; this will be the thought that you can test. However, if you are still unsure, go back to the earlier section which explains how to identify unhelpful automatic thoughts (page 179).
(2) Write the thought to be tested on the Behavioural Experiment worksheet (Appendix 2.1).
(3) With your client, identify a small step he/she can take to begin to test this thought.
(4) Get your client to identify what he/she predicts will happen and write this on his/her worksheet.
(5) Identify any potential obstacles that may prevent the client from carrying out the behavioural experiment and strategies to overcome these obstacles.
(6) Once your client has carried out the experiment, he/she should record the outcome on the worksheet.
(7) To ensure that he/she is really able to test the thought, identify with your client a number of experiments he/she could try out.
(8) Ask your client to identify what he/she has learned from these experiments and write it down under "lesson learned/take-home message".

With alternative evidence, your client can recognise inconsistencies in his/her thinking and produce more flexible alternative thoughts that will reduce passive or aggressive responses. The experiments need to be individualised to reflect your client and his/her cognitive pattern. Behavioural experiments provide your client with a chance to go into the situation, having planned in advance, and to test his/her thoughts and fears. A behavioural experiment also allows your clients to discover what will really happen in that situation, which is probably not the same as what they fear will happen (see C-BIT treatment phase 2 for more details on behavioural experiments).

Consider the following case example:

George is not happy with his medication, as it makes him feel drowsy and shaky, but he has not told his keyworker or psychiatrist about this. George believes they will not listen to him and will tell him he needs to continue taking his depot medication. George has told his family of his concerns about his medication only when drunk. At those times, he has shouted and refused to accept any medication. Until now, they have dismissed his concerns because of the circumstances in which he has raised the issue.

By now, you and your client will be aware of what the unhelpful thought is; this will be the thought that you can test.

(1) "I can't tell them how I feel about my medication without having three or four pints of lager."
(2) Write the thought to be tested on the Behavioural Experiment worksheet.
(3) With your client, identify a small step he/she can take to begin to test this thought. For example, *"Begin a discussion about your medication with your family when you are not drinking."*

If your clients believe that their opinions are not important and therefore do not express them, they will continue to respond in a passive way. Encourage them to experiment assertively, expressing their opinions in a fairly safe environment and record the response. (For example, did anyone listen, take on board their ideas or respond positively to their input? How did they feel after acting in a more assertive way? Did they experience positive internal feedback, or did they have a different outcome such as not feeling low or taken advantage of?) Over time, your clients will begin to re-evaluate their view of themselves if they receive positive feedback either internally or externally. As a result, they will begin to recognise that they are able to express opinions without using alcohol or drugs. In addition, they will feel better able to express their opinions, feelings or needs again.

George's Behavioural Experiment

Thought to be tested

"I can't discuss changing my medication without having a drink."

Experiment	Prediction	Potential obstacles	Strategies to overcome obstacles	Outcome of experiment
Experiment 1 Talk to Mum about medication without having a drink.	I won't be able to say what I mean if I don't drink.	Hard to get Mum on her own, and I might drink in the morning.	Speak to Mum on Tuesday morning because she's always home alone. Don't buy beer on Monday night.	Had one can, but then told Mum that I don't like meds and she listened.
Experiment 2 Talk to keyworker about meds without drinking.	He won't listen to me.	Might drink in the morning, and I'll be too scared to say anything.	Get Mum to look after beer. Practise what I want to say and write it down.	Mum stayed with me and encouraged me to say what I wanted and I did.

Lesson learned/take-home message

"I was able to explain what I wanted to say without having a drink, and people did listen to me."

Behavioural Skills Training

Your client may lack basic skills that would allow him/her to respond in an assertive way. Common problems are as follows:

(1) being able to say "no" to requests
(2) making requests
(3) using verbal and non-verbal communication skills effectively.

In such cases, you will need to teach your client these basic assertiveness skills and practise appropriate use of them. These can be done effectively in role-play and homework. The details of tackling these three common problems that prevent assertive responses are outlined below.

1. Saying "No"

By learning how to say "no" to requests, your client can gain some time to consider the request and make an informed decision. This will avoid "letting people down" at a later stage if your client is unable to meet all of his/her obligations. By accepting all requests, your client may be creating stress by taking on more than he/she can manage.

Some helpful strategies to teach your client the skill of saying "no":

- Rehearse scenes where your client believes it would be difficult for him/her to say "no" to a request.
- Identify his/her thoughts and re-evaluate any that seem faulty by using the strategies outlined in the cognitive strategies section in this chapter.
- Ask the client to think of alternative ways of responding to the request.
- Identify which of these responses would be considered assertive.
- Practise using this response in role-plays.
- Encourage your client to practise saying the word "no".
- For homework, ask your client to refuse simple requests with his/her family or friends, so that he/she can experience the results of using this new strategy.
- Include behavioural experiments in which your client can try out this new strategy and record the response of others and his/her own response to the new approach.

For example, take a look at the following case example:

Sue does not feel able to say "no" to her friend Mary when she asks to borrow money or cannabis. Sue begins by practising with her therapist saying the word "no". She then works out other ways that she could respond to Mary's requests, including saying, "I don't have any money with me today" or "I don't have enough money to last the week, so, I'm sorry, I can't lend you any." Sue re-evaluated her belief that her friends would like her only if she gave them money by realising that she had other friends who never asked for money and still wanted to spend time with her. Sue then tried out her saying "no" response with Mary and discovered that Mary simply asked someone else and was not greatly offended by the refusal.

2. Making Requests

Improving your client's ability to make requests will increase the chances of his/her gaining support, help and advice when needed, thereby reducing worry, concern and stress levels. Learning how to make requests does not guarantee that your client will get what he/she wants, but he/she will have made his/her needs known and will have a better understanding of why a request is granted or not. A request needs to be very specific. It is useful for your client to explain exactly why they are making the request, as this will provide a context for the listener to make a decision.

Some helpful strategies to teach your client the skill of making requests:

- Rehearse scenes where your client would find it difficult to make a request.
- Identify the thoughts he/she would have in that situation that prevent him/her from making the request and re-evaluate any that seem to be distortions or unhelpful (using the strategies described in the cognitive strategies section of this chapter).
- Ask the client to think of alternative ways of making the request.
- Identify which of these would be considered assertive.
- Practise in role-plays with your client how he/she could go about making requests in an assertive way.
- For homework, ask the client to make simple requests of family members/friends, so that he/she experiences results from using the new strategy.
- Build in behavioural experiments where your client tries out the new strategy and records the response of others and his/her own response to the new approach.

Here is a case example:

Julie does not feel able to ask her friends to accompany her in new "healthy alternative" activities that will begin to replace her previous cocaine-related activities. She would like her friend to go swimming with her and to start a creative night class at the local college. Julie believes that her friend will think that she will fail in her new activities, and that her friend would not be interested in spending time with her now that she doesn't use drugs. Julie was encouraged to remember the types of comments that her friend usually makes to her, and she realised that her friend often complimented her on her abilities and encouraged her to try new activities. She also realised that they had been friends for a long time before she started to use drugs. During a session, Julie practised asking her Community Psychiatric Nurse (CPN) if she wanted to go swimming on a specific day at a specific time, and thought about how she could respond and compromise with her friend's responses (that is, suggesting other times or activities, such as going to the gym). Julie then tried out asking her friend, and they arranged to go to the gym the following week.

3. Using Verbal and Non-Verbal Communication Skills

To promote the appearance of being assertive, it is important that your client's verbal communication and non-verbal communication are giving the same message. Saying "no" to a request will not be as effective if your client cannot make eye contact and does not speak firmly and clearly. A request will not be viewed as important if your client is not concise and does not use good eye contact.

Some useful strategies to teach your client to match his/her verbal and non-verbal communication skills are as follows:

- Get your client to identify someone he/she knows who appears confident and assertive.
- Clarify what this person's method of communicating is. What does the person look like when communicating (posture, etc.)? What non-verbal skills does the person use?
- Model communicating in an assertive way if necessary.
- Role-play with your client communicating in an assertive way. Use video for feedback if possible.
- For homework, get your client to practise using verbal and non-verbal communication skills to assist with an assertive statement.
- Use behavioural experiments so your client can try out different methods of communicating and identify the most effective and assertive strategies.

Consider the following case example:

Martin feels that his attempts to refuse alcohol are ignored by his friends, and that his requests for help with his medication from his doctor never get anywhere. When he demonstrated how he would communicate his ideas, it was apparent that he made no eye contact, was not clear and firm in what he said, and fidgeted and appeared unsure of himself. His CPN mirrored back to Martin how he came across, and they brainstormed how James Bond would communicate these ideas. Martin then planned exactly what he wanted to say and practised delivering his ideas firmly while maintaining good eye contact. Martin also worked hard on not picking his fingers and hanging his head when he spoke. At his next Care Programme Action (CPA) planning meeting, Martin asked for help with his medication and received a medi-dose wallet and p.r.n. anxiolytic medication.

So remember, to tackle a lack of assertiveness,

- use behavioural experiments to re-evaluate thoughts that prevent assertive behaviour
- teach and role-play assertive ways of saying "no" to requests, making requests and using non-verbal behaviour.

APPLYING ASSERTIVENESS SKILLS TO SPECIFIC SITUATIONS

Clients with serious mental-health and substance-use problems may be confronted by specific situations where they will need to be assertive—for example, refusing drugs/alcohol from dealers, family members and friends, and negotiating with services and organisations regarding issues such as care, treatment, housing and benefits. Your client will benefit from considering these situations specifically and applying the assertiveness skills already learned to manage these potentially extremely difficult encounters. How to apply assertiveness skills to *refusing drugs and alcohol* and *negotiating with services* will be outlined below.

Drug/Alcohol-Refusal Skills

AIM

To develop strategies to be able to refuse drugs/alcohol from a dealer, family member or friend.

Drug/alcohol-refusal skills are a specific form of saying "no" and will be essential to your client if he/she is to maintain positive changes in drug and alcohol use. Drug/alcohol-refusal skills require a combination of communication and assertiveness skills. It is vital that your client plans in advance for when he/she will need these skills and is clear about the strategy he/she will use in each situation. Your client will probably need to develop different strategies for dealing with different people. Some situations that will be particularly difficult for your client include refusing drugs or alcohol from a dealer, a family member or friends.

Refusing a Dealer

Your client may well perceive a dealer as an authority figure, dangerous or a "friend". These perceptions will all make it more difficult for your client to refuse an offer of drugs/alcohol. Moreover, a dealer will have a vested interest in reminding your client of all the reasons "for" using alcohol/drugs. Your client will probably know in which circumstances he/she is most likely to meet dealers, so he/she can avoid some confrontations with them. However, it is still important that your client plans for the eventuality of "bumping into" a dealer who could become pushy or coercive.

Some helpful strategies to teach your client how to refuse a dealer are as follows:

- Get your client to remind him/herself of all the reasons why he/she no longer wishes to use the substance. Your client may find it useful to keep a card in his/her wallet outlining the new beliefs.
- Practise, in role-play, saying "no" firmly, using good eye contact and moving away from the situation.
- Devise an explanation that could be given to the dealer, if your client wishes to.
- Decide at what point it would be best to leave the situation.

Here is a case example:

Sally says that she might meet her old dealer as she leaves the post office, having just cashed her giro. He has previously offered her crack on credit in these circumstances. Sally wrote out the reasons why she does not want to use crack and decided that she would read this as she left the post office each week. After much thought and practice with her CPN, Sally decided to respond to the dealer's offer by saying, "I don't want any drugs any more, thank you", and walking away immediately. She decided that if the dealer persisted and followed her, she would repeat the same sentence and head for her friend's house, which is very close to the post office.

Refusing a Family Member

For a client, refusing drugs or alcohol from someone within his/her own family can be extremely difficult. There may be few places to escape to if your client is surrounded by temptation. Again, a plan needs to be developed before your client is in such a difficult situation.

Some helpful strategies to teach your client how to refuse a family member are as follows:

- Get your client to remind him/herself of all the reasons why he/she no longer wishes to use the substance. The client may find it useful to keep a card in his/her wallet outlining the new beliefs.
- Practise, in role-play, saying "no" firmly, using eye contact.
- Your client is likely to want to devise an explanation that can be used consistently.
- Identify an alternative activity that your client could suggest to the family member instead of using drugs or alcohol.
- Decide at what point it would be best to leave the situation and where he/she could go.

Consider the following case study:

Delroy's father smokes cannabis and drinks alcohol with his friends each weekend at home. Delroy is working on abstaining from both of these substances. He used to join in using with his father and family on Friday and Saturday evenings. Delroy decided that he would explain to his father why he did not want to use cannabis and alcohol, and ask his father to help him to refuse offers from his father's friends. He practised this with his keyworker and was able to explain clearly to his father what he wanted. His father understood but was adamant that he would not change his own behaviour. He and his father agreed that if Delroy was repeatedly offered drugs/alcohol, his father would send him on an errand to remove him from the situation.

Refusing a Friend

Peer-group pressure can be a powerful thing, and your client may feel that he/she needs to find a new group of friends who do not use substances. However, it will still be important for him/her to have in place a strategy to deal with meeting a friend with whom your client previously used who offers him/her drugs or alcohol.

Some helpful strategies to teach your client how to refuse a friend are as follows:

- Get your client to remind him/herself of all the reasons why he/she no longer wishes to use the substance. Your client may find it useful to keep a card in his/her wallet outlining the new beliefs held about the substance.
- Practise, in role-play saying "no" firmly, using eye contact and moving away from the situation.
- Your client is likely to want to devise an explanation that can be used consistently.
- Find an alternative activity that your client could suggest to his/her friend instead of the one being refused.
- Decide at what point your client needs to leave the situation.

Inevitably, your client will come across new situations where he/she is offered drugs or alcohol and has been unable to plan for it. Your client may also experience a lapse when he/she has been unable to refuse an offer of drugs/alcohol. These situations can be used as an opportunity to reflect upon what went wrong in those situations and the skills your client has in place. You will need to review those skills and possibly look at modifying your client's beliefs about those situations or behaviour and developing further skills to use on future occasions.

Negotiating with Services

AIM

To develop skills that improve clients' abilities to negotiate with health and social services and other service providers.

It can be extremely difficult for clients to assert their opinions with staff involved in providing them with treatment or other services. There is often a power imbalance between "service users" and "service provider" and at times a perception that the "professional" knows best. The result is that often clients feel their concerns are not heard and that they may not receive optimum or appropriate treatment or services. Clients may be at a disadvantage if they are experiencing psychotic symptoms, as their opinion can often be dismissed due to concern over their lack of insight. As a result, health professionals may misinterpret assertiveness as evidence of "poor compliance". The issue of appropriate negotiation with health or social services is a difficult one to tackle, particularly as, in your role as keyworker, clients may have difficulty in expressing their views to you. It is important to discuss with your clients their feelings about asserting themselves in meetings and with staff, and to acknowledge how hard this can be.

Some helpful strategies to help your client to negotiate assertively with health or social services are as follows:

- Provide as much appropriate information (about mental health, medication, alternative treatments, self-help groups, voluntary organisations and other issues) as you can to your client, so that he/she can make informed decisions and present a reasoned argument.
- Help your client to problem solve, so that he/she is clear about what he/she wants to express.
- Encourage the client to write down what he/she wants to say.
- Discuss methods of communicating assertively and practise these.
- Suggest that the client practise expressing these methods with a relative or friend.
- Provide information about advocacy services that are available and assist the client to contact these if necessary.
- Review your client's performance and provide helpful feed-back.

A case example follows:

Frances does not want to take her medication, as she experiences distressing side effects with her current tablets. She has tried to discuss this with her doctor, who felt that they should not alter her medication, as she has been taking it for only a short time. Other staff were equally dismissive, saying that her mental health symptoms were much better and she should persevere with the tablets. Frances decided to read books and articles about antipsychotic medications and researched alternatives to her current medication. She then practised stating her case to her sister and took a friend to her next CPA review meeting for support. Frances clearly stated why she wished to change her tablets and proposed an alternative medication that she was happy to take. The team agreed to alter her medication in the next two weeks.

So remember, to help your clients apply assertiveness skills to refusing drugs/alcohol and negotiating with the health services, you can,

- identify a plan of action to deal with difficult situations
- help your clients clarify the view(s) they wish to express
- teach and role-play skills
- review performances and provide feedback.

ADDITIONAL TREATMENT COMPONENTS I—SKILLS BUILDING

Chapter 13

SELF-ESTEEM

AIMS

(1) To identify your clients' views of themselves and self-esteem.
(2) Use cognitive and behavioural strategies to improve self-esteem and self-concept.

Helpful references/resources: Argyle (1972), Drummond et al. (1995), Fennell (1997), Field (1995), Marlatt and Barrett (1994), Mueser and Bellack (1998).

"Self-esteem is the extent to which a person approves of and accepts himself, and regards himself as praiseworthy, either absolutely or in comparison with others."
(Argyle, 1972)

EFFECT OF LOW SELF-ESTEEM ON MENTAL HEALTH AND DRUG/ALCOHOL USE

Low self-esteem can create disturbances in your client's mental health by creating feelings of anger, anxiety, guilt and depression. Low self-esteem could decrease motivation for and compliance with treatment, as your client may believe that he/she does not deserve to get better or that things will never change. Self-efficacy is said to be an individual's expectation of his/her capacity to cope with a given task or situation. Thus, if a person has low self-esteem, he/she may feel unable to influence what happens or to change his/her circumstances. As a result, his/her self-efficacy will be low. It is therefore not surprising that low self-esteem and low self-efficacy negatively affect treatment outcomes (e.g., Burlington et al., 1989; Drummond et al., 1995). It has been suggested that if a person has in place what he/she perceives or has found to be effective coping strategies, he/she is more likely to have increased self-efficacy and thus less chance of future lapse or relapse to problematic drug or alcohol use (Marlatt & Barrett, 1994). In addition, people with low self-esteem are more likely to be eager to gain the approval of others and are thereby easily influenced by social pressures. This leaves them at risk of being involved in drug/alcohol use behaviours and lifestyle, and the associated social circles.

EFFECT OF PSYCHOSIS AND DRUGS/ALCOHOL ON SELF-ESTEEM

When a person receives a mental health diagnosis, his/her self-esteem will often be affected. Typically, self-esteem is decreased. This may be due to feelings of loss of control and the expectation, based on stereotypes, that he/she will now have to alter and lower his/her ambitions and life goals. It has been suggested that in such a situation people search for meaning and control over the experience and indeed the illness (Birchwood et al., 1993). For example, during a period of mania, a client may experience enhanced self-esteem through beliefs such as "I can do better than others" and "My ideas are superior." Drug and alcohol use are also a means by which people may feel that they can regain some control over their mental health difficulties ("The voices stop when I am drinking and I feel relaxed"). They may also believe that this is a route to rebuilding their self-esteem and identity ("I feel like one of the crowd when I'm using").

In the short term, alcohol and drug use may enhance self-esteem. However, the long-term consequences may actually be quite the opposite. For example, problematic use of drugs/alcohol means that there is a level of dependence upon a substance that may leave the client feeling out of control of him/herself. That is, beliefs such as "I cannot manage without it" and "I am reliant upon heroin and the dealer who supplies it" will eventually lead to a reduction in self-efficacy and self-esteem. A person may wonder how he/she came to be in considerable debt, involved in criminal activity (either using an illegal substance or to fund a habit) and not caring for his/herself, circumstances which may all serve to reduce his/her self-opinion. Perceived failure by the client or his/her family to be able to make and maintain change can be an additional blow to self-esteem.

Thus, it is important to address your clients' views of themselves and their capacity to cope, with the aim of improving self-esteem and self-efficacy. This will, in turn, improve their ability to engage in positive change in their substance use and prevent relapses to psychosis. To address self-esteem, we must investigate a person's whole lifestyle and circumstances, so that a greater understanding of his/her self-esteem and the influences on it is gained.

STARTING OUT: ASSESSING SELF-ESTEEM

To begin work, identify with your client the nature of his/her self-esteem issues. You can do this by asking the following questions.

Current Self-Esteem

- How do you perceive yourself? What words would you use to describe yourself?
- What emotions do you experience? *Some common emotions displayed by people with low self-esteem are self-doubt, insecurity, anxiety, depression, guilt, worry and being self-critical, victimised and afraid of emotions.*
- In what situations do you experience these emotions? When do you experience low self-esteem?
- How long have you experienced difficulties with self-esteem?
- What thoughts go through your mind when you experience low self-esteem? *Some common thoughts of people with low self-esteem are "I am worthless", "I am no good", "I am not deserving", "I am a victim", "I am powerless", "I am a failure", and "I can't change".*
- Is your behaviour indicative of low self-esteem? *Some common behaviours of a person with low self-esteem are indecisiveness; fearful, critical, judgmental, defensive or passive/aggressive actions; won't say "no"; won't show his/her feelings; poor communication; or holding overly positive image of self.*

If you are still unsure about a client's levels of self-esteem, ask him/her to complete the Rosenberg Self-Esteem Scale (Rosenberg, 1965) or a similar standardised questionnaire to provide you with some more information.

History

It can be important for your client to understand where his/her difficulties with low self-esteem have come from. Explore the person's history, looking at the following questions. What early experiences led to his/her low self-esteem? *These may be messages and memories from childhood, which can be spoken (for example, "Boys don't cry", "Jealousy is unattractive", "I get upset when you do") or unspoken (for example, being ignored when you disagree).* What critical incidents or situations trigger(ed) low self-esteem?

Maintaining Factors

You can identify the factors that are maintaining your client's low self-esteem by exploring the following issues:

- What is keeping your client's self-esteem low? Look at your client's pattern of behaviour:
  —Does he/she set him/herself unachievable goals or have unrealistic role models?
  —Does he/she minimise the importance of his/her own needs and take no time for him/herself?
  —Does he/she constantly put him/herself down or be self-critical?
  —Does he/she always take personal responsibility if things go wrong?
  —How does he/she view his/her use of drugs/alcohol?
  —Does he/she avoid doing things for fear of failure?
- Look at your client's pattern of thinking:
  —Does he/she minimise his/her successes, putting them down to external causes?
  —Does he/she make overgeneralisations (such as "I never get anything right")?
  —Does he/she engage in all-or-nothing thinking (for example, "My family will think I've failed again because I've started using crack again")?
- Look at your client's social network/circumstances:
  —Are friends or relatives negative in their communication with your client?
  —Could his/her social status or mental health difficulties (such as not working, having psychotic symptoms/mental health problems and experiencing medication side effects) be affecting his/her self-esteem?
  —Is there a past history of being badly treated or taken advantage of by friends, family or services?

You should now have an idea of:

- your client's current level of self-esteem
- how your client's low self-esteem developed
- the thinking patterns that maintain low self-esteem
- the behavioural and social factors that keep your client's self-esteem low.

STRATEGIES TO IMPROVE SELF-ESTEEM

Below are outlined three strategies to help your clients improve their self-esteem: *psychoeducation, cognitive strategies and behavioural strategies.*

Helping Your Client Understand Self-Esteem

It would be helpful to give your client some psychoeducational information regarding self-esteem to start with. You will find the explanation in the following box helpful.

Self-esteem is about how we perceive ourselves and feel about ourselves. We all have rules, beliefs and standards, developed during our childhood, about how things ought to be. However, sometimes these rules, beliefs or standards can become a bit rigid and prevent us from trying things for fear of "failing". The result is that they can eventually reduce our self-esteem (that is, how we value ourselves and our beliefs in our abilities). If we have low self-esteem, our performance levels and successes can decline, like a self-fulfilling prophecy, because if we don't believe we can succeed, we are less likely to do so. Another common habit of people with low self-esteem is to compare themselves unrealistically with ideals or exemplary people; thus, they typically feel a poor comparison. In these circumstances, they will never feel proud or have success. They will also eventually begin to disregard any evidence that suggests that they are OK. The important thing to remember is that self-esteem comes from within and cannot be earned from other people by being seen as "clever" or "successful" or by "being loved by others". Self-esteem is a continuum, and at different times in our lives and when we are with different people or in different settings, our self-esteem will vary.

A person with high self-esteem will think: "I believe in myself", "I trust my intuition", "I deserve the best", "I am worthy", "I respect myself", "I respect others", "I can make things happen", "I can change", "I do the best I can".

He/she will feel spontaneous, free, caring, optimistic, appreciative, balanced, positive, in touch with his/her emotions and secure.

He/she will behave decisively, effectively, trustingly, openly and assertively. He/she will take risks, say "no", show his/her feelings and have good communication skills.

Cognitive Strategies

AIM

To identify the thoughts and beliefs that are maintaining low self-esteem and re-evaluate these to produce more helpful and realistic alternatives.

Coping with Unhelpful Automatic Thoughts

Unhelpful automatic thoughts are specific, involuntary, negative, plausible, distorted, habitual, subjective, idiosyncratic, abbreviated, repetitive and situation specific. They are usually short and direct ("I'm a failure"), seem to pop into your head and are negative in content. Because of their content, these negative automatic thoughts can trigger a reduction in self-esteem. In order to help your client improve his/her self-esteem, you will need to help him/her re-evaluate and find alternatives to his/her negative automatic thoughts and beliefs.

Current pattern of thinking

Help your client to identify his/her current pattern of thinking and identify specific patterns that are maintaining low self-esteem. Use thought diaries (see Appendix 5.2) to identify when and in what circumstance thoughts associated with low self-esteem occur and what these thoughts are. *For example, Karen has experienced two psychotic episodes and has developed low mood and thoughts of suicide. She uses £30 of cocaine a day but is trying to cut down.*

Situation	Moods	Automatic thoughts
Tried to talk to CPN about feeling low in mood and upset. Ended up not saying what I wanted to and doing what she suggested for the session. Snorted cocaine after the session to pick me up.	*Low* *Frustrated* *Happy*	*"My feelings aren't important."* *"I don't deserve to feel better than this."* *"I knew I'd end up using cocaine to feel better, even though I'd promised myself I wouldn't."*

Re-evaluate and modify unhelpful automatic thoughts

Your client will then need to challenge the evidence for these automatic thoughts to produce more helpful alternatives. The impact of generating more helpful thoughts in situations that usually make your client feel low is to break the cycle of thinking that maintains low self-esteem and lift his/her mood. You can help your clients to start re-evaluating their thoughts by teaching them to use the following strategies:

- Identify any distortions in their thinking; for example, "should/ought to/ must". This type of thinking implies that there is a correct way to do things that your clients are not doing. Get them to ask themselves "Why?" after any statement like this. Note the following example:
  —" I should be able to stop using cannabis overnight."
  —"Why?"

—"*Because anyone else would be able to do that.*"

—"*How do I know that?*"

—"*I don't know that. In fact, I know my friend has tried to give up twice and has really struggled.*"

—**New thought:** "*I will make a plan to help me to give up cannabis.*"

- Go back to each thought in the thought diary and ask your client to re-evaluate each unhelpful thought by asking:

  —*What is the evidence for this thought?*

  —*Is this always the case?*

  —*Is there another way of thinking about this?*

  —*What other ways do I have of coping with this situation?*

Another helpful strategy is to write down in the thought diary the evidence for and against the thoughts and the alternative thought. Consider the following thought diary:

Situation	Moods	Automatic thoughts	Evidence that supports identified thought	Evidence that does not support the identified thought	Alternative/ balanced thought
Where were you? What were you doing? Who were you with?	*What did you feel? Rate each mood (0–100%).*	*What was going through your mind just before you felt this way? Which was the most important/ worrying thought?*			*Rate how much you believe the alternative thought (0–100%).*
Mum told me I had to get help with my drinking because she can't cope with it.	*Low/ depressed (75%) Angry at myself (80%)*	*"I should be able to give up alcohol on my own." "I don't deserve help because it's my fault I'm like this." "I've ruined Mum's life as well as mine.'*	*No one else can do it for me. I've created this problem—it's my fault. Mum is always upset.*	*Addictions are very hard to break. Everyone needs some help some- times. If I cut down, Mum looks happy.*	*I deserve help as much as other people, and it will make Mum happy if I accept help (55%).*

- From the client's thought diary, identify any beliefs/rules that seem to underlie his/her thinking style and generate with the client alternative guidelines/standards that would be more helpful and realistic.

- Direct your client's attention to any strengths/assets that he/she may have, and keep a list of each of these and any experiences that do not support the negative self-view.

So remember, to tackle the thinking that maintains low self-esteem, you can,

- identify negative automatic thoughts
- re-evaluate unhelpful thinking to produce more helpful alternative thoughts.

Behavioural Strategies

AIM

To develop practical strategies to improve self-esteem and use behavioural experiments to challenge thinking that maintains low self-esteem.

Some strategies to help your client improve his/her self-esteem include physical exercise, activities that give success, behavioural experiments, selective social networks and "me" time.

Physical Exercise

Diet, exercise and healthy lifestyle increase self-esteem by giving control. Exercise promotes a positive body image that enhances self-esteem. It also increases energy levels, a result which, in turn, allows more activity and leads to a sense of achievement in reaching exercise goals and realising personal potential.

Activities That Give Success

Any activity that gives a person a sense of mastery and control will enhance self-esteem. These activities could be practical or creative, and to any standard. Use the interests checklist (Appendix 7.2) to produce some ideas for activities your client could get involved with. However, it is important that activities are graded according to the client's skills and the stage the client is at to ensure he/she is able to do the activity successfully. Thus, you may find it helpful to carry out a goal-setting exercise with your client (see Chapter 6, C-BIT treatment phase 2).

Behavioural Experiments

A behavioural experiment is a practical opportunity for your client to test his/her thoughts and worst fear. Your client probably has an image or belief that something catastrophic will happen if he/she goes into the situation. Behavioural experiments allow your client a chance to go into the situation, having planned in advance, and to test the thoughts that maintain low self-esteem. A behavioural experiment also allows your client to discover what will really happen in that situation, which is probably not the same as what he/she fears will happen.

To help your client plan and carry out a behavioural experiment, you will find the following steps helpful:

(1) By now, you and your client will be aware of what his/her (unhelpful) thought is that reduces or maintains low self-esteem; this will be the thought that you can test. *For example, I will never be able to change my drug use. I'm a failure.*

(2) However, if you are still unsure, go back to the earlier section which explains how to identify unhelpful automatic thoughts (page 199).

(3) Write down the thought to be tested on the Behavioural Experiment Worksheet (Appendix 2.1)

(4) With your client, identify a small step he/she can take to begin to test this thought. *For example, "Don't use cocaine for a whole day."*

(5) Get your client to predict will happen and write this on the worksheet.

(6) Identify any potential obstacles that may prevent him/her from carrying out the behavioural experiment and strategies to overcome these obstacles.

(7) Once your client has carried out the experiment, he/she should record the outcome on his/her worksheet.

(8) To ensure that your client is really able to test his/her thoughts related to self-esteem, identify with your client a number of experiments to try.

(9) Ask your client to identify what has been learned from these experiments and write it down under "lesson learned/take-home message".

Consider the following example:

Doug's Behavioural Experiment

Thought to be tested

"I will never be able to change my drug use. I'm a failure."

Experiment	Prediction	Potential obstacles	Strategies to overcome obstacles	Outcome of experiment
Experiment 1 *Go for a whole day without using cocaine.*	*I will get cravings and feel awful, and use in the afternoon.*	*Friends call round most days and bring cocaine with them.*	*Spend the day at parent's house and plan lots to do.*	*Managed OK at Mum's house, used a little last thing when I got home.*
Experiment 2 *Use a little less cocaine every day for a week.*	*Once I get started, I won't be able to stop using my usual amount.*	*Being with people who will encourage me to use more.*	*Visit friends to use cocaine and go home when I have reached my limit. Speak to Mum when I get home.*	*Used more than I had planned but less than usual. Mum was really pleased.*

Lesson learned/take-home message

"I was able to alter my cocaine use, so I am not a complete failure."

Selected Social Networks

It will be important to encourage your client to include in his/her social network some people who help to maintain the client's self-esteem and reduce contact with those people who damage self-esteem or reinforce a negative self-view (see page 81 "Building Social Networks Supportive of Change"). In addition, caring about someone else often provides a way to enhance self-esteem. For example, if a person is socially isolated, consider getting a pet. A dog will not only provide company, something to care about and an increase in activity, but also open up a social circle of vets and fellow dog walkers. Other methods of building a supportive social network are through befriending schemes and encouraging the client to become involved in voluntary work or self-help groups.

"Me" Time

Encourage your client to schedule "me" time into his/her week. This is time for relaxation, and it encourages reflection and "switching off" from day-to-day issues. Because your client is prioritising time for him/herself, he/she is treating him/herself as important, and this will increase self-esteem. Our self-esteem is linked to our ways of experiencing emotions. Thus, if we deny our feelings, we deny our needs and time for ourselves. Denying our needs makes them appear unimportant, the basis of low self-esteem. To tackle this, your client needs to learn to recognise his/her feelings, accept them, express them and then let them go.

So remember, strategies to help your client improve his/her self-esteem include,

- physical exercise
- establishing goals and graded activities that give success
- behavioural experiments to face situations previously avoided
- building social networks that support a positive self-view
- encouragement of "me" time.

ADDITIONAL TREATMENT COMPONENTS I—SKILLS BUILDING

Chapter 14

LIFESTYLE BALANCE

AIM

To help your clients identify the activities they engage in and address any imbalance between their participation in self-care, productivity (that is, work) and leisure activities.

Helpful reference/resource: Sanderson and Reed (1980).

Lifestyle Imbalance

Many people will find that their life, goals and routines change completely when they experience mental health difficulties, or their use of drugs or alcohol becomes problematic. Life may become very empty, include only mental health services or focus on getting and using alcohol or drugs. People may lose their work and social role, experience a reduction or change in their chosen social networks and possibly become socially isolated.

If your client is involved in problematic drug/alcohol use, there is often an *imbalance in his/her lifestyle and in the way he/she may think*. Clients may tend to use *"should"* or *"must"* statements. For example, *"I should make the dinner now. If I can't do that I am useless."* They thus rule themselves by self-commands and duty, set unrealistic expectations and do not attend to their *"wants"* or *"needs"*. The result is that basic activities and chores give them no pleasure. This type of thinking can place a lot of pressure and stress on a client and can lead to a desire for *immediate pleasure to counteract how he/she is feeling*. This need for immediate gratification could lead to cravings for drugs/ alcohol as an attempt at instant pleasure. Your client may then give him/ herself permission to use drugs/alcohol with statements like *"I deserve it"* or *"It's my only pleasure"*.

Relapse prevention or lifestyle balance work aims to help your client to plan/ schedule pleasurable activities into his/her week. The aim is to ensure that there is a balance of "shoulds" and "wants" in your client's life. This will serve to reduce the pressure your client is under and the need for instant gratification through drug/alcohol use.

STRATEGIES TO ENCOURAGE LIFESTYLE BALANCE

Your client will probably be somewhat aware of the problems related to his/ her substance use. However, his/her day may be consumed with a drug/ alcohol-using lifestyle. At this stage, it would be useful to identify and develop with your client some structured daytime activities which are non-drug/ alcohol-related to help remove him/her from his/her typical daily activities and environment. This will, in turn, reduce his/her chances of boredom and unstructured time. The anticipated knock-on effect is that the alternative activity reduces the time, opportunity and motivation to use alcohol/drugs problematically.

If your client has made a change in his/her drug/alcohol-use pattern, either by reducing or abstaining from the substance, he/she will have created a gap in his/her life and activities. As your client makes the decision to change, he/ she needs to be encouraged to begin to introduce new activities that will not only fill the gap but also be incompatible with his/her drug/alcohol-using lifestyle. This could include developing a new network of friends, accessing new environments and developing new skills. Your client will be changing both his/her thinking and his/her behaviour and thus will benefit from identifying some constant social network support to lean on during the time of multiple changes. The strategies outlined below have been found to be helpful in promoting lifestyle balance, and include *increasing activity levels, time management and money management*.

INCREASING ACTIVITY LEVELS

It can be useful to break down activities into different areas. For example, occupational therapy theory uses the categories self-care, productivity and leisure (Sanderson & Reed, 1980). These categories allow you to identify *practical skills, education/employment needs* and *leisure* separately and give you an idea of the balance of these activities in someone's life. *If there is an excess of activities in one area, it can lead to imbalance and feelings of dissatisfaction in other areas of life.* This, in turn, can lead to cravings to use drugs/alcohol or mental health symptoms.

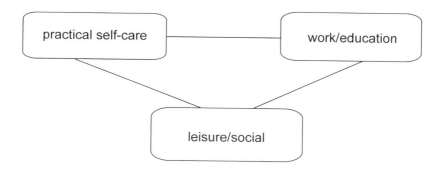

Therefore, it will be necessary for your client to increase his/her activities in all three areas to achieve some lifestyle balance if your client is to learn to manage his/her alcohol/drug use and mental health difficulties. There are three steps to increase somebody's activity levels:

(1) Establish his/her previous levels of activity, priorities and interests.
(2) Establish his/her current activity level and skills base.
(3) Facilitate decisions about what he/she would like to be doing and any deficits he/she has to help this to happen.

Some strategies that you will find helpful to increase your client's activity levels are outlined below.

Step 1: Previous Activity

Your client may find it difficult to identify any non-drug/alcohol-related activity that he/she is interested in and may say that he/she is not interested in doing anything else and quite likes his/her life as it is. Thus, to start off, take a history of education, employment and hobbies to help you get a better understanding of previous activities or interests. This can be done:

- formally during an assessment
- informally through a general conversation and discussion of previous activity
- by a specific assessment such as a roles and habits checklist (Appendix 7.1) or an interests checklist (see Appendix 7.2).

If your client identifies one activity he/she has enjoyed in the past, break this down into the various skills that are needed to complete the activity (such as patience, creativity, memory and practical skills) and identify why he/she liked the activity (e.g. end product, mentally stretching, process). Here is a case example.

James is a 24-year-old man with a 5-year history of psychosis and a 3-year history of using alcohol and cannabis problematically. He lives with his parents and brother and is currently unemployed. From discussion, it was discovered that James left school at 16 and attended a local college to do a BTEC in motor mechanics for 2 years. He planned to attend further training and possibly to get a heavy goods vehicle licence.

A "roles" checklist gave the following information. James enjoyed the practical but not the academic parts of being a student. Aged 17, he had worked casually at a local garage on the weekends. James felt an integral part of his family and felt they were "close". James had a few short-term relationships with girls, the longest of 4 months. He used to attend Birmingham City football matches with his dad.

An "interests" checklist gave the following information about James' past hobbies:

- *He used to play and watch football.*
- *He played the guitar at school.*
- *He liked art at school.*
- *He had been fishing a few times.*
- *He enjoyed watching TV and videos.*
- *He used to go to the pub regularly.*
- *He played pool and pinball at the pub.*

As you can see from the example, previous activities or interests may suggest other activities that would also be enjoyable to your client in the present and future.

By using the "interests and roles" checklists and discussing clients' past hobbies and work, you should now have an idea of:

- activities your clients have previously been involved in
- whether he/she enjoyed them.

Step 2: Current Activity

To get a picture of how your client is currently spending his/her time, use a weekly activity diary (see Appendix 5.5) for your client to record his/her daily activities. Ask him/her to include all tasks, from preparing a hot drink and food, self-care (such as bathing), to leisure and work-type activities. It can be helpful to categorise all the activities into self-care/productivity/leisure/substance-related activities and complete a timetable using colours to represent the categories. Ask your client to rate how much pleasure he/she gets from each activity on a scale of 0–10 (0 being no pleasure and 10 being the most pleasure). This gives a clearer idea of the balance of time spent on each area. Here is *James' current activity diary*:

	Mon	Tues	Wed	Thurs	Fri	Sat	Sun
a.m.	*Sleep Have shower (4)*	*Sleep*	*Sleep*	*Sleep*	*Sleep Have shower (3)*	*Sleep*	*Sleep*
p.m.	*TV (4) See mates smoke and drink (7)*	*TV Smoke and drink (5)*	*Music (5) Pub with mates, drink (7)*	*TV See mates smoke and drink (6)*	*Pub with mates, drink (5)*	*TV See mates smoke and drink (5)*	*Pub with mates, smoke and drink (8)*

The example shows that James' life has quite an imbalance; he is inactive for most mornings and is not looking after himself in terms of eating or taking showers, and his evenings are all spent using drugs or alcohol, which he finds pleasurable.

It may be that your client lacks certain skills that would help him/her to carry out certain activities. Thus, by observing your client carrying out practical activities, you will have a better idea of his/her skills level. When observing your client look out for:

- safety
- planning
- sequencing of the components of the task
- use of equipment
- hygiene
- social skills
- budgeting
- confidence
- motivation, etc.

If in doubt about assessing your client's skill level, refer him/her to an occupational therapist for an assessment. Note the following case example:

James made a hot drink and cheese on toast. He completed the task in two stages, making the drink and then the snack. He had no problems making the drink, but had difficulty in choosing what to make to eat, eventually choosing what was closest in the fridge. James did not prepare a clear area to work in or ready the ingredients, and he did not wash his hands. James was unfamiliar with the family's new cooker and could not work the grill. He was unable to follow two-stage instructions on how to use it.

James forgot to butter his bread and burnt his hand slightly when correcting himself. He left the grill turned on but remembered within safe limits. James chatted easily throughout the task. He said domestic chores were usually completed by his mum and felt this was why he needed prompting.

So remember, to get a better idea of your client's current levels of activity and their practical skills,

- use weekly activity diaries
- observe practical tasks.

Step 3: Future Activity

Personal Goals

If you have carried out C-BIT treatment phase 1, you will have identified with your client some personal goals that you have been using as "motivational hooks". Now is the time to use those motivational hooks as a means to help your client think of future activities that he/she would like to engage in. You will need to elicit a self-motivational statement about his/her interest in these activities and achieving his/her goal. You can do this by asking some exploratory and open-ended questions. *For example, "What goals have you wanted to achieve that your alcohol use has prevented you from achieving? What are the things that you have always dreamed of doing but have not got around to? If you had the opportunity, what would you spend your day doing?"*

Alternatively, by brainstorming with the Identifying Activities of Interest worksheet (Appendix 2.2), you can also use his/her completed "roles" and "interests" checklists to identify with your client what other goals he/she may have. Break down the activities into their component skills and identify any skills your client is lacking at present. Any skills deficits identified can then be addressed with a view to achieving the set goals. Note the following case example:

James identified football, being involved with cars and playing pool and pinball as his goal activities. He decided he was not fit enough to begin playing football immediately and that he was out of touch with current mechanics techniques. James decided to begin running to build up his fitness and to start buying mechanics magazines to update his knowledge. He also looked out his old college notes to refresh his memory of his skills.

It will probably be useful to liaise with education and employment agencies to ensure support for your client and to prevent difficulties with benefits. Again, an occupational therapist can point you in the right direction.

Developing Interests and Hobbies

Now that you have identified a range of activities that your client has some interest in, you will need to begin to engage his/her interest in an activity, and plan towards his/her actually doing it. Below are listed a number of steps that you may find useful to go through with your client:

(1) Rank activities in order of interest. With your client, pick two activities that he/she has identified as being of particular interest and that are feasible or practically possible.
(2) Find out more information about the activity.
(3) Identify a time in his/her week when he/she could try it.
(4) Think through the practical issues such as cost, transport, time and whether he/she would benefit from having someone to accompany him/ her.
(5) Adopt a negotiating position, that is, an attitude of "trying it out". Suggest to your client that he/she attend the first time as a "taster session".

Here is a case example:

(1) *James went to the local sports centre and found out about a football team who played in his area. He discovered that they train on Wednesday evenings and play in a league on Saturdays. The coach agreed that he could try out for the team in a month's time, when his fitness had improved. James felt he could afford the subs if he managed to cut down his drinking.*
(2) *James went to the local arcade and found that there was a pool table and a variety of pinball machines. He also discovered that there was no bar and that no smoking was allowed in the arcade. James decided to suggest to his friends that they go to the arcade instead of the pub at least once a week as part of his cannabis and alcohol-reduction plan.*
(3) *James decided to begin working on his parent's car to practise his mechanic skills. After one month of reading notes and magazines, he planned to contact the local garage where he used to work to see whether they have any part-time vacancies. He found that an ex-colleague still worked at the garage and he felt able to phone this person. He also found some vacancies in the local paper and at the job centre when he went to sign on. James decided that he would speak to the local Disability Employment Adviser with the help of his CPN to ensure that he did not lose all of his benefits if he decided to take on part-time work.*

One month later, James' week looked like this:

	Mon	Tues	Wed	Thurs	Fri	Sat	Sun
a.m.	Buy car magazines	Go for a run		Go for a run	Read college notes		Work on parents' car
p.m.	Arcade with friends	Shower and do laundry	Football training	Shower Arcade with friends	Pub with friends–drink and smoke	Play football Pub with friends–drink	Go for a run Shower and clean room

---

So remember, to engage your clients in activities,

- identify some goal or activities that they would like to be involved in
- identify any skills they will need to improve to enable them to participate in these activities.

TIME MANAGEMENT

AIM

To improve your client's ability to organise his/her activities and make the most of his/her time.

If your client is finding it difficult to manage his/her time constructively or effectively, you will find the following practical strategies helpful:

- Encourage your client to use a diary and record all appointments and arrangements.
- Encourage your client to invest in an alarm clock and ensure he/she can use it.
- Begin introducing activities later in the day and gradually make the appointments earlier. Alternatively, ask your client to identify the time when he/she feels most able to engage in activities and use that as a starting point.

- Be realistic in the goals set and begin with simple tasks. Compared with doing nothing, everything is an achievement.
- Plan tasks so that your client can see how long each component part will take and whether he/she can break the activity up to make it more manageable.
- Set time limits for each task and get your client to stop once the allotted time has been spent (For example, "I will iron for 30 minutes this morning").
- Ensure that your client has a balance of leisure, work and self-care activities in his/her routine. Get him/her to balance the activities he/she feels he/she *should* do with things that he/she *would* like to do.
- Work with your client to spread his/her activities across the whole week. Get him/her to plan at least one small task every day.
- Encourage your client to prioritise activities if he/she has too much going on. Try asking: does this have to be done today? What will happen if you do it tomorrow? Can anyone else complete this task?
- Looking back at a diary will provide motivation and esteem because it charts success and identifies helpful and unhelpful patterns of activity.

MONEY MANAGEMENT

AIMS

(1) To identify your client's difficulties in managing his/her money and how his/her finances interact with his/her drug/alcohol use.
(2) To improve your client's ability to manage his/her finances.

If your client is finding it hard, due to a lack of money, to do the activities that he/she would like to do to achieve a better lifestyle balance, it would be useful to address money management. This would enable him/her to get a sense of the things that he/she is spending money on, particularly drug or alcohol use, and to manage this so he/she is still able to engage in other activities. Outlined below are a number of steps that will help you to do this:

(1) To begin with, identify with your client all of the places where he/she has money, such as banks, building societies or post office, and whether anyone else has control of any of his/her finances (drugs supplier, family member, partner, etc.).
(2) Produce a basic budgeting plan (Appendix 1.4), that is, a breakdown of the money coming in and the money that needs to be paid out:

Money in per week/month   £ _____
Money out:

    Rent   £ _____
    Bills: electricity, gas, phone, TV, rates, council tax   £ _____
    Loans: credit cards, store cards, loans, debts   £ _____
    Food   £ _____
    Social   £ _____
    Other: childcare, clothes, kids' school, travel, etc.   £ _____
    Alcohol/drugs: current   £ _____

(3) To motivate your client to change the amount he/she spends on drugs/alcohol, ask questions such as, what would you like to buy but can't afford because of alcohol/drugs? When you had more money, what was different then?

(4) Discuss with your client the amount he/she would preferably be spending on drugs/alcohol.

(5) Does your client find that having money is a trigger for his/her use of drugs/alcohol? If so, he/she may need to find new methods of collecting his/her money or keeping his/her money.

(6) Discuss with your client ways to improve his/her finances; for example, receive weekly payments, buy all food and pay bills first, identify someone to hold spare cash, get money paid straight into the bank and have bills directly debited from account, and look for employment.

(7) If your client has serious debt problems, suggest he/she speaks to the Citizens Advice Bureau or his/her bank for further advice.

So remember, to improve your clients' lifestyle balance, you will need to,

- help your clients put pleasurable (non-substance-related) activities back into their daily routines
- help your clients make the most of their time
- help your clients balance their money.

ADDITIONAL TREATMENT COMPONENTS II—FAMILIES AND SOCIAL NETWORK MEMBERS

Chapter 15

WORKING WITH FAMILIES AND SOCIAL NETWORK MEMBERS

AIMS

(1) Provide family/social network members with psychoeducational information about the nature of severe mental health and drug/alcohol problems.
(2) Encourage family/social network members to become involved in providing support for the management of problematic alcohol/drug use and psychosis.
(3) Facilitate the development of adaptive practical coping skills and strategies to provide support.

Families and friends of people with severe mental health problems may find it hard to relate to them and cope. Such families are said to experience significant levels of emotional distress and burden (e.g., Provencher & Mueser, 1997) in relation to attempting to adjust and cope with the person's severe mental health problem. They may also find it difficult to understand why these individuals get involved in problematic drug and alcohol use. Problematic drug or alcohol use by a family member is said to contribute to high levels of stress within the family (Copello et al., 1998) due to heightened family conflict and expressed emotion (Kashner et al., 1991). Crawley (unpublished) found that families of people with combined severe mental health and substance use problems tend to cope by trying to be supportive of the person but attempt to control the drug or alcohol use. Similarly, Barrowclough et al. (2000) have also found that families tend to want to take control of their relatives' alcohol or drug use, rather than leave the responsibility for change with their relatives. The feelings of families were that to leave responsibility for change to their relatives would be an indication of support for continued substance use. Often, too, families and friends feel out of their depth in trying to provide support. They also tend to find that attempting to control a relative's drug/alcohol use only leads to further family conflict and stress.

Your client's family and friends may at this stage be at their wits' end or unclear about how best to provide support. On occasion, your clients may not see their drug or alcohol use as a problem and express no desire to change. However, a family member or friend may be constantly in contact with you, expressing a high degree of concern and worry. If so, it may be helpful to begin to work with the family member or friend in the first instance while attempting to engage the client using the strategies outlined in C-BIT treatment phase 1 (Chapter 5).

In this treatment component, we will look at a number of strategies that have been found to be helpful in improving the interactions and coping skills of families and friends of people with combined severe mental health and substance use problems. These strategies build on those described throughout all four C-BIT treatment phases (pages 65, 81, 94, 107). The strategies that will be described here fall into three areas: *provision of psychoeducational information; encouraging involvement; and facilitating the development of practical coping strategies and skills.* Some of the common questions family members and friends ask and strategies to address each of them are described.

PROVISION OF PSYCHOEDUCATION

References and helpful resources: Beck et al. (1993), Falloon et al. (1996), Liese and Franz (1996), Marlatt and Barrett (1994), Mueser and Gingerich (1994), Ch. 12.

You will probably be surprised to find that your clients' families and friends know very little about the nature of severe mental health problems, drug/alcohol use or medication. They may have a number of unanswered questions that fuel their frustration with the inability of treatment services to "make their relative or friend stop using". Some of the common questions family members/friends ask and strategies to address each of them are described below. It is preferable that psychoeducational information is provided in group settings, as families and friends will benefit from the support and experiences of other families and friends.

Understanding Drug/Alcohol Use Among Those with Severe Mental Health Problems

Why Do People with Severe Mental Health Problems Get Involved in Drug/Alcohol Use?

You will need to provide the family or social network members with some information on two main areas to get them to begin to appreciate the factors that may have contributed to their relative or friend using alcohol/drugs problematically. They may already be aware of some of this information, but it would be worthwhile to go over it again and to provide them with some leaflets.

The nature of severe mental health problems

The information you provide should cover the following areas:

(1) You should provide some general information on severe mental health problems and psychosis.
(2) In addition, you will need to explain how the onset of severe mental health problems may affect and disrupt people's life, goals and identity, particularly if it happens during their youth, and increases the likelihood of their using alcohol or drugs problematically.
(3) They may be unaware that alcohol and drug problems are common in the general population and greater for people with severe mental health problems. Therefore, you will need to inform them of some of the statistics; for example, approximately 37 per cent of people with a psychosis were found to have used alcohol/drugs problematically in the past year in the UK (Menezes et al., 1996). In the USA, it was found that 47 per cent of people with a diagnosis of schizophrenia would have a problem with alcohol/drugs in their lifetime (Rieger et al., 1990).
(4) In addition, problematic alcohol and drug use has been found to be greater among younger males with a diagnosis of schizophrenia who probably used drugs/alcohol before they experienced mental health problems.

Reasons and motives for drug/alcohol use (lifestyle)

Families and social network members may still feel confused and frustrated that their relatives or friends continue to use alcohol or drugs even though it has a considerable negative impact on them (such as increased hospital admissions, worsening of psychotic symptoms and financial cost or debts). Therefore, you will need to help families and social network members understand that their relatives or friends use these substances to obtain similar benefits to their own efforts, that is, for socialisation, as a way of coping and for pleasure. The information you provide can include the following factors:

(1) *Socialisation.* Like the general population, people with a severe mental health problem think of alcohol as commonly used in social situations. They may also think in a similar way about drugs. However, those with a severe mental health problem, particularly those who are young, may begin to feel quite socially isolated due to their mental health problems and the attached stigma. In contrast, they may feel quite socially accepted within a drinking/drug-using group. Such a group might offer a sense of belonging and a social identity that is seen as less stigmatising. In addition, if people with severe mental health problems used drugs/alcohol before they experienced mental health problems, they may not want to lose touch with friends who use and a lifestyle that they enjoyed.

(2) *Coping.* It is not uncommon for people to use alcohol or drugs to cope with particular feelings and situations. However, when people experience mental health difficulties, they may want an immediate way of coping with how they feel, particularly if they feel they have no other quick and effective method of coping. They may feel distressed by symptoms such as "voices", paranoia, depression, anxiety, low energy/motivation, or medication side effects, and may believe alcohol/drugs to be a solution to these symptoms. If they have found in the past that alcohol or drugs have been an immediate and effective way of coping, this will strengthen the likelihood of their continuing to use. Even though they may be aware of some of the negative effects of using alcohol or drugs, as these negative effects tend to occur in the long term and not in the short term, they will ignore or minimise any negative consequences of continued use.

(3) *Pleasure.* Like the general population, people with severe mental health problems may enjoy the effects of alcohol and drugs and find that it provides a diversion from feelings of boredom, depression and isolation. They may also enjoy the "taste".

These reasons and motives for using alcohol or drugs will drive continued use of the substance. Each time people use alcohol or drugs and get the effects they desire and expect, the likelihood of their using the substance again will be increased. As outlined previously, even though they may be aware of some of the negative effects of using alcohol or drugs, as these negative effects tend to occur in the long term and not in the short term, they will ignore or minimise any negative consequences. The result is that they will continue to use and focus on the positive aspects of using.

Why Does My Relative or Friend Act the Way He/She Does When Using?

Types of substances used problematically and their effects

Families and social network members will also benefit from knowing that the most common substances used problematically by those with severe mental health problems, particularly those with a diagnosis of schizophrenia, include alcohol, cannabis, cocaine powder/crack cocaine, amphetamines, heroin, benzodiazepines, ecstasy, LSD and solvents. Usually, more than one substance at a time will be used problematically. You will also need to inform families and social network members of the effects of alcohol and drugs on a person's mood, behaviour and presentation. However, the effects vary from person to person, but here is some general information you can give them:

- Substances can be classified by the effect they have on the central nervous system (brain and spinal cord).
- Substances that stimulate the central nervous system are typically called "*stimulants* or *uppers*". Some examples include cocaine/crack, amphetamines (that is, *speed* or *whizz*), and *Ecstasy*. The main effects when someone uses these substances are *increased alertness, reduced sleep, less fatigue, increased ability to be vigilant and elevated mood. In high doses, these substances can cause nervousness, anxiety and temporary paranoid psychosis*. The withdrawal effects include *fatigue, hunger and possibly low mood and anxiety*.
- Substances that depress the central nervous system are typically called "*downers*". Some examples are *alcohol, benzodiazepines* (such as *valium* and *temazepam*), *solvents* and *gases, opiates* (such as *heroin*) and *barbiturates*. The main initial effects of these substances are *alleviation of tension or anxiety, promotion of relaxation and decreased self-control. In higher doses, there can be "drunken" behaviour (slurred speech, drowsiness, poor coordination, or sleep or unconsciousness). With frequent use of high doses, tolerance and physical dependence can develop (except to solvents and gases)*. The withdrawal effects vary according to the substance, but include *increased anxiety*.
- Substances that alter the perception of reality are typically called "*hallucinogenics*". Some examples are *cannabis, LSD* (that is, *acid*) and *hallucinogenic mushrooms* (that is, *magic mushrooms*). The main effects of these substances are *perceptual distortions, increased sensitivity to sensory experiences* (such as *music*), *feelings of dissociation and sometimes anxiety or panic. These substances, particularly cannabis, can cause pseudo-hallucinations. The effects of heavy use of cannabis may include lack of energy, apathy or poor motivation, and poor performance.*

The interaction between problematic drug/alcohol use and severe mental health problems/medication

Why Does My Relative or Friend's Motivation to Change Fluctuate?

You will need to introduce the families/social network members to the concept of ambivalence by informing them of the following considerations:

- When people become involved in problematic drug/alcohol use, their attention becomes skewed and they focus primarily on the positive aspects of substance use. At other times, they may be aware of both the positive and negative aspects of drug/alcohol use, but may present as ambivalent about change or not desirous of change. That is, on the one hand, the supported person may want to change, but, on the other hand, he/she does not. The result is that the person presents with conflicting and fluctuating motivation. Therefore, families and social network members will notice that motivation fluctuates over time, depending on when their relatives or friends last used the substance, their financial situation, health, etc. For example, the day after using drugs in a binge pattern they may tell their relatives and friends that they have made a decision "never to use again", because they feel so bad. However, the next time they are seen, they may be feeling much better, have "forgotten" how bad they felt a few days before and are no longer interested in changing their drug/alcohol use.
- Their relatives or friends probably use alcohol/drugs for very good reasons in their own minds and have strong beliefs about the effectiveness of these substances. In their minds and experiences, drug and alcohol use has a helpful purpose. Therefore, to consider changing their use will mean a major lifestyle change. For any one of us, making a lifestyle change is a big step that means our motivation and resolve will often fluctuate.

Why Does My Relative or Friend Keep Relapsing to Problematic Alcohol/Drug Use?

It is highly likely that supportive others are not familiar with the ideas related to lapses or relapses to problematic drug or alcohol use. Therefore, it is fundamental that you spend time describing and explaining the idea of relapses to those who will be involved in providing support. The aim is to increase their awareness that lapses or relapses are common when people have recently changed a behaviour, and are an opportunity to learn rather than an act of weakness, a sign of failure or a sign that they are "back to square one":

- It is important to acknowledge that temptation (cravings) to use substances when trying to abstain or reduce is common in those attempting to change behaviour. For example, if supportive network members view a relapse or lapse to substance use as a failure or an act of "weakness" on the part of the person with the problem, they may withdraw support when the client needs their help the most. However, the lapse or relapse to problematic drug or alcohol use is understood as a part of the journey towards improvement, network members will be more inclined to continue to offer support.

- You will need to discuss key concepts involved in a lapse or relapse, including "activating stimuli and high-risk situations", "lapses" or "slips", and "relapse". This can include the following discussion. Cravings and urges are said to be the sense of desiring or wishing to have a substance or an impulse to seek and use alcohol/drugs. The desire to use drugs or alcohol can be triggered by people, places, things, feelings, situations or anything else that has been **associated** with alcohol/drug use in the past. If someone has decided to stop or cut down, cravings tend to be stronger in the initial period but eventually fade away over time. However, if people still focus on the positive aspects of alcohol/drug use and are in a "high-risk situation" that has been associated with previous use, cravings will intensify and the person may use. Often people will feel very bad about themselves if they have made a decision to stop using or to cut down and then have a "slip". They may see it as the end of the world or of their attempts at abstinence. The *abstinence-violation* effect is said to be the reaction that occurs when the person has made a decision to stop using, and then uses. Alternatively, a *rule-violation* effect is said to be the reaction when a person had decided to change his pattern of use (for example, to cut down or to stop injecting drugs) and he/she then has a "slip" and uses. If he/she returns to using alcohol/drugs on one or two occasions as he/she previously was, this is called a *lapse*. However, if following this "slip", the person completely returns to his/her previous alcohol/drug-using behaviour, this is called a *relapse*. If people have a lapse, it is more likely to turn into a relapse if they engage in particular distorted styles of thinking and feelings about themselves. For example, *"I've blown it"*; *"I knew I wouldn't be able to stop."* The result is that they may feel fed up and talk themselves into using again by thinking, for example, *"I've messed up already so I might as well keep going."*

Once these concepts are clear, you will have conveyed the message that lapses and relapses can be prevented. Foster a positive orientation towards the person with the substance-related problem and minimise attitudes that may foster a feeling of failure or criticism if the client does indeed lapse/relapse.

ENCOURAGING INVOLVEMENT

Helpful references/resources: Drake, Bebout and Roach (1993), Falloon et al. (1996), Galanter (1993).

Why Should I Support Them?

You will need to inform families and social network members that including them in providing support will ensure two things:

(1) that essential support is available for positive change in drug or alcohol use and lifestyle
(2) that your clients have shared their decisions to make positive changes in their drug/alcohol use with someone else, a fact which provides an added incentive to maintain changes.

Your clients may believe that *all* the people they know or can get on with use drugs or alcohol. This belief may also be one of the reasons they cite for continuing to use problematically. This belief may not be 100 per cent true. However, it is possible that over time, since your clients have been spending a significant amount of time using alcohol or drugs, they have spent increasing amounts of time with other people who also use alcohol or drugs and less time with those who do not. Accumulating evidence supports the crucial role of social networks in helping people to initiate and maintain change in their drug and alcohol use behaviour. Therefore, engaging the support of families and social networks will increase the likelihood that their relatives and friends will begin to make positive changes and be more likely to maintain any changes.

How Can I Best Support Them?

Families and social network members have probably become discouraged and despondent about their relatives or friends who use drugs or alcohol, especially if they have successfully made changes in the past and then relapsed to using problematically. An important goal when encouraging families and social network members to support clients is to encourage them to take a step back and observe or remember the following principles:

- Provide support that matches their relative or friend's stage of change.
- Identify with their relative or friend drug or alcohol goals that are realistic and easily achievable, that is, a range of short- and long-term goals that limit the harm or damage that drug/alcohol use inflicts on the person's life, rather than goals focused just on abstinence from drugs or alcohol.
- Remain optimistic that in the long term their friend or relative will in some way change his/her drug/alcohol use behaviour.
- Remember that it is normal for motivation to fluctuate, and be consistent and non-judgemental in their approach, even when their relative or friend's motivation wanes.
- Look towards identifying new ways of communicating with their relative or friend and let go of strategies used in the past that have led to arguments and conflict, and have not worked.
- Provide positive feedback whenever their relative or friend takes a step in the right direction, no matter how small, rather than focusing on "slips".
- Remind themselves that their relative or friend is actually the one who is responsible for change and that they need to provide support and a social environment that encourages steps toward change.

- Become involved in relapse-prevention/management plans to help avoid relapse or lapse to problematic alcohol or drug use.

PRACTICAL COPING STRATEGIES AND SKILLS

How Do I Handle Behaviours Related to Problem Drug/Alcohol Use?

Setting Limits and Boundaries

The members of the family who have responsibility for the property should set limits and then discuss them with the whole family. Families and friends need to decide what is acceptable behaviour within the home and what is not acceptable. Some fundamental rules could include:

- no violence to people or property
- no illegal drug use in the house
- must bathe regularly
- no shouting or intimidating behaviour.

Other rules will be peculiar to the family or social network and could regard behaviour associated with positive or negative symptoms of psychosis or drug/alcohol use. Some clients may have lost sight of what is socially acceptable or "normal" behaviour. It is useful to review this with clients before setting rules, as they may be unaware that they are not following social norms and will modify their behaviour when it is pointed out. They may also have difficulty concentrating and remembering, so, to begin with, they may need gentle reminders about the rules or decisions that have been made. For each behaviour identified, there needs to be a *reward* for changing the behaviour and a ***consequence*** for its continued existence. Rewards and consequences need to be relevant and significant enough to promote behaviour change. *For example, Stuart's family decided that they would not allow his drug-using friends to stay at the house. They decided that if no friends stayed for a week they would all go to the pictures and for a meal. However, if friends did stay, Stuart would not be allowed to use the family car for a week.*

Effective rules focus on the behaviour displayed, not on a person's personality, and are realistic (not beyond the capabilities of the person) and rational. When a rule focuses on someone's achieving something, such as doing household chores, the family or friends need to ask whether there is a time limit to completing the task, as this may make it more difficult for someone with a psychosis to achieve. *For example, Jane is able to do ironing, but only in small bursts, so it takes her a few days to complete the task. When given a few days, she succeeds, but, if rushed, she does not manage the task and the family end up arguing.*

No "Rescuing"

One of the main frustrations for family members and friends can be the client's lack of awareness of the impact of his/her drug/alcohol use on his/her mental health. Clients will often focus on the benefits of use and minimise the negative aspects. Family members and friends can help to shift clients' perceptions of their use by *helping them to see the negative impact* drug/alcohol use has on their and their family's life. Family members or friends may currently be helping to mask these consequences by bailing the client out of trouble (for example, paying off his/her debts) either for an "easy life", or to reduce the client's distress. Changing this pattern could take two forms. Firstly, it could involve explaining to the client in a calm, clear manner the effect his/her drug/alcohol use has on other family members/friends and how they feel about this. Secondly, it could be stopping behaviours which cover up or hide the unpleasant consequences of continued use. This could involve not cleaning up after incontinence or vomiting, not lending money, or not bailing the client out of police custody. These should be discussed and explained to the client so that he/she understands the change in behaviour and the motives behind it. The family and friends should also have a plan of how to cope with these consequences and any distress they cause.

How Do I Discuss Alcohol/Drug Use or Just Talk to Them?

Communication Skills

Some common mistakes of families and friends trying to communicate with clients about their drug/alcohol use include the following:

(1) making coercive statements ("You should clean up your room")
(2) mixing positive and negative statements ("Doing the washing was good, but it's all gone grey")
(3) speaking for others ("We are angry that you haven't cleaned up")
(4) mind-reading ("You think I'm nagging")
(5) name-calling ("You're lazy")
(6) dwelling on the past ("You spoilt Christmas last year too")
(7) using conflicting verbal and non-verbal messages ("Yes, I'll give you a lift", spoken while sighing and rolling eyes).

The family and friends could map out their current strategies by role-playing how they would speak to the client or tape-recording sessions in which they try to speak to clients. From the information gained, they could brainstorm more effective methods to try and then practise these. Encourage family members/friends to use a *non-threatening approach* that limits the chances of the client's becoming defensive. It could be useful to encourage families/friends to use *motivational interviewing* approaches where the client sets the agenda for any discussions. The family or friend then starts by asking the client about his/her drug/alcohol use, focusing on positive aspects of use to begin with to gain an understanding of motives to use. Discuss with families and friends the need to avoid confrontation or arguing about use, as these may encourage resistance and even further use.

Talk through with family members and friends how they can leave the responsibility for change with the client, and not take over. That is, explain to the family and friends about the stages of change that people go through and help them to match discussions about drug/alcohol use with the client's current stage of change. Remind them that the client's motivation and readiness to change will fluctuate and may appear to go backwards at times. An optimistic, long-term approach is required, and making an effort to discuss issues and understand may be the most influential contribution a family member/friend can make. Encourage family/friends to use "I" and "feelings" statements to express concerns. *For example, "I get upset when I see you drunk. It makes me feel sad that you need to do that."* Have a consistent "team approach" within the family or social network by discussing methods and approaches to speaking to the client prior to speaking to him/her.

So remember, the families/social networks aims are:

(1) Initially, help the client talk about the positive aspects of substance use.

(2) The next stage is to help clients begin to shift the focus to the problems associated with drug or alcohol use either by not rescuing them from the consequences of their use or by discussing problems as they arise.

(3) Help to challenge and re-evaluate the cognitive distortions which maintain problematic substance use.

How Do I Manage Financial Issues?

It has been shown that taking complete control over clients' finances does not encourage them to change their behaviour or reduce stress for family and friends. A more constructive approach looks at helping clients to *see the negative consequences of their substance use on their finances* and identifying items or activities that they could afford if they used less. Moreover, relatives and friends need to identify any patterns of rescuing behaviour in which they give the client money or pay debts when the client gets into financial difficulty. It may be useful to negotiate within the family about monitoring finances and sharing responsibility for them. A family member could agree to hold some money or to take rent or other expenditures as soon as the client gets his/her money. This should be agreed with the client and reviewed regularly. How to deal with finances could be a family rule that is set. Behaviour relating to stealing should definitely be resolved through setting a family rule prohibiting it and setting consequences if it occurs. It may also become apparent through discussion that the client does not have budgeting skills, and either a family member or a case worker could address this with the client (see Chapter 14, C-BIT "Lifestyle Balance", skills-building component).

How Do I Know Whether They Are Getting Unwell or Have Started to Use Drugs/Alcohol Problematically?

Early Warning Signs and Relapse Cycle

Both family members and clients will be aware of behavioural and other changes that have occurred prior to previous periods of illness or substance use, although they may not have realised that they have recognised these. It is important to include families and friends in discussions of both the substance-use relapse cycle (see Chapter 7, C-BIT treatment phase 3) and the psychotic relapse signature (see Chapter 8, C-BIT treatment phase 4). This will ensure that family and friends are familiar with the individual's signs and symptoms of relapse and can be included in producing a plan to tackle these if they occur. This will give family and friends a role within the management of psychosis and substance use, and thereby a positive role in helping their relative/friend.

With regard to substance use, it may appear to families and friends that the client relapses to using in a problematic way very quickly. Thus, it is important to educate families and friends about the client's *relapse cycle*, an explanation which will include a chain of events (that is, a trigger, personal beliefs, automatic thoughts, and thoughts giving permission to use). It is important for families and friends to be aware of the client's particular triggers and high-risk situations (such as *feeling under pressure, seeing certain people or having money*) and the person's beliefs about the substance that he/she uses (for example, *"Alcohol is the only thing that calms me down"; "I can't sleep if I don't smoke")*, because these factors are indicators that the client may be experiencing increased urges and craving to use drugs/alcohol.

If a person begins to use drugs/alcohol problematically, changes may occur in his/her:

- group of friends (for example, may return to spending time with old friends)
- appearance (unkempt or smell of alcohol)
- behaviour (lying, not eating or spending more time alone)
- available money (asking to borrow money, or failing to pay rent)
- mental health (more positive symptoms: voices, delusional thoughts or paranoia).

With regard to a mental health relapse, families and friends can brainstorm with the client the process that the client goes through when he/she becomes unwell (see Chapter 8, C-BIT treatment phase 4). This could include changes in appearance, eating and sleeping patterns, becoming isolated, positive symptoms, and so on. It is important to explain to the family that every client's relapse signature is different and that the signs will become progressively more severe, but that they can intervene at any stage to help prevent complete relapse. The required intervention should again be agreed by the family with the client, and could include pointing out the behaviour, reducing stress levels for the client, using self-help strategies or contacting the health services for support.

How Do I Get Involved in Helping Maintain Changes in Alcohol/Drug Use?

Relapse Prevention

Relapse prevention means identifying situations and thoughts that will make the person either crave substances or feel the need to use drugs/alcohol, and it means making plans for how to deal with these situations. Triggers for drug/alcohol use may be internal or external (such as stress, people or places, and money). Once people can identify situations that are high risk for them, they can make plans to avoid them or deal with them. Family members and friends may well have noticed patterns and triggers that the client is not aware of. Once they have established an environment in which they can discuss substance use, they can brainstorm triggers together and produce coping strategies. Families and friends should remember that the client needs to learn to handle these situations him/herself, and should not include in the plan rescuing behaviour (that is, hiding the consequences) or controlling behaviour (that is, removing the person or the substance) as strategies.

Positive Reinforcement for Not Using in a Problematic Pattern

People make positive changes in their behaviour because the reasons against the behaviour begin to outweigh the reasons for it. To assist clients to maintain a change in their substance-use behaviour, the family members and friends can provide positive reinforcement, praise and rewards for keeping up the changes. This will ensure that the client gets more from the new behaviour than he/she did from the previous behaviour.

How Do I Get Them Involved in Alternative Activities?

Identifying Alternative Activities of Interest

Alternative non-drug/alcohol-related activities are necessary to replace substance-use behaviours or fill the gaps when substance use has stopped or been reduced. These activities will also help to increase motivation and the self-esteem related to mental health. Activities can also distract clients from their psychotic symptoms and other mental health problems. When the alternative strategies are to replace substance-use behaviours, try to ensure that they offer *fairly immediate positive gratification*, not long-term satisfaction, as they are then more likely to be taken up and continued. In addition, make the activities as incompatible with substance use as possible. For example, when swimming it is difficult to smoke or drink!

Family members and friends can encourage the use of self-help groups. These aim to promote self-esteem and coping strategies for the client and increase his/her non-substance-using social network. It may be necessary to shop around for one that suits. Most clients are reluctant to begin new activities for many reasons (such as no motivation to plan them, happy with current activity, can't think of anything they want to do, lack of social, practical and confidence skills and no immediate gratification to be gained). Therefore, use an approach that encourages "trying out" different activities to see whether they are suitable. Families and friends will have a wealth of knowledge about the activities that their relatives or friends have previously engaged in, and they are in a great position to bring up gently the subject and reminisce about past pleasurable activities. Families and friends could try looking through old photographs or scrapbooks to recall activities they have done before or use television programmes as prompts for ideas and discussions. It may be useful to suggest that families and friends participate in the activity too. It is also necessary to ensure that clients are capable of carrying out the proposed activity, as the idea is to improve their self-esteem by helping them to succeed in and enjoy the activity.

Goal Planning

Whenever families and friends are setting goals with clients, they need to ensure that they are *realistic and specific and follow a step-by-step approach*. *For example, the overall aim may be for Ken to resume participation in a local football team.* This is not a realistic goal, as Ken may not be fit, may want to play any number of times a week, may not have the confidence to join in socially and may have no equipment. Therefore, they need to break the goal down into stages as follows:

(1) *Help Ken to buy trainers and shorts.*
(2) *Encourage Ken to go jogging alone twice a week in the evening.*
(3) *Join a gym with Ken and attend it together three times a week.*
(4) *Help Ken to contact the local football team.*
(5) *Attend training or selection with Ken.*
(6) *Encourage Ken to keep attending football training or the gym twice a week.*

Is important that families and friends encourage the client to stay at one stage until he/she is completely comfortable and provide positive feedback and praise for efforts made. There may be times when the client is unable to carry out his/her planned activity, but this should not be viewed as failure—we all have "off" days. It may be helpful for families and friends to record the participation in activities so that they can use this record to encourage and motivate the client.

Routine, Structure and Lifestyle Balance

Routines and structured use of time are very helpful in regaining order for a person who has been mentally unwell. In addition, using substances problematically can often result in a chaotic lifestyle. Someone who is using a large amount of substances may have become involved in illegal activities to finance his/her habit; to get the necessary money, some users develop extremely good organisational skills. These can be put to good use developing a new structured timetable of non-substance-related activities. Many people find that the trigger to use substances is a feeling of imbalance in their life. That is, when they are involved in lots of activities, they feel that they *"should"* be doing a few activities that they actually *"want"* to do. This can lead to feeling bored, unappreciated and overworked with few experiences of pleasure or enjoyment. This, in turn, makes people crave pleasure and for someone who uses drug/alcohol if his/her beliefs say that "Drugs make me feel interesting", "Alcohol relaxes me" this can lead to permissive beliefs to use substances such as "I deserve it." "It's a treat/reward for all the work I've done". Therefore, it is important that when a client plans new activities and structure into his/her week they include a balance of work (that is, "shoulds") and pleasure activities (that is, "wants").

How Do I Get Some Support and Help for Myself?

There are self-help agencies for relatives of people with drug/alcohol problems, such as Al-Anon, and groups set up for families of people with mental health problems. Providing families with a list of these will be helpful for peer support and time out for the family. The Behavioural Family Therapy package is also available for more formal family work; it covers education, problem-solving skills and communication (Barrowclough, 2003; Barrow-clough et al., 2000, 2001; Falloon et al., 1996). It is also important to encourage family members to pursue interests and hobbies of their own away from the family so that they get some space and do not become completely bogged down with thinking about the family member who is unwell.

So remember, when working with families and friends, you will need to encourage them to,

- set limits and boundaries
- not "rescue"
- practise positive, motivational communication skills
- monitor finances and help if appropriate
- learn the early warning signs and relapse cycles
- become involved in plans to prevent relapse
- provide positive reinforcement
- encourage alternative activities
- get help and support for themselves.

PART THREE

IMPLEMENTATION ISSUES

Chapter 16

IMPLEMENTATION ISSUES

OVERVIEW

As outlined in Part One of this treatment manual, C-BIT is most effectively implemented in settings that are capable of providing some level of assertive outreach. Nonetheless, some of the specific treatment components have been used successfully in other mental health and substance misuse treatment settings, including inpatient units. In Part Three, we discuss common issues encountered during the developmental stages of implementing an integrated-treatment approach, and elaborate on how to address them. For more details on the issues addressed and step-by-step guidance on implementation, see Department of Health (2002), Mercer-McFadden et al. (1998) and Mueser et al. (2003).

IMPLEMENTATION OBSTACLES AND SOLUTIONS

Over the past few years, a significant amount of guidance has appeared on implementing effective integrated-treatment approaches and service delivery models for people with severe mental health problems who use alcohol/drugs problematically (e.g., Department of Health, 2002; Drake et al., 2001; Graham et al., 2003). These guidelines have been important in providing a framework for the development of treatment services for this client group based on the available evidence base. The central themes have been as follows: providing integrated interventions within mainstream mental health services, training skilling staff, involving key stakeholders in the development process and the development of an effective evidence base.

In this section, we will highlight some of the implementation obstacles that can often arise during the developmental stages. From our experience, we will suggest some strategies to address these issues.

Attitudes and Philosophies of Staff

A major hurdle during times of change and service development is the attitude of staff. For many staff, change represents increased workload and responsibility. When one attempts to integrate the treatment of alcohol and drug problems into routine mental health treatment, a number of issues can arise. Many clinicians may feel that they are being asked to work in an area that they have no expertise in. Others may perceive alcohol/drug use as something clients continue to do of their own volition despite an awareness of the negative consequences; thus, they may place responsibility for change solely with the clients or with substance misuse services. Some may feel that help should be offered only to clients who are "motivated to change". Finally, staff may have concerns about their own safety in working with clients who use illegal substances. We will address each of these issues in turn.

Confidence and Skills of Staff

The results of a survey of the training and support needs of 136 community-based clinicians in our services revealed that staff were interested in working with people with severe mental health problems who misuse alcohol and drugs, and saw it as part of their role. However, they emphasised that they needed more information and training to help them work effectively with these clients (Maslin et al., 2001). Thus, training existing staff is a crucial step in the implementation process. Changing clinical practice involves developing new attitudes, knowledge and skills.

"Ownership" of the Client Group

It has been well documented that, traditionally, the experience of people with severe mental health problems who use alcohol/drugs problematically was of being "bounced" between mental health and substance misuse services, often with neither service taking responsibility for the coordination of their care. The result was that these clients often fell between the two services, either failing to receive one or both services or receiving them both in a poorly coordinated, non-integrated fashion. As a consequence, most clients had had a negative and ineffective treatment experience (e.g., Drake et al., 2001; Rorstad & Checinski, 1996). Mental health and substance misuse treatment services have had different philosophical approaches to engagement and treatment, and have traditionally addressed only those problems specific to one or the other problem area. Mental health services have typically engaged service users assertively in treatment for their mental health problems, and referred them to substance misuse services if alcohol/drug use was deemed to be the primary problem. In contrast, substance misuse services have typically required clients to be motivated for change as a prerequisite for providing treatment.

The current guidance on implementation of integrated treatment arose from an acute awareness of this tension between treatment services about "ownership" of this client group. Thus, the consensus view in the literature is that people with severe mental health problems who use alcohol/drugs problematically should receive integrated care that is delivered within mental health services (e.g. Department of Health, 2002; Drake et al., 2001). In some instances, this may include some consultation and liaison with specialist substance misuse services for facilities such as rehabilitation. An important part of the implementation process is to understand how care pathways between mental health and substance misuse services have previously worked, and to consult and work alongside both services to build a shared understanding and an alliance of mutual support.

Legal and Safety Issues

Violence and involvement in criminal behaviour are issues that often arise when working with people with severe mental health problems who use alcohol and drugs problematically. Among those with severe mental health problems, the most important predictors of violence are a history of prior violence, including aggression, dating to before the onset of the mental health problems (Hodgins & Côté, 1993), and substance use problems (Swartz et al., 1998). Integrated approaches to the treatment of this client group can be effective in preventing and managing violence. Strategies used in these approaches, such as assertive outreach and close monitoring, mean that teams are familiar with the clients they work with and are well placed to conduct risk assessments that take into account history and risk potential for future violence (including substance-related problems), and to develop responsive treatment plans that take into account the combined risk posed by both the mental health and substance use problems.

Assertive outreach to clients in community settings where alcohol/drug-related problems are significant can place staff at risk of violence. These issues require careful attention to conducting regular risk assessments, carrying out joint visits, access to mobile telephones, and having personal emergency alarms. Some clients with active alcohol and drug problems may engage in dangerous or predatory behaviours that affect other more vulnerable clients served in mental health centres or residential hostels. Clinicians and administrators should be prepared to take action to limit the access to the centre of clients who exhibit such behaviours. This should not prevent treatment, however, and home- and community-based services can be substituted.

Resource Costs and Savings

A significant concern for services that are already overstretched is how to implement integrated treatment approaches for people with severe mental health problems who use alcohol/drugs problematically. However, the evidence suggests that, although there may be some extra initial expenditure, the net result is significant savings. A number of studies have highlighted the disproportionate costs to services of this client group when compared to people with severe mental health problems who do not use alcohol/drugs problematically (Dickey & Azeni, 1996; Jerrell & Ridgely, 1995). Research studies looking at the comparative resource costs of integrated treatment versus standard practice have begun to demonstrate the significant long-term savings to services that implement integrated treatment (e.g., Jerrell 1996; Jerrell & Ridgely, 1999). In addition, the service delivery model proposed in this manual is a capacity-building one, whereby existing mental health clinicians are trained in the necessary skills and supported to deliver the integrated treatment approach. The bottom line is that C-BIT works mainly to train and enhance the expertise of existing staff rather than hiring new specialist staff.

Evaluation

The measurement of outcomes is of critical importance for services to track accurately their impact on substance use and mental health problems, and to demonstrate their effectiveness and cost-effectiveness. There is often reluctance by service providers to include an evaluation component in new service developments, perceiving it as too costly or unnecessary. Evaluation is often viewed as separate from the development process. However, we have found evaluation to be an essential component of our service and treatment development. It has helped in mapping local need, developing a strategic plan, piloting treatment approaches and refining the treatment, as well as in the development and evaluation of the resulting training programme.

Incorporating simple outcome measures of substance use, mental health functioning and symptoms, and other key areas (such as hospitalisations, relapses and contact with criminal justice system) is important in evaluating improvement on an individual client basis and for the wider services.

Detoxification and Rehabilitation Facilities and Housing

An important component of integrated treatment for people with severe mental health problems who misuse alcohol/drugs is comprehensiveness; that is, the availability of a range of interventions that address the scope of problems encountered by this client group. Integrated services will need to be directed not only at the problems of substance use and mental health but also at the broad array of other areas of functioning that are frequently impaired in clients, such as housing, and social and vocational functioning. Inattention to any one component can undermine the overall effectiveness of a treatment programme.

Our experience has highlighted, in particular, the lack of alcohol/drug rehabilitation facilities and housing appropriate to the needs of this client group. Often, alcohol/drug rehabilitation facilities that were designed for people with a primary substance use problem are not well suited to the needs of people with severe mental health problems. They are often residential placements, thus requiring a disruption in the clients' community-based mental health treatment. In addition, the treatment philosophy typically is not based on a harm-reduction approach and requires complete abstinence from all substances, sometimes including medication. All of these factors present a gap in service provision in terms of the recovery and rehabilitation process. Some consideration is needed to identify creative solutions to overcome this obstacle.

The lack of a range of housing options is a vital area of concern. For many clients with severe mental health problems who continue to use alcohol/drugs problematically, obtaining and remaining in accommodation suited to their needs is a significant challenge (Bebout et al., 1997; Drake et al., 1997). The literature and available evidence suggest that outcomes are improved for this client group when they receive integrated treatment that incorporates appropriate, supported and matched accommodation (Drake et al., 1997; Pickett-Schenk, Banghart & Cook, 2003). That is, stable housing is most successfully achieved when a range of housing options, provided by a single agency, is available, from "dry" (that is, no use of substances) to "medium" (some use of substances, but not chaotic) to "wet" (still using) housing that is matched to the client's needs and includes short- and long-term options (Mueser et al., 2003). In addition, clients need housing-support staff that are clinicians trained in substance use and mental health, as well as housing services.

TRAINING AND SUPERVISION (CAPACITY BUILDING)

Integrating the treatment of alcohol and drug problems into existing mental health services involves broadening the traditional focus of treatment. This can be accomplished by a variety of strategies, including providing staff with training in the recognition and treatment of problem alcohol and drug use in persons with severe mental health problems, forming specialised teams to support existing services in providing integrated treatment, and recruiting new staff with experience in the treatment of problem substance use to work in existing services. The result of each of these options is a mental health team that is capable of addressing substance use problems while maintaining awareness of the unique needs of people with severe mental health problems.

To shift the treatment philosophy of mental health teams to embrace the concept of integrated treatment, all clinicians on the teams need to be trained. Training each mental health team together as a unit has been fundamental, in our experience, in facilitating a change in the team's approach. This method of training offers all clinicians within the team an opportunity to be exposed to the issues at the same time and to work through, as a team, any difficulties they perceive they will encounter when implementing the treatment approach.

Once they are trained, the provision of specialist supervision to these mental health teams is an important strategy to support and encourage implementation and adherence to the integrated treatment approach. We have found that teams have benefited from receiving team supervision. The aim of supervision sessions has been to facilitate the process whereby the team is able, using the treatment approach, to think through a particular client's current problems or review his/her overall case. The end result is typically a reformulation or reconceptualisation of the client's difficulties and a clearer treatment plan, with consensus on how the team will work with the client to address the issues.

ORGANISATIONAL FACTORS

Leadership/Stakeholders

Strong leadership is crucial for the development and implementation of effective integrated treatment into existing service provision. The person(s) appointed to take on the leadership role must embrace the mission to integrate the treatment of problem substance use into all aspects of mental health services (Mueser et al., 2003). The tone for implementation must be set by the leader and a core group of key stakeholders by making clear the expectation that all clinicians need to acquire skills for assessing and treating substance-use problems. A lead commissioner will need to be identified, by the key local stakeholders in health and social care, to coordinate the planning process and carry the work forward. Middle managers must ensure that training, supervision, and monitoring are in place, and the medical director will also need to ensure that psychiatrists also acquire the requisite skills (Department of Health, 2002).

We have found it important to have a designated director charged with overseeing the integrated treatment services in order for effective services to be established and maintained. The literature on programme innovation indicates that major programme change and the maintenance of high-quality programming require a director (often called a "champion") who assumes primary responsibility for the overall quality of a new programme (Corrigan, 1995; Liberman et al., 1982; Mueser & Fox, 2000; Spaniol, Zipple & Cohen, 1991). The responsibilities of the director of integrated services include the recruitment and training of specialist staff, ensuring that services are being implemented with fidelity to the principles of the integrated treatment approach, the training and supervision of existing clinicians and teams, and research and coordinating implementation across levels of care (inpatient, outpatient and residential). The director also provides liaison with the substance misuse treatment services and other agencies.

OVERVIEW OF THE EVIDENCE BASE AND FUTURE DIRECTIONS FOR RESEARCH

Integrated Treatment Research

Over the past 15 years, as the problem of substance misuse in persons with severe mental health problems has become widely recognised, significant gains have been made in the development of effective, integrated-treatment programmes. The evolution of research on integrated treatment can be divided into three phases:

(1) evaluation of the effects of adding substance misuse treatment groups to existing mental health services
(2) feasibility studies aimed at examining the effects of fully integrated-treatment programmes on services and clinical outcome
(3) controlled trials of integrated-treatment programmes.

In this chapter, we provide a brief review of each of these phases of research on integrated treatment, with the most attention given to controlled studies of integrated-treatment programmes.

Research on Adding Substance Misuse Groups to Existing Mental Health Services

Early efforts at integrating mental health and substance misuse services involved the provision of circumscribed substance misuse services within mental health settings (Hellerstein, Rosenthal & Miner, 1995; Herman et al., 1997; Lehman et al., 1993; Mowbray et al., 1995). These services, most often in the form of substance-misuse-oriented groups, or more broad-based, 12-step, inpatient programmes, were based on interventions drawn from the substance misuse field with minimal effort aimed at adapting those services to people with severe and persistent mental health problems. Services typically involved a time-limited intervention during which a combination of educational and confrontational strategies were used to attempt to help clients develop awareness of the nature of their substance use problems. Treatment focused on abstinence rather than substance use reduction or minimisation of the harmful consequences of substance use. Although these studies were an important step forward in efforts to treat substance use problems in people with severe mental health problems, they had very limited success.

Several problems were noted with efforts to add substance misuse services to existing mental health treatment. Of greatest concern, these interventions were associated with high dropout rates, possibly reflecting their lack of assertive outreach and the negative effects of interpersonal confrontation in people with severe mental health problems. These programmes tended to provide clinic-based services without recognising the fact that many clients with severe mental health problems attend clinic-based treatment erratically. Clients with severe mental health problems who use substances problematically are frequently in and out of treatment, and are often least engaged with treatment when their substance use problems are greatest. Hence providing only clinic-based services in the absence of assertive outreach made it difficult to engage and retain significant numbers of this client group (Drake et al., 1993).

In addition, early-treatment programmes for people with combined severe mental health and substance use problems tended to use educational and confrontational approaches, but failed to take into account the need for motivation-based interventions. Furthermore, the use of confrontational approaches with this client group was problematic because of the high sensitivity of people with severe mental health problems to emotionally charged interactions. Such stressful interpersonal encounters are more likely to drive people away from treatment than to break through ambivalence and lead to motivation to work on substance use problems. These problems underscored the need for motivation-based interventions that recognise that clients differ in their levels of motivation to work on substance use problems, and that treatment must take the client's motivation to change into account (Carey, 1996; Mueser et al., 2003).

Most early attempts to add substance misuse services to mental health treatment involved the provision of a single intervention without necessarily addressing the client's more comprehensive needs. Furthermore, these services tended to be provided on a time-limited basis, placing unrealistic expectations for rapid improvement in substance misuse. These limitations made it difficult or impossible for substance misuse treatment to benefit the most severely impaired clients, who often present multiple needs and improve only gradually over long periods of time.

As may be expected, these studies had few effects on improving substance use outcomes. However, the experience gained from implementing and evaluating the effects of merely adding treatments for problem substance use to existing mental health services paved the way for the development of more comprehensive, integrated-treatment programmes. These subsequent interventions were more appropriately tailored to meet the needs of clients with severe mental health problems.

Feasibility Studies of Comprehensive Integrated-Treatment Programmes

The second phase of research on treatment for people with severe mental health problems who misuse substances involved evaluating the feasibility of more comprehensive, motivation-based, outreach-oriented interventions. These US studies, many of them supported by grant funds from the Center for Mental Health Services, National Demonstration of Services for Young Adults with Severe Mental Illness and Substance Abuse Project (Mercer-McFadden et al., 1997), involved the development of speciality services for this client group that incorporated many of the core features of integrated treatment. These studies lacked experimental controls. However, they sought primarily to evaluate whether the new approaches to integration were more successful in engaging and retaining clients in treatment, and to determine whether substance misuse outcomes improved as expected for clients who remained in treatment.

A variety of psychotherapeutic approaches were incorporated within these integrated programmes, including individual, group, and family therapy. The results of these studies provided a solid basis for optimism about the effectiveness of these services (Detrick & Stiepock, 1992; Durell et al., 1993; Meisler et al., 1997). Clients were more readily engaged in the programmes, retention was substantially higher than in programmes where substance misuse services were simply added to existing mental health services, and clinical outcomes were positive. These studies demonstrated that, through a combination of assertive outreach, motivation-based interventions, and harm-reduction philosophy, the vast majority of clients could be successfully engaged and retained in treatment. Furthermore, they underscored the fact that participation in such treatment was associated with positive clinical outcomes. These encouraging results led to the next phase of research on integrated dual disorders: controlled studies of integrated-treatment programmes.

Controlled Studies of Integrated Treatment

The identification of core ingredients of integrated treatment for people with coexisting severe mental health and substance use problems (that is, motivation-based intervention, assertive outreach, and harm-reduction approach), combined with demonstrated feasibility and promising outcomes in the second phase of research, led to controlled studies designed to evaluate rigorously the effects of integrated treatment. While there are methodological limitations to controlled research on integrated treatment, as discussed below, the results further support the effectiveness of integrated treatment, and shed some light on the relative effectiveness of different approaches to the delivery of integrated treatment. These studies are briefly described below.

Five different studies have compared the effectiveness of integrated treatment with non-integrated treatment for this client group. Two additional studies have evaluated different approaches to providing integrated treatment.

Studies of Integrated versus Non-Integrated Treatment

An early study of integrated treatment for "dual disorders" was a randomised control study conducted by Godley and colleagues (1994). This study compared the effectiveness of integrated treatment combined with intensive case management with standard services in 38 clients (44 per cent schizophrenia). Follow-up was conducted over 2 years during which time the interventions were provided; attrition was relatively low at 21 per cent. Clients who received integrated treatment had better outcomes than clients who received standard services on days of substance abuse. The two groups were of comparable effectiveness in days hospitalised and symptom severity.

Drake and colleagues conducted a quasi-experimental study on 217 predominantly African–American clients (89 per cent) with coexisting severe mental health and substance use problems (50 per cent schizophrenia) living in Washington, DC. Clients who received integrated treatment (including individual motivation-based work, group and social network intervention, and assertive outreach) also received extensive assistance on housing issues. A comparison group of clients was assessed who received routine, non-integrated services available in a similar region. Clients were assessed every 6 months for an 18-month period with a 14 per cent rate of attrition from research. At the end of treatment, clients in the integrated programme had made more progress in their treatment, and had significantly lower levels of alcohol misuse (but not drug misuse) than the non-integrated-treatment group. Clients in the integrated-treatment group also had more stable housing and spent fewer days in institutional settings over the treatment period. There were no differences between the integrated and non-integrated-treatment groups in other outcomes, such as symptoms, quality of life, or legal problems.

Carmichael and colleagues (1998) conducted an evaluation of five different sites implementing integrated-treatment programmes, including individual and group-based motivational work, assertive outreach, and competence of services. Two of these five sites conducted controlled studies, one quasi-experimental and one a randomised control trial. For both of the controlled studies, the comparison intervention was standard (non-integrated) services. A total of 208 clients were included in the two controlled studies (31 per cent schizophrenia); attrition from research was relatively high at 45 per cent. The results indicated superior outcomes for the integrated treatment over the standard services group across several domains, including alcohol and drug abuse, medication adherence, suicidal thoughts, income, arrests and satisfaction with services. No differences between the groups were found on hospital utilisation or symptom severity.

Barrowclough and colleagues (2001) conducted a randomised control trial evaluating the effects of a 9-month intervention that combined family work with individual-based treatment, and incorporated both cognitive-behavioural therapy for psychosis and motivational interviewing to address substance misuse. A total of 36 clients were studied (all with a diagnosis of schizophrenia), with the integrated-treatment programme compared to non-integrated treatment as usual. The results of the study at 1 year after initiation of the programme were striking and strongly favoured the integrated-treatment programme. Clients who received integrated treatment had more abstinent days, less severe psychiatric symptoms, and fewer hospitalisations. It appears that the focus of the cognitive-behavioural therapy on addressing psychotic symptoms, along with family intervention, may have succeeded in reducing psychiatric severity, in addition to reducing substance misuse.

Graham and colleagues (Copello, Graham & Birchwood, 2001; Graham et al., 2003) are undertaking a study based on a quasi-experimental design. Five assertive outreach teams have been randomised, three to receive an integrated-treatment package (training in C-BIT plus support to deliver the integrated treatment) and two to standard practice. A total of 58 clients have entered the study (79 per cent with a diagnosis of schizophrenia) and are being assessed at 6-month intervals for 36 months. At the 18-month period, the control teams received the integrated-treatment intervention. Preliminary results suggest some positive improvements in client outcomes, including substance use behaviour and engagement in treatment when compared to standard practice. In addition, teams are demonstrating improved confidence and ability to deliver the C-BIT approach and adherence to integrated treatment.

Comparisons of Different Models for Delivering Integrated Treatment

Two studies have examined different models for delivering integrated treatment to people with severe mental health problems who use substances problematically. Jerrell and colleagues (J. Jerrell & Ridgely, 1995; J. M. Jerrell & Ridgely, 1995; Jerrell & Ridgely, 1999; Ridgely & Jerrell, 1996) compared the effectiveness of three different approaches to providing integrated treatment: a modified 12-step approach (based on the 12 steps of Alcoholics Anonymous) (Alcoholics Anonymous, 1985), intensive case management (Durell et al., 1993) and behavioural skills training (based on social skills training) (Liberman, DeRisi & Mueser, 1989). The skills training intervention focused on improving interpersonal skills across a range of situations, including basic conversational and friendship skills, as well as skills for dealing with substance-abuse-related situations. A total of 132 clients were assigned to one of the three treatment groups (some were randomly assigned and others were not) and followed up over 18 months. Attrition from research was moderate at 31 per cent. The results indicated that, overall, the behavioural skills training group had the best outcomes, followed by the intensive case-management group, followed by the group with the modified 12-step approach. Specifically, substance use outcomes favoured the behavioural skills training group over the other two groups, which did not differ. Symptom outcomes were significantly better for the behavioural skills training group than the intensive case-management group, whose symptoms were significantly better than the group with the 12-step approach. There were no differences in other outcomes, such as social functioning and goal performance. It is unclear what proportion of the study participants had schizophrenia.

Drake and colleagues (1998) compared the effects of two different case-management methods for providing integrated treatment to clients with coexisting severe mental-health and substance use problems over 3 years across seven different mental health centres: intensive case-management teams based on the Assertive Community Treatment (ACT) model (Stein & Santos, 1998) with clinician caseload ratios of 1 to 10, versus regular case-management teams with ratios of 1 to 30. Both models included outreach, team orientation, integrated "dual-diagnosis" treatment, a longitudinal approach and supportive housing. A total of 240 clients were recruited into the study, 215 for whom follow-up data are available. Research attrition was low at 9 per cent. Outcomes were good for both approaches, with significant reductions in hospitalisation and improvement in substance misuse over the follow-up period. Outcomes favoured the ACT model, with significantly greater reductions in alcohol misuse, but no differences in other outcomes.

Summary of Research on Integrated Treatment

Research on integrated treatment for people with severe mental health problems who use substances problematically has made significant progress over the past decade. Of particular importance, five controlled studies have been completed, comparing integrated with non-integrated programmes, and all have demonstrated the advantages of integrated over traditional non-integrated care. While there is a need for more research on this topic, and the findings of effective integrated-treatment programmes need to be replicated, the results provide a solid basis for optimism concerning the effects of integrated treatment on substance misuse outcomes.

Appendix 0

ASSESSMENT PHASE: WORKSHEETS

0.1   IMPORTANCE—CONFIDENCE RULER

On scale of 0–10, how important is it right now for you to change your use _____
(insert name of substance)?

Importance: 0 ——————————————— 10

On a scale of 0–10, if you did decide to change, how confident are you that you would succeed?

Confidence: 0 ——————————————— 10

Adapted from Rollnick, Butler & Stott (1997)

0.2   DRUG DIARY

Day, date + time	Where were you? What was happening?	What were you thinking + feeling?	How much did you use and spend?	How did you think + feel after using?

0.3   ALCOHOL DIARY

	Time of drinking	Number of Units/Pints/ Singles/ Glasses of Wine, etc.*	Type of Alcohol	In company or alone	Where drinking took place	Feelings before and afterwards	Effects of drinking	Money spent on Alcohol
Mon								
Tues								
Wed								
Thu								
Fri								
Sat								
Sun								
Total units						Total Cost		

1 Unit* = Half-pint ordinary beer
            Single measure vermouth
            Single measure spirits
            1 Glass of wine
            Small glass sherry
1 + Units = 1 Standard can of lager
2 + Units = 1 Strong can of lager
4 Units = 1 Extra-strong can of lager

Name ....

Date of Completion: /   /

0.4   CASE FORMULATION TEMPLATE

HOW DID THESE PROBLEMS DEVELOP?

Early Experience(s)
→

Core Beliefs
→

Conditional Beliefs—general
(e.g., if . . . then statements)
→

Drug/Alcohol-Related Beliefs
(e.g., if . . . then statements)
→

Trigger Event(s)
→

CURRENT PROBLEM(S) +
RELATIONSHIP BETWEEN THEM?

MAINTAINING FACTORS?

DRUG/ALCOHOL USE   SEVERE MENTAL HEALTH PROBLEM(S)   OTHER(S)

TRIGGERS FOR DRUG/ALCOHOL USE: _____

SOCIAL NETWORKS: _____

REASONS FOR USING/DRUG ALCOHOL BELIEFS _____

EFFECTS/PROBLEM ASSOCIATED WITH USE: _____

SEVERE MENTAL HEALTH PROBLEM: _____

OTHER(S): _____

0.5   C-BIT: SCREENING ASSESSMENT OF DRUG AND ALCOHOL USE AND RELATIONSHIP WITH MENTAL HEALTH

1. CURRENT FUNCTIONING

To initially engage the client, build rapport and assess current functioning, information should initially be gathered about current mood, sleeping patterns, appetite/eating patterns, concentration, general motivation and level of interest, daily activities/ employment, social support, physical health, suicidal ideation/self-harm behaviours, medication.

2. FOR EACH SUBSTANCE ASK THE CLIENT ABOUT TYPICAL (PAST WEEK) USE AND CURRENT USE (PREVIOUS DAY)

Pattern of Use
- What substances does he/she use?
- How much does he/she use? (i.e. cost, quantity, units of alcohol)
- Financial cost? (i.e. per day/week) How does he/she fund his/her substance use? (What time does he/she first use in the morning and then how is it spaced throughout the day?)
- Route of use (i.e. smoked, oral, injected, snorted, etc.)? (whether he/she has ever injected/shared injecting equipment)
- Triggers for use or cravings (e.g. moods, psychosis symptoms, social settings)
- Moderating factors (i.e. what factors seem to make his/her substance use generally worse/better?)
- How long has he/she used in this pattern? Any recent changes (e.g. increases/ decreases, change of route of administration)
- Social networks (who does he/she use with? And what proportion of the people he/ she currently spends time with use substances? How often does he/she use alone?)

Effects of Use/Other Problems
- Withdrawal symptoms experienced when he/she does not have the substance (e.g. first thing in the morning or if he/she were unable to get hold of the substance, after at least several days of continued use, how would he/she feel?)
- Assess if client experiences or has experienced any problems resulting from or related to his/her substance use in the following domains:

    Mental health/psychotic symptoms
    Financial/debts
    Social relationships
    Physical/health
    Housing
    Legal/forensic
    Occupational
    Childcare
    Getting aggressive/argumentative
- Has there been a narrowing of the person's usual repertoire of behaviours, activities or types of substances used?

3. REASONS FOR USING AND BELIEFS ABOUT SUBSTANCE USE

- Ask the client what are his/her reasons for using the substance(s) (e.g. pleasure, social/cultural, coping), what are some of the things he/she enjoys about using and how has he/she found using substances helpful?
- To help identify beliefs about alcohol/drug use, ask: "What usually goes through your mind just before you use?
- What are the attitudes of key people in the client's family/social network to drug/alcohol use?

4. TAKE A DRUG/ALCOHOL HISTORY

- Development history: brief outline of developmental milestones, childhood experiences, family atmosphere, psychosexual, education and occupational/work history
- Family history: brief outline of parents and siblings including age, occupation, relationship with client and family history of substance use and/or mental health problems.
- Age of first use of each substance and how substance use progressed over time
- When did he/she think that his/her alcohol/drug use became problematic and what was the nature of such problems?
- Periods of abstinence or any changes in use (ask about the most recent period of abstinence and if he/she has a period of abstinence, ask what helped him/her to stop and what helped him/her to remain abstinent)
- Periods of treatment for drug/alcohol use (what types of treatment did he/she find helpful?)

5. ASSESS THE RELATIONSHIP BETWEEN SUBSTANCE USE AND MENTAL HEALTH

Assess whether the mental health problems/symptoms exist in the absence or presence of substance use:

- If the mental health problem/symptoms are current, identify if the client has recently used a substance, is the mental health problem due to an acute toxic reactions or is the client experiencing withdrawal effects from the substance?
- When did he/she first experience the mental health problem/symptoms? Was he/she using substances at that time?
- Does the mental health problem or symptoms only occur during or following recent use of the substance?
- Are there times when the mental health problem/symptoms have improved/worsened? What has helped or made it worse?
- When he/she is using the substance are the mental health problems/symptoms worsened? How?
- If he/she has been abstinent from the substance for a few weeks, has he/she continued to experience the mental health problems/symptoms or have these difficulties subsided?
- Are this person's reasons for using substances related to his/her mental health problems/symptoms or his/her experience of taking medication etc.?

6. MOTIVATION TO CHANGE AND GOALS

- Does the client see his/her substance use as a problem and want to change or not?
- What does the client see as his/her treatment goal?

BELIEFS ABOUT ALCOHOL/DRUG USE

Instructions: The aim of this question is to elicit the clients' main belief about the substance they use more problematically (in the case of polydrug users, beliefs should be elicited for the two most problematic substances). Below are a series of questions to establish the client's belief/s. Some clients may require additional prompting to uncover their belief/s about the substance/s they use rather than their thoughts about the substance/s they use.

Q1) Let's think about the last occasion you used_____(insert name of substance). What was going through your mind about_____ (insert name of substance) just before you used it?
(N.B. Interviewer needs to prompt until client's belief about the substance is elicited (i.e. a conditional statement such as "I won't be able to sleep without this drink"). An example of a prompt to help elicit the belief is "How did you think that X would help you?").

_____
_____

Q2) Is that the usual thought that goes through your mind about _____(insert name of substance) just before you use it?   YES/NO

(If no, ask): What is the usual thought that goes through your mind just before you use _____ (insert name of substance)?

Q3) On scale of 0 to 100, how much do you generally believe this to be true?

0%   25%   50%   75%   100%

(If the client is polydrug user, ask Q4 in order to elicit beliefs about other problematically used substances).

Q4) Is this the same thought that goes through your mind just before you use
_____ (insert name of second substance)?   YES/NO
(If no, ask): What is the usual though that goes through your mind just before you use_____(insert name of second substance)?

Q5) On scale of 0 to 100, how much do you generally believe this to be true?

0%   25%   50%   75%   100%

IMPORTANCE AND CONFIDENCE ASSESSMENT
Ask client: "On a scale of 0–10, how *important* is it right now for you to change your use of _____(insert name of substance)?"

Importance
    0_____10

Ask client: "On a scale of 0–10, if you did decide to change, how *confident* are you that you would succeed?"

Confidence
    0_____10

Appendix 1

TREATMENT PHASE 1: WORKSHEETS

1.1   CLIMBING MOUNTAINS: GOAL SETTING AND PROBLEM SOLVING

Where I would like to be?

STEP 5

What can I do to achieve this step?
What obstacles might there be and how can I overcome these?

STEP 4

What can I do to achieve this step?
What obstacles might there be and how can I overcome these?

STEP 3

What can I do to achieve this step?
What obstacles might there be and how can I overcome these?

STEP 2

What can I do to achieve this step?
What obstacles might there be and how can I overcome these?

STEP 1

What can I do to achieve this step?
What obstacles might there be and how can I overcome these?

Where I am now?

Self-motivational statement of intent to change

1.2   ADVANTAGES–DISADVANTAGES ANALYSIS

Name: _____

Date: _____

Behaviour: _____

	Ads (FOR)	Disads (AGAINST)
SHORT TERM		
LONG TERM		

Self-motivational Statements:

Concern: _____

_____

Intent to Change: _____

_____

1.3   DECISION BALANCE SHEET

Name: _____

Date: _____

Behaviour: _____

	'PROS' (FOR)	'CONS' (AGAINST)
SHORT TERM		
LONG TERM		

1.4   BUDGETING WORKSHEET

INCOMING	*OUTGOINGS*	
Weekly and Monthly £_____	*Electricity*	£_____
	Gas	£_____
	Council Tax	£_____
	Rent	£_____
	Food	£_____
	Spending Money	£_____
	Travel	£_____
	Cigarettes	£_____
	Activities	£_____
	Other (?Drugs/Alcohol)	£_____

Appendix 2

TREATMENT PHASE 2: WORKSHEETS

2.1   BEHAVIOURAL EXPERIMENT WORKSHEET

THOUGHT TO BE TESTED: _____

_____

EXPERIMENT	PREDICTION	POTENTIAL OBSTACLES	STRATEGIES TO OVERCOME OBSTACLES	OUTCOME OF EXPERIMENT
EXPERIMENT 1				
EXPERIMENT 2				

LESSON LEARNED/TAKE-HOME MESSAGE:_____

_____

_____

From Greenberger & Padesky (1995)

2.2   IDENTIFYING ACTIVITIES OF INTEREST

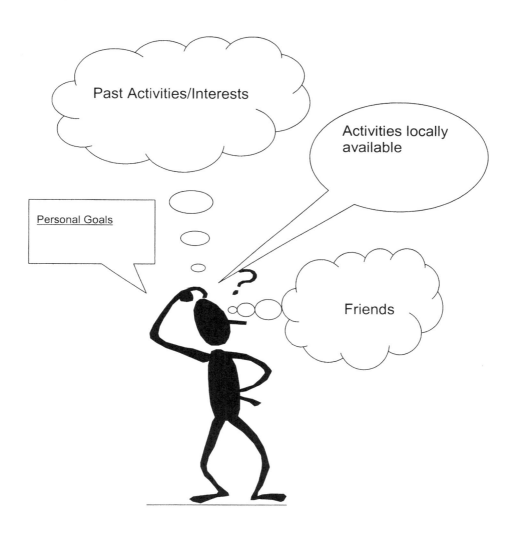

I WILL PLAN TO DO^(Activity) _____ **ON**^(Date) _____

WITH ^(Name) _____

Appendix 3

TREATMENT PHASE 3: WORKSHEETS

3.1   RELAPSE CYCLE OF PROBLEM SUBSTANCE USE

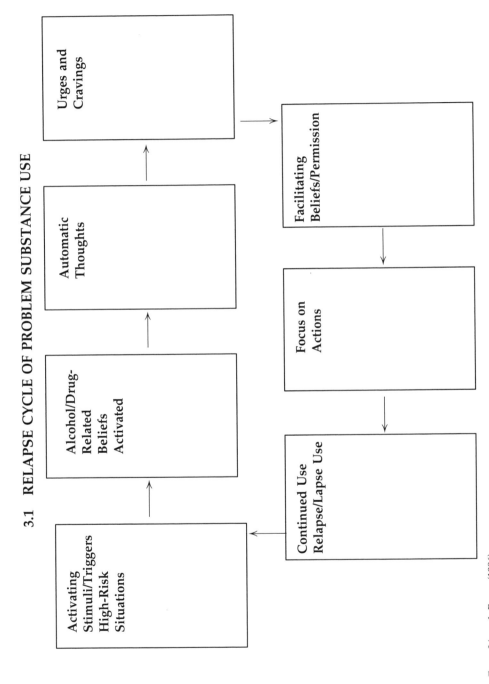

From Liese & Franz (1996)

3.2 RELAPSE-PREVENTION PLAN

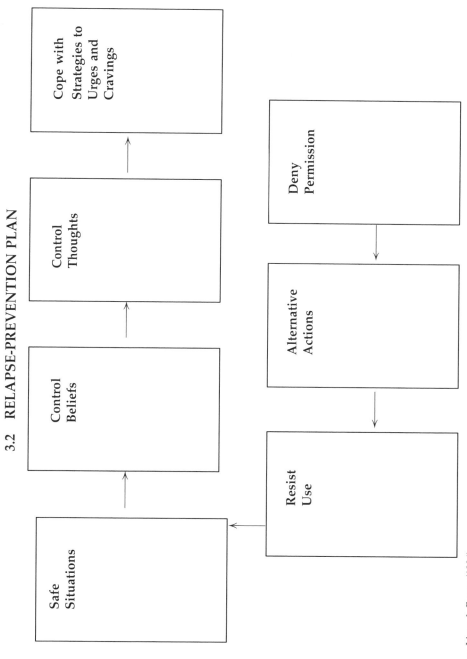

From Liese & Franz (1996)

Appendix 4

TREATMENT PHASE 4: WORKSHEET

4.1   EARLY WARNING SIGNS OF PSYCHOTIC RELAPSE

Thinking/Perception	Feelings	Behaviours
• Thoughts are racing • Senses seem sharper • Thinking you have special powers • Thinking that you can read other people's minds • Thinking that other people can read your mind • Receiving personal messages from the TV or radio • Having difficulty making decisions • Experiencing strange sensations • Preoccupied about one or two things • Thinking you might be somebody else • Seeing visions or things others cannot see • Thinking people are talking about you • Thinking people are against you • Having more nightmares • Having difficulty concentrating • Thinking bizarre things • Thinking your thoughts are controlled • Hearing voices • Thinking that a part of you has changed shape	• Feeling helpless or useless • Feeling afraid of going crazy • Feeling sad or low • Feeling anxious and restless • Feeling increasingly religious • Feeling like you're being watched • Feeling isolated • Feeling tired or lacking energy • Feeling confused or puzzled • Feeling forgetful or far away • Feeling in another world • Feeling strong and powerful • Feeling unable to cope with everyday tasks • Feeling like you are being punished • Feeling like you cannot trust other people • Feeling irritable • Feeling like you do not need sleep • Feeling guilty	• Difficulty in sleeping • Speech comes out jumbled and filled with odd words • Talking or smiling to yourself • Acting suspiciously as if you are being watched • Behaving oddly for no reason • Spending time alone • Neglecting your appearance • Acting like you are somebody else • Not seeing people • Not eating • Not leaving the house • Behaving like a child • Refusing to do simple requests • Drinking more • Smoking more • Using alcohol • Using drugs (e.g., cannabis, cocaine and amphetamines) • Using more alcohol • Using more drugs • Movements are slow • Unable to sit down for long • Behaving aggressively

Adapted from Birchwood, Spencer & McGovern (2000)

Appendix 5a

ANXIETY: WORKSHEETS

5.1 RELAXATION TECHNIQUE

Please set aside 20 minutes each day to practise relaxation

There are three general things, which you should remember:

(1) Find a quiet place away from distracting noises where you will not be disturbed.
(2) Don't try to do your relaxation practice when you are in a hurry or when you have an appointment to keep.
(3) Don't do your relaxation practice just after a meal, as you may not get as relaxed then as at other times.

When you are ready to start your relaxation practice, sit down in a comfortable position. Then go through the 16 muscle groups. First tense each muscle group for a few seconds and notice the feelings of tension; then let the muscles relax completely. Focus your attention on the feelings of relaxation in each muscle group and let the muscles become really relaxed before moving on to the next group. Here, to remind you, are the 16 muscle groups and the way to produce tension in each one.

(1) Right hand and lower arm—make a tight fist.
(2) Right upper arm—pull your elbow against your hip bone.
(3) Left hand and lower arm—make a tight fist.
(4) Left upper arm—pull your elbow against your hip bone.
(5) Forehead—frown.
(6) Eyes—screw up your eyes tight. When you relax, leave them closed.
(7) Jaw—clench your teeth and pull back the corners of your mouth.
(8) Neck—push your chin down and pull back your head at the same time.
(9) Shoulders and upper back—take a deep breath and hunch your shoulders. Let your breathing become slow and regular as you relax.
(10) Stomach—brace the muscles of your stomach.
(11) Right thigh—concentrate on tensing both the muscles at the top and the one underneath the thigh.
(12) Right calf—point your toes upwards.
(13) Right foot—curl your toes.
(14) Left thigh—concentrate on tensing both the muscles at the top and the ones underneath the thigh.
(15) Left calf—point your toes upwards.
(16) Left foot—curl your toes.

5.2   THOUGHT DIARY

Situation Where were you? What were you doing? Who were you with?	Moods What did you feel? Rate each mood (0–100%)	Automatic thoughts What was going through your mind just before you felt this way? Which was the most important/ worrying thought?	Evidence that supports automatic thoughts	Evidence that does not support automatic thoughts	Alternative/ balanced thought Rate how much you believe the alternative thought (0–100%)

5.3 HIERARCHY OF FEARED SITUATIONS WORKSHEET

FEARED SITUATION	PREDICTION AND ANXIETY RATING (0–100)	TASK	ACTUAL ANXIETY (0–100)	OUTCOME OF TASK

Appendix 5b

ANGER AND IMPULSE CONTROL: WORKSHEET

5.4 ANGER DIARY

Situation Where were you? What were you doing? Who were you with?	Moods What did you feel? Rate each mood (0–100%)	Automatic thoughts What was going through your mind just before you felt this way? Which was the most important/ worrying thought?	Evidence that supports automatic thoughts	Evidence that does not support automatic thoughts	Alternative/ balanced thought Rate how much you believe the alternative thought (0–100%)

Appendix 5c

DEPRESSION: WORKSHEET

5.5   WEEKLY ACTIVITY DIARY

Note: Rate activities **P** for Pleasure **0** (not at all pleasurable) $\rightarrow$ 10 (extremely pleasurable)

	M	T	W	TH	F	S	S
9–10							
10–11							
11–12							
12–1							
1–2							
2–3							
3–4							
4–5							
5–6							
6–7							
7–8							
8–12							

Appendix 6

COMMUNICATION—SOCIAL SKILLS AND ASSERTIVENESS: WORKSHEETS

6.1   COMMUNICATION STYLES CHART

Situation Where, who with, what were you doing?	Response What did you do?	Style Passive/aggressive/ assertive

6.2   THOUGHT DIARY (ASSERTIVENESS)

Situation Where were you? What were you doing? Who were you with?	Moods What did you feel? Rate each mood (0–100%)	Style of response Passive/ aggressive/ assertive	Automatic thoughts What was going through your mind just before you felt this way? Which was the most important/worrying thought?	Evidence that supports automatic thoughts	Evidence that does not support automatic thoughts	Alternative/ balanced thought Rate how much you believe the alternative thought (0–100%)

Appendix 7

LIFESTYLE BALANCE: WORKSHEETS

7.1   ROLES AND HABITS CHECKLIST

Please indicate which roles you have previously had, whether you enjoyed them; and which roles you would like to have in the future.

ROLE	PAST	PRESENT	FUTURE
Homemaker/childcare			
Student			
Voluntary worker			
Paid worker			
Unemployed			
Member of family			
Partner in relationship			
Member of group/organisation			
Participant in hobby/interest			

Which activities do you do regularly?

Do you wish to continue with these?

7.2   INTERESTS CHECKLIST

Please indicate whether you have done (did you like it?) or would like to do any of the
following activities.

ACTIVITY	PAST	PRESENT	FUTURE
Cooking			
Team sports			
Photography			
Playing music			
Going to a gym			
Art			
Languages			
Museums/art galleries			
Church activities			
Dancing			
Listening to music			
Individual sports (e.g., running, cycling)			
Yoga			
Fishing			
Member of club			
Collecting objects (e.g., stamps)			
Car maintenance			
Crafts (e.g., knitting, jewellery making)			
Watching TV/videos			
Meeting friends			
Day trips			
Pottery			
Reading			
Pubs/clubs			
Learning skills (e.g., DIY, aromatherapy)			
Penpals/letter writing			
Computer games			
Board games (e.g., scrabble)			
Shopping			
Pets			
Cinema			
Rambling/walking			
Voluntary work			
Gardening			
Dress making			
Sports events (e.g., football match)			
Self-care (e.g., bath, visit salon)			
Restaurants			
Pub-related games (e.g., darts, pool)			
Other			

REFERENCES

Alcoholics Anonymous (1985). *Twelve Steps and Twelve Traditions*. New York: Alcoholics Anonymous World Services.

Argyle, M. (1972). *The Psychology of Interpersonal Behaviour*. London: Penguin.

Barrowclough, C. (2003). Family intervention for substance misuse in psychosis. In H. L. Graham, A. Copello, M. J. Birchwood & K. T. Mueser (eds), *Substance Misuse in Psychosis: Approaches to Treatment and Service Delivery* (pp. 227–243). Chichester: Wiley.

Barrowclough, C., Haddock, G., Tarrier, N., Moring, J. & Lewis, S. (2000). Cognitive behavioural intervention for severely mentally ill clients who have a substance use problem. *Psychiatric Rehabilitation Skills*, **4**, 216–233.

Barrowclough, C., Haddock, G., Tarrier, N., et al. (2001). Randomized controlled trial of motivational interviewing, cognitive behavior therapy, and family intervention for patients with comorbid schizophrenia and substance use disorders. *American Journal of Psychiatry*, **158**, 1706–1713.

Bartels, S. J., Drake, R. E. & McHugo, G. (1992). Alcohol use, depression, and suicidal behavior in schizophrenia. *American Journal of Psychiatry*, **149**, 394–395.

Bebout, R., Drake, R., Xie, H., McHugo, G. & Harris, M. (1997). Housing status among formerly homeless dually diagnosed adults. *Psychiatric Services*, **48**, 936–941.

Beck, A. T. (1976). *Cognitive Therapy and the Emotional Disorders*. New York: International Universities Press.

Beck, A. T., Wright, F. D., Newman, C. F. & Liese, B. S. (1993). *Cognitive Therapy of Substance Abuse*. New York: Guilford.

Bellack, A. S. & DiClemente, C. C. (1999). Treating substance abuse among patients with schizophrenia. *Psychiatric Services*, **50**, 75–80.

Bellack, A. S. & Gearon, J. S. (1998). Substance abuse treatment for people with schizophrenia. *Addictive Behaviors*, **23**, 749–766.

Bellack, A. S., Mueser, K. T., Gingerich, S. & Agresta, J. (1997). *Social Skills Training for Schizophrenia: A Step-By-Step Guide*. New York: Guilford.

Birchwood, M. & Tarrier, N. (1994). *Psychological Management of Schizophrenia*. London: Wiley.

Birchwood, M., Fowler, D. & Jackson, C. (2000). *Early Intervention in Psychosis: A Guide to Concepts, Evidence and Interventions*. London: Wiley.

Birchwood, M., Spencer, E. & McGovern, D. (2000). Schizophrenia: early warning signs. *Advances in Psychiatric Treatment*, **6**, 93–101.

Birchwood, M., Mason, R., Macmillan, F. & Healy, J. (1993). Depression, demoralization and control over psychotic illness: a comparison of depressed and nondepressed patients with a chronic psychosis. *Psychological Medicine*, **23**, 387–395.

Birchwood, M., Smith, J., MacMillan, F. & McGovern, D. (1998). Early intervention in psychotic relapse. In C. Brooker & J. Repper (eds), *Serious Mental Health Problems in the Community: Policy, Practice and Research* (pp. 204–237). London: Baillière Tindall.

Blanchard, J. J., Brown, S. A., Horna, W. P. & Sherwood, A. R. (2000). Substance use disorders in schizophrenia: review, integration and a proposed model. *Clinical Psychology Review*, **20**, 207–234.

Burlington, T. A., Reilly, R. M., Moltzen, J. O. & Ziff, D. C. (1989). Self-efficacy and relapse among inpatient drug and alcohol abusers: a predictor of outcome. *Journal of Studies on Alcohol*, **50**, 354–360.

Carey, K. B. (1996). Substance use reduction in the context of outpatient psychiatric treatment: a collaborative, motivational, harm reduction approach. *Community Mental Health Journal*, **32**, 291–306.

Carmichael, D., Tackett-Gibson, M., O'Dell, L., Jayasuria, B., Jordan, J. & Menon, R. (1998). *Texas Dual Diagnosis Project Evaluation Report 1997–1998*. College Station, TX: Public Policy Research Institute/Texas A&M University.

Clark, D. & Steer, R. A. (1996). Empirical status of the cognitive model of anxiety and depression. In P. M. Salkovskis (ed.), *Frontiers of Cognitive Therapy* (pp. 75–96). London: Guilford.

Cooper, M. L., Russell, M., Skinner, J. B. & Windle, M. (1992). Development and validation of a three-dimensional measure of drinking motives. *Psychological Assessment*, **4**, 123–132.

Copello, A., Graham, H. & Birchwood, M. (2001). Evaluating substance misuse interventions in psychosis: the limitations of the RCT with 'patient' as the unit of analysis. *Journal of Mental Health*, **10**, 585–587.

Copello, A., Orford, J., Hodgson, R., Tober, G. & Barrett, C. (2002). Social behaviour and network therapy: basic principles and early experiences. *Addictive Behaviours*, **27**, 345–366.

Copello, A., Templeton, L., Krishnin, M., Orford, J., Velleman, R. & Merriman, C. (1998). Recruiting primary care professionals to develop and pilot a package to improve effectiveness in working with family members of problem alcohol and drug users. *New Directions in the Study of Alcohol Group*, **22**, 412–450.

Corrigan, P. W. (1995). Wanted: champions of rehabilitation for psychiatric hospitals. *American Psychologist*, **50**, 514–521.

Cournos, F., Empfield, M., Horwath, E., et al. (1991). HIV prevalence among patients admitted to two psychiatric hospitals. *American Journal of Psychiatry*, **148**, 1225–1229.

Creek, J. (1990). *Occupational Therapy and Mental Health Principles, Skills and Practice*. London: Churchill Livingstone.

Day, E., Georgiou, G. & Crome, I. (2003). Pharmacological management of substance misuse in psychosis. In H. L. Graham, A. Copello, M. J. Birchwood & K. T. Mueser (eds), *Substance Misuse in Psychosis: Approaches to Treatment and Service Delivery* (pp. 259–280). Chichester: Wiley.

De Leon, J., Dadvand, M., Canuso, C., White, A. O., Stanilla, J. K. & Simpson, G. M. (1995). Schizophrenia and smoking: an epidemiological survey at a state hospital. *American Journal of Psychiatry*, **152**, 453–455.

Department of Health (2002). Mental Health Policy Implementation Guide: *Dual Diagnosis Good Practice Guide*.

Detrick, A. & Stiepock, V. (1992). Treating persons with mental illness, substance abuse, and legal problems: the Rhode Island experience. In L. I. Stein (ed.) *Innovative*

Community Mental Health Programs (New Directions for Mental Health Services, No. 56, pp. 65–77). San Francisco, CA: Jossey-Bass.

Dickey, B. & Azeni, H. (1996). Persons with dual diagnosis of substance abuse and major mental illness: their excess costs of psychiatric care. *American Journal of Public Health*, **86**, 973–977.

Dixon, L., Goldman, H. & Hirad, A. (1999). State policy and funding of services to families of adults with serious and persistent mental illness. *Psychiatric Services*, **50**, 551–553.

Dixon, L., McNary, S. & Lehman, A. (1995). Substance abuse and family relationships of persons with severe mental health problems. *American Journal of Psychiatry*, **152**, 456–458.

Drake, R. E. & Brunette, M. F. (1998). Complications of severe mental health problems related to alcohol and other drug use disorders. In M. Galanter (ed.), *Recent Developments in Alcoholism* (Vol. 14, *Consequences of Alcoholism*, pp. 285–299). New York: Plenum.

Drake, R. E., Bebout, R. R. & Roach, J. P. (1993). A research evaluation of social network case management for homeless persons with dual disorders. In M. Harris & H. C. Bergman (eds), *Case Management for Mentally Ill Patients—Theory and Practice* (pp. 83–98). Pennsylvania: Harwood Academic Publishers.

Drake, R. E., Brunette, M. F. & Mueser, K. T. (1998). Substance use disorder and social functioning in schizophrenia. In K. T. Mueser & N. Tarrier (eds), *Handbook of Social Functioning in Schizophrenia* (pp. 280–289). Boston, MA: Allyn & Bacon.

Drake, R. E., Mueser, K. T. & McHugo, G. J. (1996). Clinician rating scales: Alcohol Use Scale (AUS), Drug Use Scale (DUS) and Substance Abuse Treatment Scales (SATS). In L. I. Sederer & B. Dickey (eds), *Outcomes Assessment in Clinical Practice* (pp. 113–116). Baltimore, MD: Williams and Wilkins.

Drake, R. E., Wallach, M. A. & Hoffman, J. S. (1989). Housing instability and homelessness among aftercare patients of an urban state hospital. *Hospital and Community Psychiatry*, **40**, 46–51.

Drake, R. E., Gates, C., Whitaker, A. & Cotton, P. G. (1985). Suicide among schizophrenics: a review. *Comprehensive Psychiatry*, **26**, 90–100.

Drake, R. E., Bartels, S. B., Teague, G. B., Noordsy, D. L. & Clark, R. E. (1993). Treatment of substance abuse in severely mentally ill patients. *Journal of Nervous and Mental Disease*, **181**, 606–611.

Drake, R. E., Yovetich, N. A., Bebout, R. R., Harris, M. & McHugo, G. J. (1997). Integrated treatment for dually diagnosed homeless adults. *Journal of Nervous and Mental Disease*, **185**, 298–305.

Drake, R. E., Essock, S. M., Shaner, A., et al. (2001). Implementing dual diagnosis services for clients with severe mental health problems. *Psychiatric Services*, **52**, 469–476.

Drake, R. E., McHugo, G. J., Clark, R. E., et al. (1998). Assertive community treatment for patients with co-occurring severe mental illness and substance use disorder: a clinical trial. *American Journal of Orthopsychiatry*, **68**, 201–215.

Drummond, C. D., Tiffany, S. T., Glautier, S. & Remmington, B. (1995). Cue exposure in understanding and treating addictive behaviours. In D. C. Drummond, S. T. Tiffany, S. Glautier & B. Remmington (eds), *Addictive Behaviour Cue Exposure, Theory and Practice* (pp. 1–46). Chichester: Wiley.

Durell, J., Lechtenberg, B., Corse, S. & Frances, R. (1993). Intensive case management of persons with chronic mental illness who abuse substances. *Hospital and Community Psychiatry*, **44**, 415–416.

Dusenbury, L., Botvin, G. J. & James-Ortiz, S. (1989). The primary prevention of adolescent substance abuse through the promotion of personal and social competence. *Prevention in Human Services*, **7**, 201–224.

Falloon, I., Mueser, K., Gingerich, S., et al. (1996). *Behavioural Family Therapy—A Workbook*. Buckingham Mental Health Service, UK.

Fennell, M. (1994). Depression. In K. Hawton, P. Salkovskis, J. Kirk & D. Clark. *Cognitive Behavioural Therapy for Psychiatric Problems: A Practical Guide* (pp. 167–234). Oxford: Oxford University Press.

Fennell, M. J. V. (1997). Low self-esteem: a cognitive perspective. *Behavioural and Cognitive Psychotherapy*, **25**, 1–25.

Field, L. (1995). *The Self-Esteem Workbook*. Shaftsbury: Element Books.

Fowler, D., Garety, P. & Kuipers, E. (1995). *Cognitive Behaviour Therapy for Psychosis*. Chichester: Wiley.

Freeman, R., Gillam, S., Shearin, C. & Plamping, D. (1997). *COPC Depression and Anxiety Intervention*. London: Kings Fund.

Galanter, M. (1993). Network therapy for substance abuse: a clinical trial. *Psychotherapy*, **30**, 251–258.

Galanter, M. & Kleber, H. D. (eds) (1999). *Textbook of Substance Abuse Treatment* (2nd edn). Washington, DC: American Psychiatric Press.

Gambrill, E. D. (1977). *Behaviour Modification—Handbook of Assessment, Intervention and Evaluation*. Chapter 12. California: Jossey-Bass.

Glass, I. B., Farrell, M. & Hajek, P. (1991). Tell me about the client: history-taking and formulating the case. In I. B. Glass (ed.), *The International Handbook of Addiction Behavior* (pp. 216–224). London: Tavistock/Routledge.

Godley, S. H., Hoewing-Roberson, R. & Godley, M. D. (1994). *Final MISA Report*. Bloomington, IL: Lighthouse Institute.

Gossop, M., Drake, S., Griffiths, P., Hando, J., Powis, B., Hall, W. & Strang, J. (1995). The Severity of Dependence Scale (SDS): psychometric properties of the SDS in English and Australian samples of heroin, cocaine and amphetamine users. *Addiction*, **90**, 607–614.

Graham, H. L. (1998). The role of dysfunctional beliefs in individuals who experience psychosis and use substances: implications for cognitive therapy and medication adherence. *Behavioural and Cognitive Psychotherapy*, **26**, 193–207.

Graham, H. L. (2003). A cognitive conceptualisation of concurrent psychosis and problem drug and alcohol use. In H. L. Graham, A. Copello, M. J. Birchwood & K. T. Mueser (eds), *Substance Misuse in Psychosis: Approaches to Treatment and Service Delivery* (pp. 74–89). Chichester: Wiley.

Graham, H. L., Copello, A., Birchwood, M. J. & Mueser, K. T. (eds) (2003). *Substance Misuse in Psychosis: Approaches to Treatment and Service Delivery*. Chichester: Wiley.

Graham, H. L., Maslin, J., Copello, A., et al. (2001). Drug and alcohol problems amongst individuals with severe mental health problems in an inner city area of the UK. *Social Psychiatry and Psychiatric Epidemiology*, **36**, 448–455.

Greenberger, D. & Padesky, C. (1995). *Mind Over Mood*. Basingstoke: Guilford.

Hall, R. G., Duhamel, M., McClanahan, R., et al. (1995). Level of functioning, severity of illness, and smoking status among chronic psychiatric patients. *Journal of Nervous and Mental Disease*, **183**, 468–471.

Hawton, K., Salkovskis, K. J. & Clark, D. M. (eds) (2001). *Cognitive Behaviour Therapy for Psychiatric Problems: A Practical Guide*. Oxford: Oxford University Press.

Heather, N., Wodak, A., Nadelman, E. & O'Hare, P. (1993). *Psychoactive Drugs and Harm Reduction: From Faith to Science*. London: Whurr.

Heather, N., Luce, A., Peck, D., Dunbar, B. & James, I. (1999). Development of a treatment version of the Readiness to Change Questionnaire. *Addiction Research*, **7**, 63–83.

Hellerstein, D. J., Rosenthal, R. N. & Miner, C. R. (1995). A prospective study of integrated outpatient treatment for substance-abusing schizophrenic outpatients. *American Journal on Addictions*, **4**, 33–42.

Hemming, M., Morgan, S. & O'Halloran, P. (1999). Assertive outreach: implications for the development of the model in the United Kingdom. *Journal of Mental Health*, **8**, 141–147.

Herman, S. E., Boots-Miller, B., Jordan, L., et al. (1997). Immediate outcomes of substance use treatment within a state psychiatric hospital. *Journal of Mental Health Administration*, **24**, 126–138.

Hodgins, S. & Côté, G. (1993). The criminality of mentally disordered offenders. *Criminal Justice and Behavior*, **28**, 115–129.

Hughes, J. R., Hatsukami, D. K., Mitchell, J. E. & Dahlgren, L. A. (1986). Prevalence of smoking among psychiatric outpatients. *American Journal of Psychiatry*, **143**, 993–997.

Hunt, G. E., Bergen, J. & Bashir, M. (2002). Medication compliance and comorbid substance abuse in schizophrenia: impact on community survival 4 years after a relapse. *Schizophrenia Research*, **54**, 253–264.

Jerrell, J. M. (1996). Cost effective treatment for persons with dual disorders. In R. E. Drake & K. T. Mueser (eds), *Dual Diagnosis of Major Mental Illness and Substance Abuse*. Vol. 2. *Recent Research and Clinical Implications* (pp. 79–92). San Francisco, CA: Jossey-Bass.

Jerrell, J. & Ridgely, M. (1995). Evaluating changes in symptoms and functioning of dually diagnosed clients in specialized treatment. *Psychiatric Services*, **46**, 233–238.

Jerrell, J. M. & Ridgely, M. S. (1995). Comparative effectiveness of three approaches to serving people with severe mental illness and substance abuse disorders. *Journal of Nervous and Mental Disease*, **183**, 566–576.

Jerrell, J. M. & Ridgely, M. S. (1999). Impact of robustness of program implementation on outcomes of clients in dual diagnosis programs. *Psychiatric Services*, **50**, 109–112.

Kashner, M., Rader, L., Rodell, D., Beck, C., Rodell, L. & Muller, K. (1991). Family characteristics, substance abuse, and hospitalization patterns of patients with schizophrenia. *Hospital and Community Psychiatry*, **42**, 195–197.

Kemp, R. & David, A. (1996). Compliance therapy: an intervention targeting insight and treatment adherence in psychotic patients. *Behavioural and Cognitive Psychotherapy*, **24**, 331–350.

Kemp, R., Hayward, P., Applewhaite, G., Everitt, B. & David, A. (1996). Compliance therapy in psychotic patients: randomised controlled trial. *British Medical Journal*, **312**, 345–349.

Kemp, R., Kirov, G., Everitt, B., Hayward, P. & David, A. (1998). Randomised controlled trial of compliance therapy: 18-month follow-up. *British Journal of Psychiatry*, **173**, 271–272.

Kessler, R. C., Nelson, C. B., McGonagle, K. A., et al. (1996). The epidemiology of co-occurring addictive and mental disorders: implications for prevention and service utilization. *American Journal of Orthopsychiatry*, **66**, 17–31.

Kingdon, D. G. & Turkington, D. G. (1994). *Cognitive-Behavioural Therapy of Schizophrenia*. Hove: Psychology Press.

Kushner, M. G. & Mueser, K. T. (1993). Psychiatric co-morbidity with alcohol use disorders. *Eighth Special Report to the U.S. Congress on Alcohol and Health* (Vol. NIH Pub. No. 94—3699, pp. 37–59). Rockville, MD: U.S. Department of Health and Human Services.

Kushner, M. G., Abrams, K. & Borchardt, C. (2000). The relationship between anxiety disorders and alcohol use disorders: a review of major perspectives and findings. *Clinical Psychology Review*, **20**, 149–171.

Lehman, A., Herron, J., Schwartz, R. & Myers, C. (1993). Rehabilitation for adults with severe mental illness and substance use disorders: a clinical trial. *Journal of Nervous and Mental Disease*, **181**, 86–90.

Liberman, R. P., DeRisi, W. J. & Mueser, K. T. (1989). *Social Skills Training for Psychiatric Patients*. Needham Heights, MA: Allyn & Bacon.

Liberman, R. P., Eckman, T., Kuehnel, T., Rosenstein, J. & Kuehnel, J. (1982). Dissemination of new behaviour therapy programs to community mental health centers. *American Journal of Psychiatry*, **139**, 224–226.

Liese, B. S. & Franz, R. A. (1996). Treating substance use disorders with cognitive therapy: lessons learned and implications for the future. In P. Salkovskis (ed.), *Frontiers of Cognitive Therapy* (pp. 470–508). New York: Guilford.

Linszen, D., Dingemans, P., Van der Does, A. J. W., Scholte, P., Lenior, R. & Goldstein, M. J. (1996). Treatment, expressed emotion and relapse in recent onset schizophrenic disorders. *Psychological Medicine*, **26**, 333–342.

Marlatt, G. A. (ed.) (1998). *Harm Reduction: Pragmatic Strategies for Managing High-Risk Behaviors*. New York: Guilford.

Marlatt, G. A. & Barrett, K. (1994). Relapse prevention. In M. Galanter & H. D. Kleber (eds), *The Textbook of Substance Abuse Treatment* (pp. 285–299). Washington, DC: American Psychiatric Press.

Marlatt, G. A. & Gordan, G. R. (1985). *Relapse Prevention: Maintenance Strategies in the Treatment of Addictive Behaviors*. New York: Guilford.

Maslin, J., Graham, H. L., Cawley, M. A. C., et al. (2001). Combined severe mental health and substance use problems: what are the training and support needs of staff working with this client group? *Journal of Mental Health*, **10**, 131–140.

Meisler, N., Blankertz, L., Santos, A. B. & McKay, C. (1997). Impact of assertive community treatment on homeless persons with co-occurring severe psychiatric and substance disorders. *Community Mental Health Journal*, **33**, 113–122.

Menezes, P. O., Johnson, S., Thornicroft, G., et al. (1996). Drug and alcohol problems amongst individuals with severe mental illness in South London. *British Journal of Psychiatry*, **168**, 612–619.

Mercer-McFadden, C., Drake, R. E., Brown, N. B. & Fox, R. S. (1997). The community support program demonstrations of services for young adults with severe mental illness and substance use disorders 1987–1991. *Psychiatric Rehabilitation Journal*, **20**, 13–24.

Mercer-McFadden, C., Drake, R. E., Clark, R. E., Verven, N., Noordsy, D. L. & Fox, T. S. (1998). *Substance Abuse Treatment for People with Severe Mental Disorders: A Program Manager's Guide*. Concord, NH: New Hampshire-Dartmouth Psychiatric Research Center.

Meyer, R., Babor, T. & Hesselbrock, V. (1988). An alcohol research center in concept and practice: interdisciplinary collaboration at the UConn ARC. *British Journal of Addiction*, **83**, 245–252.

Meyers, R. J., Dominguez, T. P. & Smith, J. E. (1996). Community reinforcement training with concerned others. In V. B. Van Hasselt & R. Hersen (eds), *Sourcebook of Psychological Treatment Manual for Adult Disorders* (pp. 257–294). New York: Plenum.

Miller, W. R. & Rollnick, S. (1991). *Motivational Interviewing: Preparing People to Change Addictive Behavior*. New York: Guilford.

Miller, W. R., Zweben, A., DiClemente, C. C. & Rychtarik R. G. (1995). Motivational Enhancement Therapy Manual: A Clinical Research Guide for Therapists Treating Individuals with Alcohol Abuse and Dependence. Vol. 2. Project Match Monograph Series, National Institutes of Health Publication.

Mowbray, C. T., Solomon, M., Ribisl, K. M., et al. (1995). Treatment for mental illness and substance abuse in a public psychiatric hospital. *Journal of Substance Abuse Treatment*, **12**, 129–139.

Mueser, K. T. (1998). Social skill and problem solving. In A. S. Bellack & M. Hersen (eds), *Comprehensive Clinical Psychology*, Vol. 6 (pp. 183–201). New York: Pergamon.

Mueser, K. T. & Bellack, A. S. (1998). Social skills and social functioning. In K. T. Mueser & N. Tarrier (eds), *Handbook of Social Functioning in Schizophrenia* (pp. 79–96). Needham Heights, MA: Allyn & Bacon.

Mueser, K. T. & Fox, L. (2000). Family friendly services: a modest proposal. *Psychiatric Services*, **51**, 1452.

Mueser, K. T. & Fox, L. (2002). A family intervention program for dual disorders. *Community Mental Health Journal*, **38**, 253–270.

Mueser, K. T. & Gingerich, S. L. (1994). *Coping with Schizophrenia: A Guide for Families*. Oakland, CA: New Harbinger.

Mueser, K. T., Bennett, M. & Kushner, M. G. (1995). Epidemiology of substance abuse among persons with chronic mental disorders. In A. F. Lehman & L. Dixon (eds), *Double Jeopardy: Chronic Mental Illness and Substance Abuse* (pp. 9–25). New York: Harwood Academic.

Mueser, K. T., Drake, R. E. & Noordsy, D. L. (1998). Integrated mental health and substance abuse treatment for severe psychiatric disorders. *Journal of Practical Psychiatry and Behavioural Health*, **4**, 129–139.

Mueser, K. T., Drake, R. E. & Wallach, M. A. (1998). Dual diagnosis: a review of etiological theories. *Addictive Behaviors*, **23**, 717–734.

Mueser, K. T., Yarnold, P. R. & Bellack, A. S. (1992). Diagnostic and demographic correlates of substance abuse in schizophrenia and major affective disorder. *Acta Psychiatrica Scandinavica*, **85**, 48–55.

Mueser, K. T., Noordsy, D. L., Drake, R. E. & Fox, L. (2003). *Integrated Treatment for Dual Disorders: Effective Intervention for Severe Mental Illness and Substance Abuse*. New York: Guilford.

Mueser, K. T., Essock, S. M., Drake, R. E., Wolfe, R. S. & Frisman, L. (2001). Rural and urban differences in dually diagnosed patients: implications for service needs. *Schizophrenia Research*, **48**, 93–107.

Mueser, K. T., Nishith, P., Tracy, J. I., DeGirolamo, J. & Molinaro, M. (1995). Expectations and motives for substance use in schizophrenia. *Schizophrenia Bulletin*, **21**, 367–378.

Novaco, R. W. (1993). Clinicians ought to view anger contextually. *Behaviour Change*, **10**, 208–281.

Padesky, C. A. (1993). Socratic questionning: changing minds or guiding discovery? A keynote address delivered at the European Congress of Behavioural and Cognitive Therapies, London.

Padesky, C. & Greenberger, D. (1995). *Clinician's Guide to Mind Over Mood*. New York: Guilford.

Pandina, R. J., Labouvie, E. W., Johnson, V. & White, H. R. (1990). The relationship between alcohol and marijuana use and competence in adolescence. *Journal of Health and Social Policy*, **1**, 89–108.

Persons, J. B. (1989). *Cognitive Therapy in Practice: A Case Formulation Approach*. New York: Norton.

Phillips, P. & Johnson, S. (2001). How does drug and alcohol misuse develop among people with psychotic illness? A literature review. *Social Psychiatry and Psychiatric Epidemiology*, **36**, 269–276.

Pickett-Schenk, S. A., Banghart, M. & Cook, J. A. (2003). Integrated treatment outcomes for homeless persons with severe mental illness and co-occurring substance use

292 COGNITIVE-BEHAVIOURAL INTEGRATED TREATMENT

disorders. In H. L. Graham, A. Copello, M. J. Birchwood & K. T. Mueser (eds), *Substance Misuse in Psychosis: Approaches to Treatment and Service Delivery* (pp. 321–331). Chichester: Wiley.

Pokorny, A. D., Byron, M. D., Miller, M. S. W. & Kaplan, H. B. (1972). The Brief MAST: a shortened version of the Michigan Alcoholism Screening Test. *American Journal of Psychiatry*, **129**, 342–345.

Postma, P. & Kumari, V. (2002). Tobacco smoking in schizophrenia: the self-medication hypotheses. *Journal of Advances in Schizophrenia and Brain Research*, **3**, 81–86.

Powell, J. E. & Taylor, D. (1992). Anger, depression and anxiety following heroin withdrawal. *International Journal of the Addictions*, **27**, 25–35.

Prochaska, J. O., DiClemente, C. C. & Norcross, J. C. (1992). In search of how people change: applications to addictive behaviors. *American Psychologist*, **47**, 1102–1114.

Provencher, H. L. & Mueser, K. (1997). Positive and negative symptom behaviours and caregiver burden in the relatives of persons with schizophrenia. *Schizophrenia Research*, **26**, 71–80.

Razzano, L. (2003). Issues in comorbidity and HIV/AIDS. In H. L. Graham, A. Copello, M. J. Birchwood & K. T. Mueser (eds), *Substance Misuse in Psychosis: Approaches to Treatment and Service Delivery* (pp. 332–346). Chichester: Wiley.

Ridgely, M. S. & Jerrell, J. M. (1996). Analysis of three interventions for substance abuse treatment of severely mentally ill people. *Community Mental Health Journal*, **32**, 561–572.

Rieger, D. A., Farmer, M. E., Rae, D. S., et al. (1990). Comorbidity of mental disorders with alcohol and other drug abuse: results from the Epidemiologic Catchment Area (ECA) study. *Journal of the American Medical Association*, **264**, 2511–2518.

Roberts, L. J., Shaner, A. & Eckman, T. (1997). *Substance Abuse Management Module (SAMM) Skills Training for People with Schizophrenia Who Are Also Addicted to Drugs and Alcohol*. West Los Angeles VA Medical Center and the Department of Bio-behavioural Science, UCLA.

Rogers, C. R. (1991). *Client-Centred Therapy*. London: Constable.

Rollnick, S. & Miller, W. R. (1995). What is motivational interviewing? *Behavioural and Cognitive Psychotherapy*, **23**, 325–334.

Rollnick, S., Butler, C. & Stott, N. (1997). Helping smokers make decisions: the enhancement of brief intervention for general medical practice. *Patient Education and Counselling*, **31**, 191–203.

Rorstad, P. & Checinski, K. (1996). *Dual Diagnosis: Facing the Challenge*. Kenley, UK: Wynne Howard.

Rosenberg, M. (1965). *Society and Adolescent Self-Image*. Princeton, NJ: Princeton University Press.

Rosenberg, S. D., Goodman, L. A., Osher, F. C., et al. (2001a). Prevalence of HIV, hepatitis B and hepatitis C in people with severe mental health problems. *American Journal of Public Health*, **91**, 31–37.

Rosenberg, S. D., Trumbetta, S. L., Mueser, K. T., et al. (2001b). Determinants of risk behavior for HIV/AIDS in people with severe and persistent mental illness. *Comprehensive Psychiatry*, **42**, 263–271.

Roy, A. (ed.) (1986). *Suicide in Schizophrenia*. Baltimore, MD: Williams & Wilkins.

Salkovskis, P. (1996). *Frontiers of Cognitive Therapy*. London: Guilford.

Salyers, M. P. & Mueser, K. T. (2001). Social functioning, psychopathology, and medication side effects in relation to substance use and abuse in schizophrenia. *Schizophrenia Research*, **48**, 109–123.

Sanderson, S. & Reed, K. L. (1980). *Concepts of Occupational Therapy*. Baltimore, MD: Williams and Wilkins.

Saunders, J. B., Aasland, O. G., Babor, T. F., de la Fuente, J. R. & Grant, M. (1993). Development of the Alcohol Use Disorders Identification Test (AUDIT): WHO collaborative project on early detection of persons with harmful alcohol consumption. *Addiction*, **88**, 791–804.

Schneier, F. R. & Siris, S. G. (1987). A review of psychoactive substance use and abuse in schizophrenia. *Journal of Nervous and Mental Disease*, **175**, 641–652.

Sheils, R. & Rolfe, T. J. (2000). Towards an integrated approach to a family intervention for co-occurring substance abuse and schizophrenia. *Australia and New Zealand Family Therapy*, **21**, 81–87.

Sisson, R. W. and Azrin, A. H. (1989). The community reinforcement approach. In R. L. Hester & W. R. Miller (eds), *Handbook of Alcoholism Treatment Approaches: Effective Alternatives* (pp. 242–258). New York: Pergamon.

Skinner, H. A. (1982). The Drug Abuse Screening Test. *Addictive Behaviours*, **7**, 363–371.

Spaniol, L., Zipple, A. & Cohen, B. (1991). Managing innovation and change in psychosocial rehabilitation: key principles and guidelines. *Psychosocial Rehabilitation Journal*, **14**, 27–38.

Steadman, H. J., Mulvey, E. P., Monahan, J., et al. (1998). Violence by people discharged from acute psychiatric inpatient facilities and by others in the same neighborhoods. *Archives of General Psychiatry*, **55**, 393–401.

Stein, L. I. & Santos, A. B. (1998). *Assertive Community Treatment of Persons with Severe Mental Illness*. New York: Norton.

Stein, L. I. & Test, M. A. (1980). Alternatives to mental hospital treatment: conceptual model, treatment program and clinical evaluation. *Archives of General Psychiatry*, **37**, 392–397.

Strakowski, S. M., DelBello, M. P., Fleck, D. E. & Arndt, S. (2000). The impact of substance abuse on the course of bipolar disorder. *Biological Psychiatry*, **48**, 477–485.

Swartz, M. S., Swanson, J. W., Hiday, V. A., Borum, R., Wagner, H. R. & Burns, B. J. (1998). Violence and mental illness: the effects of substance abuse and nonadherence to medication. *American Journal of Psychiatry*, **155**, 226–231.

Swendsen, J. D. & Merikangas, K. R. (2000). The comorbidity of depression and substance use disorders. *Clinical Psychology Review*, **20**, 173–189.

Swofford, C. D., Kasckow, J. W., Scheller-Gilkey, G. & Inderbitzin, L. B. (1996). Substance use: a powerful predictor of relapse in schizophrenia. *Schizophrenia Research*, **20**, 145–151.

Tarrier, N. & Calam, R. (2002). New developments in cognitive–behavioural case formulation. Epidemiological, systemic and social context: an integrative approach. *Behavioural and Cognitive Psychotherapy*, **30**, 311–328.

Thase, M. E. & Beck, A. T. (1993). An overview of cognitive therapy. In J. H. Wright., M. E. Thase, A. T. Beck & J. W. Ludgate (eds), *Cognitive Therapy with Inpatients: Developing a Cognitive Milieu* (pp. 3–34). New York: Guilford.

Torrey, W. C., Drake, R. E. & Bartels, S. J. (1996). Suicide and persistent mental illness: a continual clinical and risk-management challenge. In S. M. Soreff (ed.), *Handbook for the Treatment of the Seriously Mentally Ill* (pp. 295–313). Seattle, WA: Hogrefe & Huber.

Trumbetta, S. L., Mueser, K. T., Quimby, E., Bebout, R. & Teague, G. B. (1999). Social networks and clinical outcomes of dually diagnosed homeless persons. *Behavior Therapy*, **30**, 407–430.

Trull, T. J., Sher, K. J., Minks-Brown, C., Durbin, J. & Burr, R. (2000). Borderline personality disorder and substance use disorders: a review and integration. *Clinical Psychology Review*, **20**, 235–253.

Venables, P. H. (1964). *Input Dysfunction in Schizophrenia: Progress in Experimental Personality Research*, Vol. 1. New York: Academic Press.

Warner, R., Taylor, D., Wright, J., et al. (1994). Substance use among the mentally ill: prevalence, reasons for use, and effects on illness. *American Journal of Orthopsychiatry*, **64**, 30–39.

Weiss, R. D., Mirin, S. M. & Griffin, M. L. (1992). Methodological considerations in the diagnosis of co-existing psychiatric disorders in substance abusers. *British Journal of Addiction*, **87**, 179–187.

Weiss, R. D., Najavits, L. M. & Greenfield, S. F. (1999). A relapse prevention group for patients with bipolar and substance use disorders. *Journal of Substance Abuse Treatment*, **16**, 47–54.

Yesavage, J. A. & Zarcone, V. (1983). History of drug abuse and dangerous behavior in inpatient schizophrenics. *Journal of Clinical Psychiatry*, **44**, 259–261.

INDEX

Compiled by Indexing Specialists (UK) Ltd